HOW TO STUDY SOCIAL LIFE

HOW TO STUDY SOCIAL LIFE

Russell Hitchings
Alan Latham

1 Oliver's Yard
55 City Road
London EC1Y 1SP

2455 Teller Road
Thousand Oaks
California 91320

Unit No 323-333, Third Floor, F-Block
International Trade Tower, Nehru Place
New Delhi 110 019

8 Marina View Suite 43-053
Asia Square Tower 1
Singapore 018960

Editor: Charlotte Bush
Editorial assistant: Pippa Wills
Production editor: Rabia Barkatulla
Copyeditor: Mary Dalton
Indexer: Avril Ehrlich
Marketing manager: Ben Sherwood
Cover design: Shaun Mercier
Typeset by: KnowledgeWorks Global Ltd
Printed in the UK

© Russell Hitchings and Alan Latham 2025

Apart from any fair dealing for the purposes of research, private study, or criticism or review, as permitted under the Copyright, Designs and Patents Act, 1988, this publication may not be reproduced, stored or transmitted in any form, or by any means, without the prior permission in writing of the publisher, or in the case of reprographic reproduction, in accordance with the terms of licences issued by the Copyright Licensing Agency. Enquiries concerning reproduction outside those terms should be sent to the publisher.

Library of Congress Control Number: 2024939700

British Library Cataloguing in Publication data

A catalogue record for this book is available from the British Library

ISBN 9781529763676
ISBN 9781529763669 (pbk)

CONTENTS

About the authors   vii
Acknowledgements   ix

1 Introduction: what is the point of this book and how to use it   1

2 Warrants: starting with what you want your study to achieve   11

3 Observing: on learning to learn from different social scenes   21

4 Taking part: considering the benefits of getting involved ourselves   43

5 Staging talk: how to do and imagine interviews   61

6 Engaging people: seeing social research as a relationship   81

7 Asking questions: exploring a basic act that features in many methods   101

8 Playing with words: strategies for seeing and exploring patterns   123

9 Looking at pictures: ways of getting drawn into social worlds   143

10 Choosing: how thinking about cases and samples can make for innovative projects   167

11 Writing: how to present the material we've collected   191

Coda: The people who inspired us and ideas for further reading   211
References   219
Index   229

ABOUT THE AUTHORS

Russell Hitchings is a Professor of Human Geography at University College London. His research focuses on everyday practice, energy consumption, and nature experience, and he's been lucky to study these themes in a variety of contexts all around the world. He's particularly interested in how we use talk to examine these topics, having done a lot of interviewing about them. He's also used focus groups, solicited diaries, observation, and survey methods when that seemed like a good idea. Originally from South Wales, he's now been in London, and UCL, for longer than he generally likes to think about.

Alan Latham is another Professor of Human Geography at University College London. His research focuses on sociality, social infrastructure, and the public life of cities more generally. He's studied those themes in all sorts of places around the world too. In undertaking this work, he's explored a range of research approaches – including the use of photo-diaries, diary-interviews, social contact logs, and video recording and analysis. He's interested in doing whatever works to get as close as possible to the realities of people's experience. Originally from New Zealand, he's also been in London, and at UCL, for quite a long time too.

ACKNOWLEDGEMENTS

This book came out of our teaching at UCL. We think research methods are important. But we also think social research is fun. Over the years we've tried to convey that sense of enthusiasm to our students. We'd like to thank all the students who've taken our undergraduate field class, or our graduate methods course, or otherwise been taught these topics by us. We've tried out some challenging and unusual exercises with them. The less successful ones we're very happy not to share in the book! We really appreciate the openness with which they've taken on these ideas, and we hope they've come away with a similar sense of the methods adventure. We've also learnt a lot about the nitty-gritty of social research from our PhD, MSc, and undergraduate dissertation students, and we appreciate the continued support of our colleagues, some of them bravely visiting us as special 'guest stars' in our methods class. In developing our thinking around method, the work we've done with the geography journal *Area* has been a pleasure. Thanks to their support we've really enjoyed thinking about the importance of how we handle different method dilemmas with various friends and colleagues at the Royal Geographical Society conference. Alan would like to thank Derek McCormack with whom he taught a very early version of our current field class. He'd also like to thank Rita, Luisa, Thomas, and Lacey for their support whilst finishing the book. Russell would like to thank Rhod, Jane, and Larry for helping him out in a similar capacity. Thanks also go to our editors at SAGE, first Jai Seaman and then Charlotte Bush – professional and supportive throughout with some excellent nudging to help us get it done.

1
INTRODUCTION: WHAT IS THE POINT OF THIS BOOK AND HOW TO USE IT

SAYING HELLO

Hello!

That felt strange to write. Books don't often start by addressing the reader so directly. But, as you'll soon see, a large part of what this one is about is sharing tips and ideas about how to do enjoyable and effective social research. And the best way, we think, of doing that is with a little informality. So, we'll be writing in this way throughout. Whilst we're being informal, we should probably also introduce ourselves. We're two professors who do social research at a university in London. We've been in this line of work for a while now and, as you'll also soon see, we've experimented with various approaches along the way. We've also taught social research methods for several years, to both undergraduate and postgraduate students, and we've supervised quite a few related projects. You'll hear plenty about all those experiences too. That's because working with all of these students has pushed us to think harder about how to do effective social research and about how to persuade them (and now potentially you) of the value of thinking carefully and creatively about the activities involved.

ANXIETY, INDIFFERENCE, ADVENTURE

Our teaching experience is also partly why we wanted to write this book. As social researchers, we like to think of ourselves as fairly attentive to how particular situations are handled. Something that we've noticed over the years is how some of our students respond to the idea of spending time thinking about methods with us. For some, methods are a worry. When they get to the point when they must consider the practicalities, they get anxious about the idea of going out and engaging with people, maybe speaking to some of them, perhaps even taking part in some of their activities. Imagining people's reactions can make this prospect seem daunting and that can disincline these students from thinking much more about what they'll actually do. Others are just kind of uninterested when, since they're required to take our course, we suddenly barge into their lives and attempt to enthuse them about the joys of cooking up interesting and effective projects. They'd been debating some weighty issues in some of their other courses, and practical research matters can seem a bit dull after that. Both reactions have sometimes frustrated us, we'll admit. That's partly because, for us, the real excitement of our job as researchers is often all about working out, and then testing out, an original and effective strategy for studying aspects of social life. To those who are anxious, we say that, with a little thought, they'll do a very enjoyable and effective project. To those who are indifferent, we remind them that they'll never represent people with authority in their debates if they don't think hard about their methods.

Instead of brushing methods aside – seeing them as something to avoid because they're intimidating or to downplay because they're unexciting – we ask them to think in terms of an adventure, both intellectual and practical. As we see it, with methods we're on a journey in which we're gradually figuring out how to do a project that is interesting, worthwhile, and also delivers on our objectives. We don't always see this kind of approach in the readings we give to our students. Often the focus there is on the procedures involved in carrying out a method. That's certainly helpful. But the excitement of experimenting with different techniques and approaches to find out how we can make them work for us can get a bit lost. In this book, we want to put these ideas of adventure and experimentation front and centre. We'll be using lots of examples of studies we've been involved with ourselves, interesting studies we've read about, and various exercises we've cooked up for our students, to underline and explore the potential of reflecting on the essential activities involved in a social research project. When we do social research, we meet people we might not have otherwise met. We learn the realities of how things are working out for them. We find out about how they see things. We get to see what they think of, and how they respond to, various others and different situations. This is exciting stuff.

WHO IS THIS BOOK FOR?

We like to think this book has something for social researchers at all levels. We've both done plenty of social research. But we're also constantly learning about how to do this work from others, including the undergraduate and post-graduate students we teach. So, as well as an adventure, we also see social research as a craft. It takes time to learn and become skilled at it. Even if you're an experienced researcher there are always new ways of approaching your work. Seeing social research as a craft has actually been a godsend for us too. One of the groups to which we teach methods is a cohort of students doing master's level research focused on various problems (how to think about migration, the implications of urbanisation, how to handle environmental issues). One of the challenges we've faced there was that whilst some of these students had already done methods courses – some had, in fact, previously done all sorts of excellent social research projects – others are entirely new to the whole idea. To cater to this diversity, we decided to organise our course around the idea that we can all benefit from taking a fresh look at the different concrete activities involved in doing a social research project. And that's what we've tried to do in this book. We hope this will give you a candid and helpful introduction if you've never done any social research before whilst also giving those with more experience some new ideas about how to tackle their next project. So, this is, we like to think, a book for anyone interested in social research. We're all figuring out the right ways of studying people. And thinking about the essential activities can help us all to pull off original and effective projects.

But what is studying social life? Well, for us, this is anything to do with understanding what groups of people do and think. They may have come up with these ways of living and thinking themselves. Equally, broader processes of social change and influence might be working through them. Which you prioritise depends on how you want to see things. Lots of academic disciplines do it too. We're human geographers, so that obviously shapes how we go about our work. But our disciplinary boundaries are pretty loose, and we've learnt a lot from sociologists, political scientists, educational researchers, environmental scientists, anthropologists, and others. You may also be wondering why you'd want to study people. Well, there are many possible answers here too. If you're passionate about particular issues elsewhere you might be keen on influencing what they do, perhaps so that you can encourage them to join you in tackling these issues. And that might mean learning about their perspectives first, or getting an appreciation of what they are already doing in certain contexts so that you can come up with better ways of engaging with them there. It could be about understanding where groups of people are coming from more broadly so that you can help them out. It could even be because you're just interested in learning more – being curious about others is generally a big part of this too. There are all sorts of research techniques we can draw on in response to these motivations. We'll cover many of them in the following chapters. And we'll also encourage you to think about how the methods you choose, and how you apply them, are linked to your wider purpose.

AND HOW SHOULD YOU USE IT?

How should you use this book? That sounds like a familiar response from a time-pressured researcher. Fair enough! We'll admit that we're lucky in having the time to reflect on the practicalities. But we'd still encourage you to read the whole thing and to mull over the various ideas we'll introduce as we go along. It's the sort of book we'd quite like you to gradually work through as you develop your research plans. Our intention is not so much about quickly getting you up to speed with recognised methods – there are plenty of excellent books on that already. This book, as we see it, is more about comparing and considering the available options at the start. And even though you may already have some experience with particular methods – in the way that, as we've said, our students sometimes do – it's always a good idea to think about them all before you get too wedded to particular approaches. And so, even though this book is called 'How to study social life', we'd argue that the best answer to that question is to start by pondering all the different activities you might get stuck into, rather than picking a method that appeals and following the apparent rules associated with it. We've picked our title to emphasise that we're thinking through the options more than telling you what to do!

We'll admit that this book is not exhaustive either. There are many ways of doing social research. Some techniques are excluded. Others are covered in a particular way. What this book does do, however, is take a fresh look at some of the most popular social research activities and consider how we might tackle the challenges associated with each of them in original and effective ways.

THE CHAPTERS

Chapter 2. Warrants: Starting with What You Want Your Study to Achieve

People do social research for many reasons. Let's start with that. Still, it's not all that common that researchers reflect on their essential purpose in this way, though there's often a background hope that their work will be somehow helpful. Perhaps we should instead begin by working backwards from the impacts we hope to have in order to see what that means for our methods? Our first chapter is about getting you thinking about what could be called the 'warrant' of your study. We'll also work through how people might react to the results of different methods. Which kind of method fits with which kind of audience and what does that suggest about which methods are right for you? Our first chapter is a bit of a pep talk to get you thinking about the whole point. But it makes sense to start like this. After all, we'll never do a good job if we're unclear with ourselves about what we're trying to do.

Chapter 3. Observing: On Learning to Learn from Different Social Scenes

Then we get down to business with our first practical activity. If you're new to a place and you've no idea how to engage with the people there, watching what some of them are doing can be a very good start. That's why we've put it first. Plenty of researchers take this approach too. But how exactly does it work? Observation sounds exciting. But you could soon feel rather differently if you go somewhere and start freaking out because you don't seem to be seeing anything either interesting or relevant. Our second chapter considers the value of studying social life through observation, gives you some tips about how to do it well, and works through some interesting case studies to help you see how you'd make it a success: how to notice, and then usefully analyse, some of the actions of people *in situ*.

Chapter 4. Taking Part: Considering the Benefits of Getting Involved Ourselves

OK, so we can benefit from watching what people are up to. Hopefully, Chapter 3 has persuaded you of that. But could we get ourselves even closer to the action? Plenty of other researchers do that too. So, what might we learn if we personally get involved in a social setting or practice that interests us and how exactly do we put this interesting method into practice? In our fourth chapter, we'll consider these issues along with the various motivations for taking part in the first place. For some researchers, it might involve gaining a basic sense of the practicalities involved in structuring activities or places. For others, it might be more about building trust. And for yet others, taking part allows them to really appreciate the embodied experience of an activity or environment. Drawing on examples from various researchers who thought they should get involved themselves, we'll consider how you can enjoy taking part in social life whilst also ending up with insights you wouldn't otherwise get.

Chapter 5. Staging Talk: How to Do and Imagine Interviews

Talk is fundamental to much social research – humans are defined by their use of language, after all. However, the talk that social researchers 'stage' comes in many forms. Our fifth chapter starts by highlighting the many things that are going on when we speak with someone in a social research project. Then we'll give you a heads-up about how to make interviews work and the issues we'd encourage you to consider so as to pull off an effective interview. With those tips in place, we'll then think a bit harder about what to focus on in our talk with people.

Are interviewees responding to a challenging interaction that must be managed in certain ways as a means of handling this situational strangeness? Are we asking people to surface aspects of their lives they might not otherwise think very much about? Perhaps people are telling us the stories they live by when we talk to them – narrating an account of how they came to act or think in some ways instead of others? Interviews are sometimes framed as an opportunity to get 'rich' data from our respondents. Though this may be true at a general level, there are also different kinds of richness and different ways of getting it.

Chapter 6. Engaging People: Seeing Social Research as a Relationship

Next, we consider the benefits of seeing social research as a relationship. What kinds of 'roles' might we assume when forging new, albeit often temporary, relationships with people as part of this? And what are the implications of assuming different ones? These themes are prominent within interviews, but also common across many research techniques. In our sixth chapter, we'll consider the different ways that researchers might go about 'engaging' others – both to enrol them into our research endeavours and to encourage them to show or tell us useful things about what we are researching. We explore these issues not just because we should treat people appropriately and respectfully and in ways that show suitable gratitude. We do so because this can also suggest some tricks for working most productively with them. Some researchers play up their differences. Others aim to find common cause with people as a means of gaining trust. Drawing on examples, we'll think through the value of different strategies at different stages and show how an awareness of their impacts can make for better studies.

Chapter 7. Asking Questions: Exploring a Basic Act that Features in Many Methods

Like talk, it's pretty obvious that social researchers might be keen on asking questions. But the many ways in which they might do that can sometimes be overlooked because of exactly this obviousness. So, how should we pose our questions and what does that mean for how people will likely respond? How are we reproducing particular ideas, when we compose our questions, that sometimes means we don't end up learning all that much in our studies? We have questions about questions! In exploring them in Chapter 7, we'll stray across the borders between traditional method distinctions – this time, that which is often erected between methods like social surveys and others like interviews and focus groups. We'll work through particular styles and types of questioning to think about what's happening when we draw on each of them. We'll also, as with most of our chapters, give you some tips and suggestions about how you might think creatively about the kinds of questions that could really work for you.

Chapter 8. Playing with Words: Strategies for Seeing and Exploring Patterns

Often the result of asking all our questions or writing lots of notes is banks of words. What to do with all of those? This chapter turns to how we can organise our response to the written word. We'll look at both the words we've produced ourselves and the many possible sources of writing already out there in the world that social scientists might want to examine. We'll give you a sense of how this can work, consider the importance of paying attention to what exactly you're doing, and give you some ideas about how you might do it in different ways. Chapter 8 is partly about what practitioners often call 'coding', which might sound a bit scarily scientific. But our point is more that this is essentially about slowing down so you can see the patterns. So, what patterns should we look for? And where does that take us? We're playing with words here. But this kind of play is serious because, done well, it gives a new depth to our work. And without it, we can't really speak with confidence and authority about what we've found in our studies.

Chapter 9. Looking at Pictures: Ways of Getting Drawn into Social Worlds

This chapter focuses on how and why photographs and photography might be used in social research. The aim here is not to summarise established protocols but rather to look across a range of techniques to consider the different benefits of using photography. Chapter 9 focuses on three main themes. Firstly, the ways that photography might help you to develop and deepen your sense of the social sites you're studying. How can photos lead us into a better appreciation of how these contexts function and are dwelt in by people? Secondly, how photographs might help to draw some of the people you're studying into productive and revealing conversations. This might involve us as researchers asking people to produce photographs as a means of allowing us to momentarily see the world as they do and appreciate the environments they encounter. Thirdly, how we might use photos in our final research reports.

Chapter 10. Choosing: How Thinking about Cases and Samples Can Make for Innovative Projects

Having addressed the ways in which social researchers can work with people, Chapter 10 then steps back to consider how we choose what or who to look at the first place. What are the dilemmas involved in choosing the right selection of people, or interactions, or practices, or moments to study? For some researchers, choosing happens 'on the hoof' as they think on their feet in response to the opportunities associated with the research site at hand. For others, there are some fairly fixed conventions about how these selections should be made. Comparing traditions and questioning some common sampling assumptions allow us to think inventively about how you might design your own project. We'll also give you a few ideas about how to deal with the sampling anxieties our students often harbour.

Chapter 11. Writing: How to Present the Material We've Collected

Our final chapter considers how we translate what we've found into accounts and arguments that address particular audiences. We need to think about what we want to achieve – from making persuasive points to triggering emotions – in writing up our results. What kind of final research account do we want to produce? How long should our quotes be? What are we really doing when we present a vignette? By comparing examples of different writing strategies – and reflecting on how they'll likely be received by different readers – we go back to the 'warrants' we introduced in Chapter 2. The basic idea is that, in order for us to do the studies that are right for us, we need to think about what we want to achieve with our written outputs. We'll also explore some of the most common issues of concern at this stage. What words to use to describe those we've studied and what should we call ourselves? How might we use theory to help us out? What are references for and when should they be used? And, finally, how do we even write the thing?

Coda: The People Who Inspired Us and Ideas for Further Reading

For those interested in digging further into the methods discussed in the preceding chapters, or who are curious about our inspirations, we finish up with some further readings. Taking each chapter in turn, we provide an annotated list of some of the books and articles we've either drawn on extensively or see as good starting points for getting into the literature on each topic.

Let's Get Exploring!

You'll remember what we said at the start about social research being an adventure. Well, let's get on and do some exploring then. In the chapters that follow we'll be drawing on our experiences with a variety of fellow explorers. You'll hear quite a bit about our undergraduate field class on ways of studying everyday life in cities, that master's level course we've already introduced, and a variety of student and PhD projects we've helped out with, and our teaching with undergraduates to prepare them for doing dissertations also gets a mention. As we also said earlier, this book isn't intended to be exhaustive. But it does aim to demystify the activities that social researchers most often do and help you to put them to use in effective and innovative ways. It's the book we wish we'd read before we started out ourselves. We hope it helps you as you plan for and embark upon some of your own social research adventures.

2

WARRANTS: STARTING WITH WHAT YOU WANT YOUR STUDY TO ACHIEVE

THREE PIECES OF EVIDENCE

The ball bounces towards Polo with the mouth of the goal wide open in front of him. His team is down by one goal and time is running out in the pick-up soccer game in a West Los Angeles park. He winds up to smash the ball into the back of the net. But perhaps reveling in his game-tying goal just a little too soon, he pulls back and sends the ball over the cross bar.

'¡Barusa!' (Garbage!)
'¡Estúpido!' (Stupid!)
'¡Viejito!' (Old timer!)
'Jugador de parque!' (Park player!)

These are the opening lines of David Trouille's *Fútbol in the park: Immigrants, soccer, and the creation of social ties* (2021), a study of working-class, Latin American, migrant men in Los Angeles. This description of a moment at the end of a casual football – okay, soccer if you must – game introduces readers to the key characters in Trouille's study. It also introduces them to its key themes: community, masculinity, and how public parks sustain social networks for Latino migrants. His description presents a distinctive illustration of a certain style of social research, an empathetically oriented style of engaged research that invites readers into the world of those being written about.

Now look at the map in Figure 2.1. This presents some results from a rather different research mode. The map is from Eric Klinenberg's *Heatwave: A social autopsy of disaster in Chicago* (2002). It compares the relationship between violent crime rates and death rates during the 1995 Chicago heatwave and shows how that varies. The map reveals to the reader – and Klinenberg – that there's some kind of relationship between a neighbourhood's crime rate and the number of deaths likely to happen within it during this kind of extreme weather event. But it also hints that there is much more evidence that is going to need to be examined before any conclusion might be reached on the nature of this relationship. So, though we know less of the lived experience, Klinenberg's map suggests that patterns of inequality or injustice might be entangled with who lives and dies in a heatwave.

Other pieces of evidence might more bluntly speak to an injustice in different societies. Take our third piece of evidence. The following interview quote comes

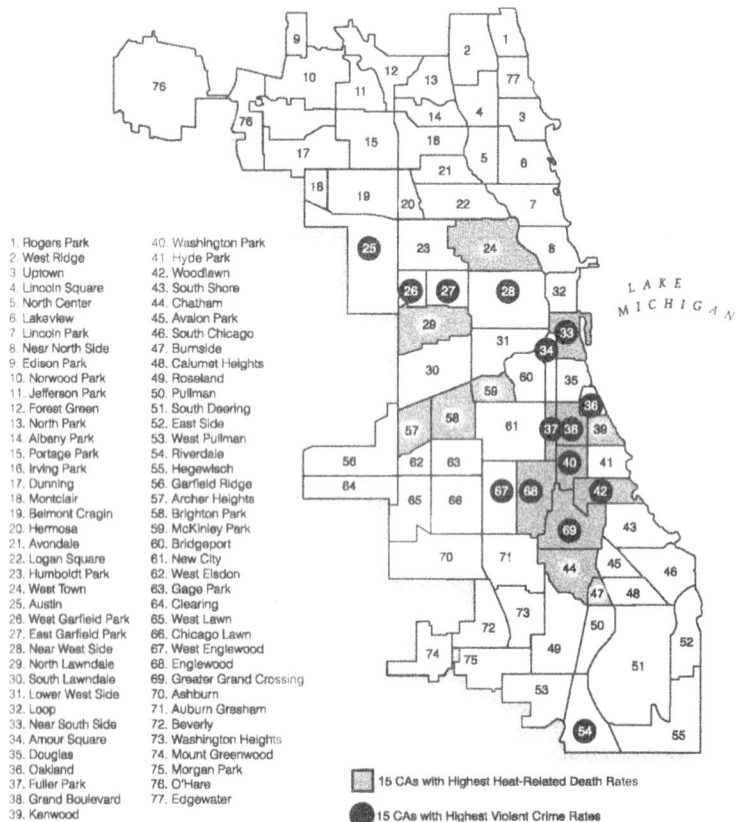

Figure 2.1 Comparing heat-related mortality and crime rates across Chicago
Source: Klinenberg, 2002, figure 24, p. 83

from Sarah M. Hall and colleagues' report: *Intersecting inequalities: The impact of austerity on Black and minority ethnic women in the UK* (2017):

> 'At uni there's not many people from my background – most of them don't have to work, I have to work to put myself through. The opportunities they get, if there's like an internship to New York, they can just go, because they don't have to worry about money, whereas that is a problem for me.'
>
> (Interview, Manchester) (p. 36)

The reader is immediately confronted with the stark reality of how university study can be experienced quite differently by those from economically straitened families compared to those from wealthier ones. We feel the resignation of the interviewee about what others can easily do but is impossible for them. This interview extract – like many of the others collected in the report – helps to hammer home how certain groups particularly must contend with the inequalities that run through UK life.

We'll return to these three examples to help us develop some suggestions about how we can make sure we do social research that fits with our underlying aims. As social researchers, we often start out with rather grand ideas about what we're going to do. There's nothing wrong with that – doing good social research is hard, so you'd expect people to have a powerful sense of purpose to get them through the challenges they'll inevitably face. But that does make it especially important to be sure about what you're trying to achieve, especially when there are many underlying motivations to choose from.

At the start of our master's level methods course, we ask the students why we might want to do social research in the first place. And we get a lot of different answers. Our students are a smart and lively bunch and they always impress us with the variety of answers they come up with. Still, the exercise can also sometimes be challenging for them at the start, as it can be for many of us. We've often a background mix of purposes that we don't always subject to scrutiny. Our students eventually tell us that we might do social research to shape policy, explore the world, create new knowledge, test theories, find solutions to problems, see what's going on, question vested interests, debunk false ideas, solve disputes, tell new stories, generate new theories, verify concepts, give voice to others, and even to understand ourselves. There's quite a lot going on there – quite a lot of possible purposes.

These are all good reasons for doing social research. But this variety also poses questions for the budding social researcher: How should they decide which is the right reason for them? And how do different approaches fit with different ambitions? From their list of ambitions, it's tempting – comforting certainly – to conclude this is probably about personal preference; that the answer depends on the kind of person that we are. That's helpful and true up to a point. However, we tell them that we want to dig into things a bit more deeply. If there are a range of ways of doing social research – in terms of how we both undertake our projects and present our results – perhaps we need to start by identifying our essential aims since different aims can take us towards different methods.

THE WARRANTS OF SOCIAL RESEARCH

Some years ago, Jack Katz (1997) wondered about how researchers might justify their way of studying social life when speaking with others. Katz does a similar kind of research work to the soccer study in seeking to make sense of a group, institution, organisation, or place through detailed descriptions of the everyday practices and understandings of those involved. The research accounts – journal articles, books, policy reports – produced through such research run the risk of presenting nothing more than what the insiders under investigation already know. And if they simply tell us what those on the ground already know, then the reader might reasonably ask, 'So what?' This is an important challenge for social researchers, especially when the power of the research method into which they've trained means they often overlook these 'so what' questions, since to them the value of their endeavours is obvious.

For Katz, we'd be wrong to dismiss such 'so what' questions. Why? Because considering such basic questions forces us, as social researchers, to explicitly consider the 'warrants' that underpin our work. As you might know, a warrant is a justification for an action or belief. In law, a warrant is often a legal document that sets out the legality of an action – a warrant for someone's arrest, or a search warrant for the police to search a property. In social research, warrants, the justifications for why our research is being carried out, are rarely so explicit. More commonly they're part of the assumed shared understanding of what makes for worthwhile research within different research communities. Katz's argument is that if a researcher is aiming to convince others of the value of their efforts – which they should – they need to reflect on the warrant of their study when presenting their work, not least because different warrants speak to different justifications, and potentially different audiences.

Pretty much all social research tends to take its warrant for granted. This can be an issue not just for uninitiated readers who may find themselves confused about the point. But it's also one for experienced researchers. It's important to think carefully about this because there are many possible warrants – and many ways of justifying the value – of the research done. Our student poll suggested that these warrants can run from informing government policy to questioning vested interests, from articulating the challenges faced by others to generating new theories of social life. Different warrants can pull us in different directions, demanding different styles of investigation, of analysis, and of final presentation.

It can be tempting to take a maximalist approach – to claim that the research delivers on many warrants at the same time. After all, what researcher wants to be pigeon-holed? The pitfall in taking such a stance is that, by trying to claim too many warrants, a piece of research, be that the whole project or an individual piece of writing, may be less effective in addressing any one of them.

There are some places within the social sciences where the purpose and methods for doing research are more or less non-contentious – everyone does broadly the same thing in a way that is reassuringly familiar. Economics, with its particular interest in econometric models is one, the part of social psychology that undertakes tightly defined experiments is another. But, in many other areas, and certainly in the worlds of human geography and environmental studies that we inhabit, there is no single agreed general warrant for undertaking social research, rather there are multiple overlapping warrants. We think we can see three broad types of warrants circulating through the work of social researchers.

Just Understanding Something

A first group of warrants focuses on the basic idea of deepening our understanding of an issue or topic. This is perhaps the classic understanding of what social researchers are about. We – and by the way we are assuming you are also a social researcher or someone with aspirations to be one – are motivated to study the social world because we want to understand it better. This might be motivated by pure curiosity. More often, however, such social research is also motivated by a parallel warrant: that by understanding something we can improve things in some way. Klinenberg's *Heatwave* is in many ways an exemplary case study. *Heatwave*'s overall aim was to use the tools of social research to understand who dies during hot weather events, and why some people died whilst others survived. Through a well-designed combination of area-based analysis, in-depth interviews, and on-the-ground observation, he discovered that age, social isolation, economic deprivation, high local crime rates, and poor neighbourhood amenities interacted in various ways to put people at risk. In tracing out the relationships between individual and neighbourhood vulnerability, he didn't just provide an improved understanding of the effects of extreme weather events like heatwaves in cities. He also pointed to a range of policies to mitigate the effects of such events in the future.

Witnessing or Giving a Platform to a Group

A second warrant is about witnessing or giving voice to a group. Contemporary societies are complex and hierarchical. Yet it is easy to think that the way we go about organising ourselves or making sense of life is the same as everyone else's. Actually, the everyday lives of other groups are often puzzling. Often the ways of life of minority groups are framed by the majority as anti-social, deviant, or destructive. Equally, other practices or groups may simply be overlooked or ignored, meaning they receive inadequate societal recognition and resource. Addressing this, a second warrant for many social scientists is to bear witness to or to bring forward such marginalised groups or practices. Through a careful and respectful engagement with the people involved, these researchers are animated by the idea of demonstrating the nature and value of the way of life being researched. The Latino migrants in Trouille's *Fútbol in the park*, for example, are often seen as problematic by neighbourhood residents and other park uses. This is perhaps unsurprising when the pitch on which they play is in an affluent, middle-class area that is overwhelmingly white. For many, the presence of so many boisterous, Spanish speaking, working-class men is intimidating. Trouille's study shows the importance of daily park soccer matches for participants. It also demonstrates the effort the soccer players make to be responsible park users, and how they're adjusting their actions in response to the existing park use rules. What can seem from outside to be a somewhat chaotic setting is, in fact, carefully – if informally – regulated. In writing about the migrant soccer players he's spent a great deal of time with, Trouille provides a window into the lives of a frequently stigmatised group. He also shows how the men in the study have become a part of the everyday fabric of a Los Angeles community, along with the work they've put into this.

Highlighting Injustice

A final group of social researchers sees social critique as the key warrant for its research. This kind of critical researcher is motivated by highlighting or revealing inequalities and injustices. The aim, for example, of the report by Hall et al. is to show how exactly Black and ethnic minority women have been disproportionately affected by changes to the United Kingdom's social benefit system after the recession that started in 2008. It does this through both presenting a statistical analysis of the differential impact of cuts to a range of benefits, alongside excerpts from focus group interviews with Black and ethnic minority women. Interview quotes, like the one we presented towards the start of this chapter, highlight the experience of living as a Black or ethnic minority woman at this time. It reveals how it feels to be the subject of the injustices of these cuts. The point of revealing or highlighting injustice is not simply to provide a dispassionate account of what is going on. For researchers working with the warrant of social critique, they hope to move the reader into some kind of action to change or transform the world. In fact, the warrant of social critique almost always reaches past the scope of the material presented. Revealing cases of injustice doesn't just expose what is wrong in the case in hand, it also points to the ways society is more broadly unjust. The report doesn't just tell the reader about the unequal impacts of a decade of benefit cuts on Black and ethnic minority women in the UK, it also highlights how these women are fundamentally disadvantaged in British society.

Before we go further, it's important to emphasise that these three groups often overlap. And there are also – as our students told us – others. In that sense, this is more about thinking through those to which we are drawn. For now, the point is to recognise that different warrants can lead to different approaches. If we want to give people a platform, then we can start by seeing how their lives go on. If we want to understand how something works, we can collect data and then hopefully that will help us to do that. If we want to document injustice, perhaps we can simply ask about how that is experienced.

WHAT DATA DOES

So far, we have emphasised how it's important to get your warrant straight when you are starting off with a social research project. This isn't always clear to many researchers when they do their studies. But knowing what you want to achieve will help you achieve it. Another way of thinking through these issues is about reflecting on different ways of engaging with audiences. Different methods present different possibilities for connecting with those who we hope will take an interest in our work. With that in mind, let's return for a final time to our three evidence examples to reflect on how they speak to us and to others who might, if the researchers have done their job thoughtfully, take an interest. Many, though not all, researchers would call this their 'data'; it represents the raw material out of which we develop our accounts of the social world. So, what do different forms of 'data' do?

The Footballer's Friend

Let's return to the soccer match. It's worth saying here that this excerpt comes from a book. Books presuppose a particular kind of engagement on the part of the reader. We know we are in for the long haul with a book. We're settling down to a slow, hopefully expert exposition. This fits well with the kind of data that Trouille has produced. He is telling us a kind of story, and the authority to speak about his soccer group is granted gradually by the reader as we are drawn into a world described so well that we cannot help but believe this is the truth of the situation. Writing quality really matters here, so that it is worth thinking about if we hope to emulate such a study. But it's also about the material that Trouille has assembled. Being there, and paying attention to the detail, provide the nuances and asides that colour his account and bring it alive. We're living that moment on the soccer field along with them. We're gradually coming to know individuals within the book pages – Polo, Motor, Roberto, Valderrama, Mi Chavo, Titi – and perhaps even coming to care about them. Different audiences will respond in different ways to Trouille's invitation into their lives. Other researchers will perhaps enjoy the feeling of being taken along on such a journey, but they'll also be wanting to know sooner rather than later what that means for how they should think about masculinity or park management. Perhaps members of the public might have more time. They might enjoy certain forms of writing where the aim is to entertain as much as to impress intellectually, and the way in which the writing transports the reader into the situation could be especially exhilarating. If we put them into other people's shoes, they might learn to think in new ways about broader political issues and question their standpoints. Finally, it could also be worth addressing those who are in a position to effect change – government officials, charities, campaigning groups. But can we see them reading this book in the office when they need to be working efficiently and effectively? Perhaps if the author is lucky and the policymaker really cares about their work, the book might find its way onto their bedside table where it could help to solidify their passion for change and thereby eventually seep into their working lives back in the office.

The Graph or Map Maker

The graph or map is easy to handle even if it took a great deal of effort to produce. These devices feel authoritative. It seems hard to contest them because the workings are hidden away as we are drawn into particular ways of seeing the issue. We can also present it quite easily. We can imagine the graph going down better in the policymaker's office because they need to know the facts more than read a book. In that sense, the graph or map maker is partly showing respect to their audiences by going to the trouble of making something that clearly illustrates some finding or another. They don't want to waste people's time with depictions that don't tell them anything. There are no doubt emotional stories in the experiences that eventually gave rise to the data that informed the graph or map. Indeed, if we allow ourselves to dwell upon the meaning of the graph or map, the lived experiences that made some of the black circles bigger than others are harrowing to imagine. Still, the tone here is professional, and the numbers and scales suggest a confident platform for action – we know where they had it worst and we should target our efforts there if we want to avoid more deaths as climate change continues to kick in. The mechanism seems clear and the course of action seems obvious. A statistic about how location shapes the death toll might also be easier to circulate on social media platforms in ways that elicit a response partly based on how statistics such as these are imbued with a sense of authority.

The Report Writer

Contemporary societies have many institutional layers. This means that there often isn't a single policy audience, but many. Still, to write effectively for your chosen audience requires thinking carefully about the characteristics of the particular audience you wish to address. Take the report on ethnicity (Hall et al., 2017). This directly addresses policymakers; it's a report after all, and a report has different conventions to a book or an academic paper. As with the graph and map, the idea is that the reader may not have too much time to delve into the social world under scrutiny and therefore needs to be told the facts of the matter quickly and efficiently. The report has an executive summary at the start – a set of bullet points, or 'headline findings' for the imagined executive who has lots of other things on her desk. Some of the most important and arresting facts are written in red inside boxes with borders that attract the eye. But rather than being directed at central government – those politicians and civil servants who had fashioned the policies of austerity in the UK – the report aims to inform other organisations working in social policy, such as NGOs and local authorities, of the unequal impacts. To reach this audience the report draws on well-known social research techniques and uses quotes from interviewees to speak for themselves. It doesn't complicate its discussion with intricate academic arguments either. If as a social researcher your warrant is to speak directly to those making policy, then writing simply and directly is crucial. But in presenting these quotes, the report sits somewhere between the soccer study and the heatwave map in the sense that there is an attempt to address the reader on an emotional level – by showing how the respondents spoke of their challenges in their own words, with the resignation we highlighted just a moment ago – whilst also speaking directly to possible responses.

As a quick side note, it is perhaps worth stressing at this point that we're interested in this chapter in different 'tropes' of presenting social research, using the three evidence examples to consider how they address specific audiences. Though our students often end up using single methods, Klinenberg's *Heatwave* presents a nuanced argument that, as well as using maps and statistics, draws on many in-depth interviews. Hall et al's. report also includes a wide range of different forms of evidence.

CONCLUSION

Many researchers don't spend all that much time thinking about the warrant that underpins their research. Rather they often end up being well versed in specific approaches and techniques, either because those are the techniques that appealed to them at the start of their careers, or because they have been recruited into particular cultures of working that predominate in their fields. In this primer chapter, we've argued that, perhaps especially when you're starting out on your social research journey, it's worth reflecting on what you want to achieve with your work and how effective particular forms of data may be in helping you with that. Many researchers are guided by multiple warrants but that doesn't mean we shouldn't think about them. Perhaps that means that we particularly should.

Ultimately, whether a social research project is good or bad rests on whether it delivers on its warrant – whether it provides the evidence that allows it to speak in the right ways to its intended audience. And, whilst the discipline you work in will have certain rules and expectations, hopefully you're interested in studying social life not just to reassure them that you've learnt their rules. You're also trying to do something in the world. So, before we get stuck into the techniques you might feasibly use in your studies, thinking about these issues can help with that. In effect, we've asked you to think backwards to your fundamental ambitions and forwards to how different audiences might respond to your results. We'll say more about writing in Chapter 11. But before we get started on the nitty-gritty of specific techniques, it's good to check in regularly with yourself about these questions. In this book we'll attempt to enthuse you about a variety of practical tools for doing social research. But the right way of studying social life for you ultimately rests on the warrants that underpin your research.

3
OBSERVING: ON LEARNING TO LEARN FROM DIFFERENT SOCIAL SCENES

LOOKING AT OTHER PEOPLE FROM A BENCH

Imagine yourself sitting on a bench somewhere near the centre of a town or city you know. There are plenty of people around. You've chosen a spot inside a busy train station perhaps and you've started to notice bursts of activity just after the platforms are announced. Maybe you're imagining a sunny day and you've taken advantage of that by picking somewhere pleasant in a park where others are enjoying the weather too. In both situations, the people around you will be doing all sorts of things. Some are pushing buggies along whilst they talk animatedly with accompanying friends. Others may be hurrying with their luggage as they attempt to navigate an environment full of obstacles. There's often a great deal going on in these places when we allow ourselves to pause for a second and take it all in. These various goings-on can provide rich pickings for the budding observational researcher.

But how exactly do you do it? Though there may be a great deal of interesting things happening around us, it isn't always easy to move from a kind of aimless people watching to observing in the more systematic and rigorous way that allow us to say we've done a 'proper' study afterwards. Researchers can't simply jump from noticing something interesting to making convincing statements about how social life goes on in the places that interest them. Just because we've seen something arresting happen once doesn't mean that such an event is common or necessarily significant to how things work there. So, if we want to be rigorous social researchers – as opposed to say social commentators or opinion columnists – we need to develop effective ways of doing something more. This chapter explores how social researchers use observation as a research technique and how you can make it work for you.

We'll start with an example to hopefully convince you about the value of this approach. Then we'll consider why social researchers use observation – starting with its usefulness for getting to know research settings. Then we'll consider the challenges associated with effectively pulling it off. As you'll see, that's all about where you go, how you take your notes, and how you'd tackle the various issues and anxieties that follow when you put this approach into practice. Finally, we'll consider how observation can sometimes also mean listening and end with some words of encouragement when this method can help us to notice the importance of things we'd never thought much about before.

BEFORE OUR VERY EYES

Let's return to that scenario in which you're sitting on a bench in a familiar city. Imagine how you'd divide up the people around you into two groups, each of which has a reasonable number within it, and each of which is moving around. This would be easier to do if you were actually there, of course. Indeed, we'd encourage you to go out to do the various exercises described throughout this book if you can – becoming an effective social researcher, after all, is, we think, about trying out different techniques to see whether you find them enjoyable, rewarding, and effective. Still, it's not impossible to picture the experience too. Either way, this is an exercise we've often done with our undergraduate field class students shortly after arriving in a new city together. This is what we've asked them to do next:

> *First, generate a basic diagram of the site that you have chosen, depicting the essential features of the setting. Then find, and settle into, a place that provides you with a comfortable, but reasonably unobtrusive, point from which to track people's movements. Then start depicting the flows of your two chosen groups, using two coloured pens to annotate your diagram. Each of your two groups should be allocated a different colour. The idea is to follow the members of each group with the relevant pen. Then we'll see what the exercise suggests.*

But what two categories? What kinds of people should be assigned to each colour? We tell our students at this point that it can pay to be creative with their choices. Some decide to compare men and women or those who seem to be alone and those who are clearly part of groups – couples and so forth. Another popular choice is to compare younger and older people, though for that you'd need to think quite hard about your working definitions: is this based on whether they have grey or white hair, for example, and, if not, how would we do it? Running with our advice about being creative, they sometimes decide to compare those who are, or are not, wearing certain kinds of clothing. Could there be differences between those in trainers and those in smarter shoes? Or those wearing coats and those without? Because we've often done this in sight-seeing spots, a popular choice has often been tourists and non-tourists. But the problem there again is being confident about who the tourists are.

Figure 3.1 is a diagram that one of our students produced (we've changed it so it works in black and white). The big black star represents where the student sat. You can see from their diagram – just about – that they'd decided to go to some sort of park. That's why there are flower beds at the bottom. There's also a bridge they were facing at the top and a convergence of paths that some – though not all – stuck to. In the evening, we'd showed diagrams like these to the rest of the class, asking them to guess what the two line-types were indicating: who are the full-line people and who are the dashed? Why don't you take a moment now to have a go yourself. Perhaps the dashed lines might indicate older people who are more reticent about straying too far from more stable walking surfaces. Could the full lines be showing how children are too inquisitive to care about social conventions to do with sticking to paths?

The answer was that the full lines were for people interacting with smartphones in some way. The dashed lines represented everyone else. The eddies that take you unthinkingly out of the main current of movement when you get engrossed in a call immediately spring to mind when we look at how some of the dashed lines peel off and isolate themselves from the others immediately after crossing the bridge. Perhaps the single phone user who ventured into the flower

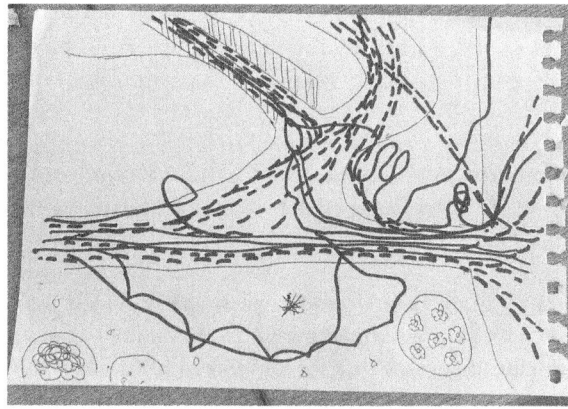

Figure 3.1 Watching two kinds of people move around an urban park
Source: Russell Hitchings

beds was inspecting the specimens and taking snaps for social media. Regardless of the mental pictures we could paint in attempting to explain this diagram, the point is that, by picking two categories we might not have previously thought a great deal about, we're starting to notice things we'd likely otherwise overlook.

As inquisitive social researchers we attend more closely to certain details of human experience than we otherwise would. It's an exciting feeling when we start to notice things that were 'before our very eyes' all along, but we hadn't yet forced ourselves to explore. What's also appealing about this approach is that we're not jumping the gun with premature explanation – for example, looking for evidence that fits with our preconceived ideas about how park life works. Rather we're allowing the context to open itself up to us. It might be interesting to look at how phone practices in parks are different at different times. Maybe this aspect of social life works out differently in other parks you know? Either way, there seemed to be something going on with how smartphones influence the ways in which people moved around that part of the park. And it's something we'd probably not have noticed before.[1]

But why might we want to notice these things? That's a question that's often asked by our students on the field class, sometimes in an exasperated way after being forced to look at something banal for longer than they'd otherwise like or enjoy. We say to them that the implications of 'trusting the process' in this way will become apparent afterwards, but that there are generally interesting implications that follow. Perhaps, for example, being stuck on your phone means that you don't get the relaxing experience you hoped for from the park, even though that's exactly why you'd gone!

FIVE REASONS TO USE OBSERVATION

That was just one way of doing observation in social research. But now we've whetted your appetite about its potential with our smartphone example, let's step back to consider some of the main reasons why social researchers do it.

1   *They don't know what's important yet.* Perhaps the most common reason for turning to observation is to get an initial handle on the contexts we want to understand. At the start of a project, we might have a sense from reading

---

1 Svarre and Gehl's (2013) *How to study public life* provided inspiration for this activity. They spent a lot of time observing and cataloguing what goes on in public spaces; often producing diagrams that looked like sophisticated versions of the one our student produced. Another source was Bissell (2009) whose diagrams of passenger movement in train stations gave him an initial sense of human movement there.

existing research of why a particular context might be interesting – perhaps we've decided that parks are important, but we don't know yet what people are doing there. So, if you've a sense that people could be doing something interesting in a particular situation or place or just want a better grasp of how certain social contexts work – who knew that smartphones shaped human movement around parks!? – observation can be a very good way to begin. The idea here is that you can't yet claim to know the most interesting and important questions to ask about the social context at hand. You'd rather wait and see what turns out to be important and interesting once you've spent some time there.

2 *They think the detail will help later.* The idea that observation is something that we do at the start of a research project suggests that, for many researchers, as they get deeper into them, observation will become less important. For many projects this is indeed the case. However, detail from fieldwork observations can also be helpful when researchers come to write up their results. As we said in Chapter 2, one of the tricks for engaging people with the research we've done is to provide the readers of our outputs – be it a dissertation, a report, or a book – with an intimate sense of the people and places we've studied. We'll say more about all that in Chapter 11 when we turn to writing. But if your research is going to depend at least in part on demonstrating that you were in a place, and on engaging your chosen audiences with how life goes on there, then having some observational detail on file can turn out to be quite helpful.

3 *They don't want to disturb things.* One of the most common rationales is about minimising the effect of us being there. If we do that, perhaps we're in a better position to see and explore the reality of how life goes on in particular places. By fading into the background through various means – we'll discuss those shortly – and allowing ourselves to concentrate on what exactly is happening around us, we can eventually understand people's lived realities better. This is called 'naturalistic' research since it's based on the idea that the best understandings come from watching things happen as they 'naturally' would with people going about their business in ways that are ideally undisturbed by our presence as researchers.

4 *They suspect people can't talk about certain things.* Much of how social life goes on is relatively automatic for the people involved. Certainly, we don't always attend to the detail of how we act in familiar environments. That's often a good thing when you think about it. Imagine if you had to reflect on everything that you physically did as part of your morning routine. That would be exhausting, and you'd be late. If our student asked a smartphone user why they had deviated from the main path, they'd probably look at them quite strangely! Yet perhaps these are exactly the things that should interest us as social researchers. Once something has become

'taken-for-granted' in this way it might be particularly powerful since those involved no longer really think about it anymore. And so, for some social researchers, understanding how cultural contexts work is all about noticing what the people there don't often notice themselves.

5   *They suspect people won't talk about certain things.* A final cornerstone argument for observing is that what people do and what they say they do can often be very different things. In other words, and going beyond the idea that our actions are often unconscious, people might want to present themselves in particular ways were we to ask them about what they do. We'll discuss that in more detail in Chapter 5. But people certainly often do have all sorts of ideas about how they want to present their experience to us and ideally be portrayed in our reports. With that in mind, if we really want to examine the reality of how things work out in different social contexts and situations, it makes sense to go and have a look ourselves.

We've chosen this as our first method because it's the least interventionist of approaches. It's also here because, as we've said, many studies start with some observation – why not go and have a look first if you can? Certainly, observation can often be particularly good at helping us to identify aspects of social life that might need to be more fully researched through some of the other methods we'll discuss (say you notice something that you'd like to ask those involved about). Observation can be excellent for generating new ideas to explore in more detail, and maybe through other methods.

If all that sounds good, let's consider some tricks for doing observation well. We're going to start with where you might do your observation and then move to thinking about how you take notes.

WHERE TO GO?

Our initial smartphone example was all about how observation can help you think in new ways about what's immediately before you. And that's certainly one of the strengths of the approach. Naturalistic observation is a kind of systematic 'people watching' – which many of us enjoy – that allows us to uncover, and then examine, patterns of social life. But we also need to think carefully about where and when observation works. Spradley (1980) talks about identifying a 'social scene'. For him, this is a place where people come together on a repeated basis such that it makes sense to spend time watching what they do there before mulling over the details. But beyond that, as we see it, there are essentially two things to be sure about when picking a viable 'social scene' for observation. We'll exemplify them now, each with reference to a study focused on how societies attempt to keep their members healthy.

Top Tip 1. Go Somewhere You Don't Mind Being

Zaman (2008) was a medical doctor before turning to the pleasures of social research. He thought to combine his professional background and current academic interest by spending time on some hospital wards in Bangladesh. His hunch was that things worked differently there to hospitals elsewhere. Perhaps local cultural issues of status and gender, along with beliefs about the importance of the family, might be seen in the mundane detail of Bangladeshi hospital life? And perhaps examining that might lead to some valuable conclusions about how, despite the ambitions of managers hoping to emulate efficiency models from elsewhere, hospital cultures are not all the same. He persuaded people to let him hang out in some hospitals and, partly because of his background, was allowed to wander the wards and shadow staff who might be interacting with patients in ways that might help him to explore these issues. He tried different techniques as the project went on, gradually identifying the social situations that were most interesting to him and thinking about how to take notes on those.

The point we want to make though is that the project worked partly because this was a context in which he could legitimately linger and in which he knew he wouldn't mind spending some time based on his professional past. If you are thinking about using observational techniques, give some thought in advance to contexts that could work for you. Places where you already go can be good choices here; though you might need to work a little harder to notice the details when it's already familiar. Places where you could get a job or volunteer in some way can be smart choices too because then you can wait for the most interesting things to happen whilst also having a socially recognised reason to be there – bars, canteens, cafés, hairdressers, and gyms can all work well for this.

Top Tip 2. Go Somewhere Interesting Things are Happening

In Iran, Sadati et al. (2016) were less keen on following their noses in terms of gradually exploring how life goes on in the hospital in the way that Zaman was. They'd already decided that they needed to understand how doctors interacted with their patients. Theirs was a different kind of observation in the sense that they knew they wanted to enumerate how many times the doctor mentions the patient's name, how often they established eye contact, and the amount of time they allowed themselves to discuss patient concerns. So, this was less about waiting to see what is interesting and more about taking some much more targeted notes. In this case, they'd already defined their focus and were motivated by a sense that things might not be working as well as they ideally would. The result was a table that exposed the truth of what really went on there in stark numerical terms; this was more than about saying this 'often happened', it was about offering precise figures on the frequency of actions.

For our purposes, the point here is that they went somewhere they knew that interesting patterns of interaction were waiting for them. Whilst they couldn't so readily say they were allowing the context to slowly reveal its secrets, they did know they would be able to analyse important issues to do with levels of patient care through their observation.

So where might certain patterns of interaction or movement be observed and examined in detail? There are lots of excellent examples that researchers have come up with in the past. Looking at how meetings work or what takes place in courtrooms has gone well because there are unwritten rules to these interactions that those involved may be too busy to notice. These represent rich pickings for observation researchers. You could also look at how people go through doors or what they do together – where they look, when and whether they interact, how they manage their bodies to avoid any 'social discomfort' – on busy commuter trains. For those of us who are studying at universities, lecture theatres and classrooms have proved productive places for observation too: Who sits where and why? In what sequences do different groups tend to interact or engage? Of course, whilst it's good to have a background sense that the context to which you'll go might be amenable to the method, another strategy would be to go and see whether some of the techniques we'll talk about in this chapter could help you to spot things. So, whilst you should think about this before, a good observer can often spot something intriguing, and you'll never know if something interesting is going on if you haven't looked.

INSIDE THE NOTEBOOK: DIFFERENT WAYS OF WRITING FIELDNOTES

We've talked about why you might want to observe, and we've now given you some ideas about where it might work for you. But how to do it? This book is called 'How to study social life', after all, so how do you do effective social research observation? For many practitioners, this means 'notebooks': commonly imagined as durable books that aren't too big in which the researcher can jot down thoughts and observations either when they are there or soon afterwards. Beyond that, these notebooks can, however, seem rather mysterious in many accounts, partly because researchers don't often like to say too much about all the messy details and dead ends that are frequently buried within them. We don't always like to admit that we've written things down that proved useless or started to develop hunches in our notebooks that ended up unexplored. But the basic idea is that the observer is jotting down all sorts of things. Hopefully through doing so, they'll be getting new ideas about what's going on there, and over time they'll start to more systematically explore features that could be important.

Some observers don't have a notebook. Or, at least, they don't take their notebook out until they're somewhere more comfortable. According to their thinking, if one of the reasons for doing observation is about letting things happen as they 'naturally' would, having someone writing notes in the corner might encourage people to behave – at least a little – differently. But can we reasonably be expected to remember it all when this method is partly about attending to the detail? Either way, we think it's worth looking inside some notebooks because how we decide to take observational notes is never a matter of effortless recording. We must always make decisions about what is worth making notes on now and thinking about later, much as we might like to present ourselves as simply 'soaking up' the scene before effortlessly recording our insightful observations. Mason (2002) makes no bones about how this aspect is often discussed. As she stresses, 'simply "hanging around" in an unfocused way can be notoriously time-consuming, unproductive, exhausting and sometimes embarrassing or risky' (p. 90).

One good way of getting a sense of how we might effectively use a notebook is to compare examples. So, let's do that! We'd now like you to imagine yourself in another urban context. Now you're in a Berlin café. It's on the edge of a large park not too far from the main parliament building. Both features have made it quite attractive to tourists, which is probably why the café is busy. Selling a range of German favourites (think lots of sausages) and with a large outdoor seating area, our café is proving to be an attractive place for visitors to stop for a snack. Perhaps it's also a good spot for some social research observation? There's a lot going on and it's a nice place to be for a while (both of which are often important features in making observation work for you). Here's a picture to give you some context:

Figure 3.2 A café in Berlin that could be good for observation
Source: Russell Hitchings

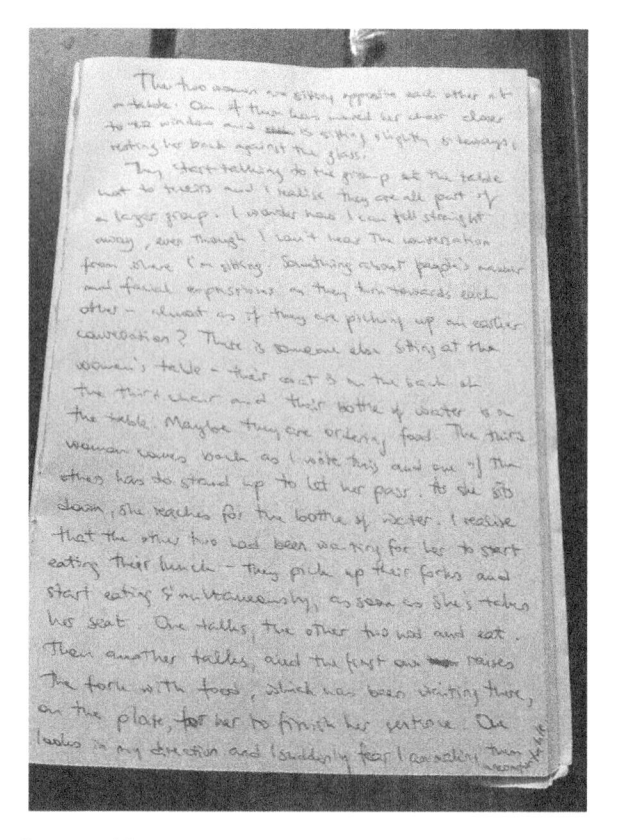

Figure 3.3 The first set of field notes from the café courtyard
Source: Russell Hitchings

With all that in mind, during a very welcome break from a busy day of teaching on a field class, two researchers thought to do some observation whilst seated in the outside area of the café. They bought a coffee and a slice of cake to share, settled in, and took out their notebooks. But what did they end up focusing on? And what did their notebooks look like as a result?

Figure 3.3 is an example. We know it's hard to pick out the detail. But you can see that we've sentences here. Or, at least, some sentences. This researcher is writing down sequences of interactions between those they see around them. There is a sense in which this is a stream of consciousness – for now they are just writing down what they are seeing in terms of how certain actions follow others. Someone's 'reaching for a bottle of water' in a way that apparently signals to the wider group that others can now start eating. In one way, these notes could be serving as a memory jogger for the researcher. They might wisely be thinking that it could be worth having some of these details to hand later to teleport themselves, and potentially the readers of their work, back into the moment mentally and remember how life in this Berlin café went on at lunchtimes. Perhaps the idea is to read through these notes later to decide upon what they might want to pay more attention to next time or to look at all the notes collected at the end and spot particular recurring themes or issues. But there is also the start of something a little more analytical happening here: they are starting to identify certain interesting processes too. Maybe there's something interesting about café etiquette here? Or, perhaps more accurately, conflicting 'etiquette cultures' when customers at this café clearly came from many different countries, bringing with them varied ideas about how they should negotiate food counters, other diners, trays, cutlery troughs, and so on. Maybe there could be something interesting to learn from how they collaborate to get food together. It's in such moments of interaction, after all, that we develop and test out our opinions on other groups – which groups wait their turn in ways that somehow feel right to us, and which ones have less of a problem with leaning over for the sausages? So, the detail of what different groups do together in cafés might be more important than we might have previously thought. Perhaps this café food counter can be seen – or, at least, studied – as a microcosm of international collaboration! Either way, given that we can't note everything down, this researcher, consciously or not, has become interested in how people interact and manage the dining situation with various degrees of success. They're making observation work for them in studying how a diverse group of people come together to eat.

Figure 3.4 is another example. This one is more diagrammatic than the first. Our second researcher is less interested in painting a picture or telling a story that allows them to spot processes that could be interesting. They've already started to identify some hunches they're now trying to test out and explore in their observational notetaking. At the top we have something not unlike the diagram with which we started this chapter. But the movement lines are not people with smartphones now. They're birds! The aim here is seemingly to examine the bravery of the local sparrows who'd discovered this café could be a rewarding place to visit. Then they could get crumbs and other treats from the floor, the tables, and even the plates, if they were quick enough to dodge defensive manoeuvres from the humans who'd paid for their own food. How far were they willing to stray from the safety of the trees that surrounded the café garden in which the researchers sat? Perhaps observation could also help us learn about how people and birds live together in cafés? That could help us to understand what people feel about birds – and how they handle us too! This researcher also became interested in etiquette. In the drawing in the middle of the page they're looking at how plates are arranged and, more specifically, how shared cakes are consumed. Where do the forks and the spoons go, and how is the potentially bonding experience of cake sharing staged in ways that keep any hint of competition at bay? And how is the cutlery placed on the plate to show when you're still involved in the eating

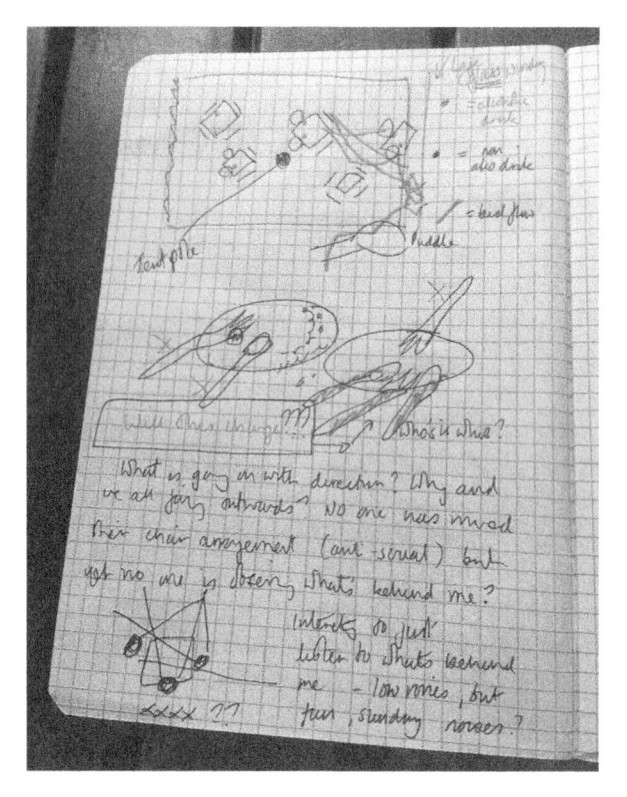

Figure 3.4 The second set of field notes from the café courtyard
Source: Russell Hitchings

and when you've had your fill? This tells us something about the social niceties that make for an enjoyable social experience in the café.

Both researchers were allowing themselves to run with the idea that, by attending through observation to details, we might start to develop a fresh appreciation of how some big issues play out in practice (how different cultural groups learn to live with one another; how people and animals interact in urban life) and with what implications (how we might help different cultures co-operate; how we might encourage people to care for city natures). So, the method would seem to be working for both of them. But if part of our job here is to identify how we make methods work for us – we're mindful of our book title here – let's linger for a little longer over the relative benefits of each approach.

Notebook 1

Strengths: Good on scene setting – as we immediately get a flavour of what's happening. This could be useful later in terms of presenting an account of our research because we can draw the reader into the social scene before zooming in on the most interesting features. That could also be good for the researcher who wants a memory jogger (or 'aide-mémoire') for later. Then, hopefully as they read through them, they'll gradually start to appreciate what the 'notes' they've taken in the café are showing them. These notes also encourage the researcher to attend to the importance of sequencing: how actions follow one another, how often certain things happen, and with what implications.

Weaknesses: Whilst it's good to set the scene – both for us when we return to our notes and for the readers who we might hope later to interest with our studies – we'll probably want to become more focused at some point. Perhaps this kind of approach is better at the start when we still want to attend to a variety of factors and not close things down. But we would need to think next about how the ideas of etiquette could be looked at in more depth. Is this about doing a diagram? Is this about training our attention onto certain interactional sequences and looking at those in more detail? Perhaps the process of sitting down to eat together as a group could be worth taking more detailed notes on? Maybe we'd want to look next at how different tour groups develop different ways of queuing together?

Notebook 2

Strengths: This researcher has more of a plan. They've already settled on a particular approach, and they're executing it. This is potentially less stressful as we don't need to think in the moment so much about what to write next as we simply follow the procedure that we've established for ourselves. So, once we've decided on a doable note-taking approach, this can be quite straightforward and can quickly generate a good sense of patterns of social – and also, in this case, bird – action.

Weaknesses: The flipside to the above strength, however, is about whether this is the right procedure. One of the downsides to a more structured approach is that we could be 'jumping the gun'. Another approach might feasibly tell us more about the relationship between sparrows and café life, but we'll never know if we settle too quickly on a particular way of examining how that works. Perhaps we should ask what is left out when we focus on movement only? What about the immediate reactions that flow diagrams can't capture – squeals, laughter, shooing the birds away? Who is reacting, and in what ways? That's missing here, and we can't capture that so well by simply tracking movements with our lines on the paper. So, this researcher needs to be willing to take stock of what is captured and missed by their approach, since they might benefit from tweaking things as a result. Then, after a while, they might decide that the time is right to try out something slightly different.

Our overall point though is straightforward: different approaches provide different insights. It's, to borrow a phrase we often use with our students, a matter of 'horses for courses' – backing the method that works in the context of what you are trying to do, like the punter who needs to think about which racehorse will respond best to the effects of specific weather conditions. There are no rights or wrongs here, which, as we'll discuss, can be both frustrating and liberating depending on how we're feeling and how our studies are going. Either way, you can learn a lot by playing around with different note-taking styles. This is partly because the very act of writing something down (or doing diagrams, even drawings) forces us stay with the details long enough to see, and then start to explore, the importance of otherwise easily overlooked issues. In a way, this is partly about thinking hard about what you're doing whilst you're doing it. But it's also partly about trusting the process – just writing something down makes you think about what to write and that makes you notice the detail. And when different note-taking strategies naturally train your attention onto different aspects of what's happening around you, it makes sense to try a few and then see whether they're taking you anywhere interesting.

A TRICK IF YOU ARE STUCK: TRY A LIST AND THINK ABOUT THE WORDS

Getting to a point when you trust the process can be difficult. In the smartphone example, the suggestion was that, by forcing ourselves to consider easily overlooked differences, we'll start to see how particular contexts are inhabited by people in new ways. In effect, this was about finding ways of making ourselves notice. But, as we've just suggested, noticing can be difficult when, just as this is often the case for the people we may be watching, many aspects of what's happening can easily fade into the background for us too. A café is just a café. A park is just a park. A train station seems so dispiritingly familiar that there really seems nothing more to say about it.

These feelings are to be expected. But they can also be a problem for the budding research observer who, after all, has gone there to notice – and then find some way of analysing – the detail. One way of pushing through is to force ourselves to acknowledge the many things that surround us. With that in mind, and rather like the discipline of our initial diagram exercise, we've sometimes asked our students on our field class to make a list. We ask them to sit down somewhere – most end up in cafés or fast-food restaurants – and then write a list of at least 600 words of things they see around them. Single words. They could be nouns. They could be adjectives. The point is to notice as much as you can. Then, when we get together in the evening after their coffees are long finished and the lists have been written, they read them out to us. We ask them to do it slowly, like a kind of performance poetry. The idea is to think, as we move from one word to the next, about how each word could be further observed to understand the role that it plays in the social life of places. This is another trick to try if you're starting out and considering whether an observational study is for you. Some words work. Others turn out to be duds. That is to be expected – not all features of a place are suitable for this kind of study. We'll talk about some of their themes in later chapters, but in the past, their lists have included words like 'feet', 'seats', 'hands', 'signals', 'crossings', 'bags'. These things are all around us, but we've never forced ourselves to think about the role they play in the life of places.

Take bags, as an example. Thinking about social life from the perspective of objects can generate novel research questions. With some of the master's students, one year we asked them to observe a particular category of object in everyday life where they lived and then allow their minds to wander around what they saw (this was a year when we were teaching remotely because of the Covid-19 pandemic). Perhaps they'd then see the importance of that object. Again, a lot of them understandably did this in public spaces. One year, we asked them to observe 'bags'. Here's a summary of what they came up with:

> *In the evening in the park, I see women carrying bags on the front of their bodies and wonder whether the bags migrated there as the sky turned dark. Some bags elsewhere in London are more acknowledged than others and some backpacks seem largely ignored on the ground. That might make them easier to steal from. Some Birmingham shoppers collect all their bags together in one hand. Perhaps this is a way of keeping hands free for phones and handles as they move efficiently around town. Elsewhere bags are distributed around the body so perhaps this varies between contexts as some shoppers might have more hand activity than others. Sometimes bags attract other bags in train stations – bags can sit on top of other bags and some bags seem attracted to similar bags. Bags are sometimes handled differently by the old and the young, by men and by women, by taller and by shorter people. Bags can become a barrier when we sit down and want to be a safe or certain distance from others. They can allow us to mark our territory and to police how we interact with others. Putting them down signals something to others about how long we will interact with them. Plastic bags seem to be comparatively uncared for based on where they get placed, and smaller bags seem to be more loved or, at least, kept closer to the person who sometimes holds and caresses them when pausing and speaking with other people.*

Like our smartphone diagram, what we can see here is how you start to develop new hunches if you allow your mind to wander whilst observing. Simple observational comparisons are a neat trick to get you thinking about how to study a particular type of person, object, or phenomenon. But we only started to see how bags were part of social life when we forced ourselves to ponder them. They were there all along – but we had never allowed ourselves to run with the idea that how people handled them could be quite revealing: what they do for us, how they help city life to go on, and in what circumstances they shape how we interact in intriguing ways. Our exercise spanned different UK cities, but we are sure there will be interesting similarities and differences to spot in other places around the world.

LISTENING IN AT THE SAME TIME

So far in this chapter, we've discussed observation as if we're purely 'looking' at what happens. To be fair, this is generally a big part of it since the point is partly to 'open our eyes' to how particular social contexts work. But social life is never merely a sequence of embodied movements as people gesture and signal in particular ways or interact in a purely physical manner with various objects, creatures, and other humans. And especially if we're interested in the 'social' aspect, namely how exactly people come together, then various forms of speech are an important part of these interactions. One of the reasons why the words can be downplayed when thinking about how observational methods are used in social research is because it can feel creepy to be too up front about how you are actually listening to people. Observation has a reassuringly scientific ring to it: we are observing, we aren't eavesdropping.

The truth of the matter, however, is that much of social life is an interesting mix of physical movement and spoken exchange. And, as many have argued, we can learn a lot from 'learning the language' (Crang and Cook, 2007) in terms of being open to the power of certain phrases or words – or what some would call 'utterances', namely exclamations, 'uh-huh's, and so on – in structuring the experience of social contexts. So how should we handle that? Here's another pair of examples to reflect on. These are a little more developed in terms of their focus, so you'll get to see how things might look when you've moved a few stages beyond the rookie observers we found in that Berlin café. These studies have a sense of what they're hoping to explore by attending to combinations of words and actions in context.

Understanding Social Life Online

In this excerpt from Reeves et al. (2016), the researchers are hoping to understand social life online, more specifically how online gaming is made more enjoyable by doing it together. Observation has often been used to examine how new technologies are lived with because it allows a direct view into the challenges people face in doing so. In this case, the researchers are keen to explore how players are not just playing the game, but also talking about the game as they go. Communicating through the computer interface is just one part of the experience of playing together in a room. By observing how talk 'in real life' and on-screen play

```
Players: G, in view, and D,
as well as six other players, (A,B, C,E, F, H)
Game: Warcraft III - Dota

1     G.    ((engages enemies with his hero))
2           (5 s.)
3     G.    ((turns head towards the other players))
4     G.    But what'll happen later
             Me va händer sen när
5           when you get ganged= >yeah
             du blir gangad= >a:
6           now< for example?
             nu< till exempel?
7     D.    Yea but why would I do that cause
             A men va skulle ja de för
8           cause I used the ulti?     [really     ]
             för att ja lagt ulti? [egentligen]
```

Figure 3.5 Gaming together to make it more fun
Source: Reeves et al., 2016: 316

Image 1, excerpt 1:
Player G leaning towards the other players

combine, a more sophisticated sense of the social experience, along with what players get out of it, follows. Drawing on 'conversation analysis' research, talk for them should be examined in terms of the immediate social situation, not something that we should stage in an interview afterwards. You'll have noticed perhaps that they did this by installing video cameras to record some of the gamers whose playing practices they wanted to understand. That allowed them to pay especially close attention to how certain patterns of talk were part and parcel of their game playing – as in the above figure where they shared tips and suggestions about strategies as the game went on – and to understand what people got out of playing together. This is not always an easy method to organise in terms of persuading people to be recorded. There'll be ethical issues to consider here too. Still, it certainly takes the pressure off in terms of the researcher noticing and recording that all-important detail in the moment. The idea is that, by watching the videos afterwards, we should start to get a sense of the informal rules that shape interaction and how these interactions shape the experience. And it's probably true that collaborating around tasks whilst gaming can be a big part of the fun.

Handling Identity in Group Situations

Suddenly Chloe knocks her pint glass over the edge and spills most of a pint onto the table. In an instant, the beer has run over the edges to wet both her lap and Jenny's. Jenny gets up quietly and goes off to the bathroom to dry herself. I give Chloe a couple of tissues. She dries herself off and moans that her clothes are soaked, and they are going to smell of beer. However, she is more concerned with what the others in the group will think of her. As soon as she knocked over her glass, her eyes darted up towards Lisa and Claire and they do so a couple of times over the next minute or two. (First thought turned to Claire and Lisa, not Jenny who got the spillage. Chloe is worried about status with colleagues – when the relationships are unsure, validation comes from popular, attractive people?)

Here we have another study of how groups interact (see Lim, 2003). This time the focus is on how those with different ethnic backgrounds, different gender identities, and different sexual orientations socialise together. Perhaps issues of sexism and racism might be present in these interactions even though those involved might not always be aware of this and they might also be reticent to talk about them to us. That was exactly why our next researcher (Jason) set about exploring these issues by hanging out with 'mixed' friendship groups with a variety of relevant attributes – some women, some men, some gay, some straight, and from a range of ethnic backgrounds – in London. He wanted to understand how they managed this experience and what that says about 'multicultural' society in terms of how and whether particular social hierarchies and patterns of deference were persisting. The above are some of his notes that, in this case, were sometimes written on the night-bus that took him home after spending time with these groups (though he tells us this wasn't always easy because of the bumpy roads). You can immediately see how he's starting to explore how particular, potentially internalised, ideas about who should be 'the judge' of appropriate conduct came forward (the writing in the brackets is him starting to develop his analysis). You'll also notice that, even though he's interested in the interactions, he, understandably enough, can't recall the precise phrases they used (Chloe 'moans' about the beer on her clothes but we don't get more detail than that). He's also starting to develop some hunches to explore further at the end of his entry.

Reflecting on the Two Examples

What defines this approach to studying the role of speech is that, unlike how – as we'll discuss – they're often examined by social researchers, these words are words *in situ* in the sense that they are being studied 'naturalistically' as they place the individuals involved in certain roles or reproduce particular ideas in the moment. Jason took his notes about what was said afterwards (good for not disturbing the social scene, but will you remember all the detail?). The first group installed cameras: good for ensuring you get that detail and good for those who don't like notebooks, but potentially quite a lot of work to organise. So, think about what might work for you. Either way, this kind of analytical eavesdropping gets us closer to the reality of how it is to experience particular social contexts when, going back to some of our earlier points, people might not be able or willing to work through the detail that observers especially prize.

FEELING A BIT FUNNY

Whilst we're talking about eavesdropping, it's worth saying something about the sense of nervousness and of potentially betraying trust, along with some of the anxieties about how people may react, that often accompany observational methods. Our master's students have often told us they worry about these matters. That's understandable. Here are some of their thoughts on doing observation in public spaces (after doing a one-hour observation exercise):

- Stressful to both be potentially judged as a voyeur and to stay on track with following all these people – I worried about their reactions to me as much as doing my own work.
- Different ways of taking notes might solicit different kinds of reactions which might be worth thinking about – taking notes on my phone was less stressful for me because people didn't react.
- I didn't really like watching people and making judgements about them – I felt I was making all sorts of assumptions and I'd much rather hear about their actions from them.

Their concerns amounted to a general idea of 'feeling funny' about it that was often expressed, and which is, we think, quite common when starting out with observational research. How you tackle these feelings depends on the relationships that you develop with those you are observing. Do they gradually become friends as your continued presence in a place means you inevitably get to know them a little? Or do you endeavour to keep your distance by blending into the background in a way that allows you to focus more fully on what you are observing and means they don't become too inquisitive?

This is about actively managing the situations that lead you towards certain relationships with those found in the contexts of your observational research. A lot has been written about these issues because researchers want to do right by those who they study. This kind of 'worry writing' (Crang and Cook, 2007) is widespread. We think that, before we reach the point when we can work through these concerns, we need to think about the practicalities of making our study work. We'll talk more about the relationships that develop between ourselves and those who we study in Chapter 6. For now, though, and to end this section on a more positive note, our students have found that people were more often indifferent – or likely to take a passing interest – than personally offended by what they were doing when they did their short observation exercises for us. In many places, most people, if you explain what you're doing if they ask, will let you get on with your work as they get back to their lives.

NOTHING'S HAPPENING!

We've mentioned already that some of the practicalities of doing observational research are infrequently discussed. Why? Emmerson et al. (2011) suggest that the idea of taking observational notes as a craft doesn't sit easily with how this kind of work is commonly presented:

> At one extreme, many field researchers assume that almost any literate, adventurous person can simply go into the field and do fieldwork; technical skills can be learnt on the spot in a 'sink or swim' vein. At another extreme, others contend that ethnographic research, particularly writing field-notes, involves God-given talents and sensitivities that simply cannot be taught. (p. xvii)

In this chapter, we've tried to demystify the process by working through some of the steps in an observational study. Observation isn't easy. A lot of the time it feels like 'nothing's happening'. We often hear this anxious refrain when our students have invested a great deal of time and energy into preparing for their projects – carefully establishing with reference to existing studies why they want to do some observing somewhere. The problem is that all that effort can, in fact, make it harder to slow down and give yourself the mental space to relax into the social scene so that you're open to letting it gradually reveal its secrets. If you're really invested in the idea of doing it well, that can mean that you'll easily 'freak out' – as a student recently put it to us in class – such that you can't immediately spot anything that seems worth systematically observing over a longer period: 'Oh my God, this isn't working, even though I've spent all that time reading first!' It may, of course, be the case that there really isn't anything much of interest going on – or, perhaps better, nothing much that is amenable to the processes of observing and analysing that we've discussed in this chapter. If that's the case, there might be good reason to just leave and then chalk this up to experience. Or you could come back another time when things are busier or more interesting interactions are more likely to happen. Perhaps you need to think about observing elsewhere. It's also quite possible that, after trying some different approaches to observing, you need to turn to another method. Equally it could be a matter of perseverance and experimentation, of trying some of the tricks we've presented in this chapter and of acknowledging that sometimes you must wait a while in order to start developing your hunches. We'll say a little more about this in

Chapter 10, but this method is generally based on the idea that being there a long time will lead to better insights, or as Small and Calarco (2022) put it, maximising your 'exposure'. So be ready to trust the process a bit, slow down, and let what's interesting emerge (Rivoal and Salazar, 2013). Consider some of the above ideas, try to relax, hold your nerve.

CONCLUSION

It's tempting to think of observation as the most straightforward approach to social research. In some ways it is – we are doing a structured sort of people watching here and that sounds easy. But there are plenty of challenges involved in doing effective observation partly because, compared to many of the other techniques we'll talk about in the following chapters, you're much less in charge of the process. In other words, you can't force things to happen that relate to what you hoped to explore when the point is to watch how things 'naturally' work out. Acknowledging that means being careful about where you go, often being experimental and open-minded with your notetaking, and effectively just being a bit patient if nothing relevant seems to be happening. Having said all that, observation can be really exciting because it allows us to see and explore important topics and processes that – as social researchers or indeed as everyday people – we may never have thought very much about before.

4
TAKING PART: CONSIDERING THE BENEFITS OF GETTING INVOLVED OURSELVES

SOME DIFFERENT WAYS TO SHOP

Walking through his neighbourhood the other day, Alan noticed a new convenience store. Nothing amazing about that. It looked pretty modern, so he thought he'd give it a try. To get inside, however, first he needed to scan his smartphone, which was unusual. Once inside, he collected a black plastic shopping basket and started filling it. He needed bananas, breakfast cereal, oat milk. After finding them, he tried to find the check-out. There didn't seem to be one. He looked everywhere, circling around the store a couple of times. It was all very disorienting. Was Alan missing something? There were no employees there to ask about what to do next either. Not understanding what was supposed to be happening here, he left his basket in the middle of the store and walked out.

Alan felt stupid to leave empty handed; not to say anti-social for dumping the basket like that. Not being able to negotiate a convenience store seems like a fairly basic failing. But it did get him thinking about how everyday spaces like convenience stores work, along with how their customers learn how to use them. So, he decided to do a little project on how convenience stores work – he's a social researcher so that's how he rolls! To start, Alan went to the Algerian grocery store near his house (Al Bahai). This is a narrow store with a long counter behind which two men in white coats serve out bread, pastries, and butchered and cooked meats. On entering, the older of the two storekeepers – a slim guy with short, slightly greying, hair – greeted him: 'How are you, Sir? What can we help you with?' To buy things at our second store, Alan needed to ask first. In fact, he had to pass over his shopping bag, which the storekeeper then gradually filled with the chosen items before congratulating him on his purchases and, after he'd paid, wishing him luck in life. After that, Alan tried a national chain supermarket store (Sainsbury's Metro, if you're curious). Here the norm seemed to be to not talk to others. He found baskets on one side of the security scanners just past the entrance. A guard in a dark blue uniform with 'security' embroidered in yellow on the lapels was standing on the other side. Alan smiled in greeting this time, but the guard didn't acknowledge him. He gathered his items, found two automatic check-outs, both with green lights above them to indicate they were both working and available, placed his basket to the side and followed the on-screen instructions, paying at the end with his contactless credit card. Still being ignored by the guard, he then left the store.

In the ordinary flow of social life, we often learn from copying or imitating others. This is a very common way in which people learn about how particular social settings work, and indeed how to become competent at all kinds of practices. It's also a facility that social researchers can plug into to do excellent projects. Some call this 'participant observation'. Participation suggests we're right in the midst of things; that the researcher, body and all, is mixed in with the research setting and those they're researching there. Observation suggests that, at the same time, this researcher is also trying to stand back and take note of what's going on around them. Though, as we discussed in the last chapter, an observational piece of research doesn't always require us to participate in local social life, now let's consider what we can learn from getting more fully involved in the flow of things ourselves.

This chapter focuses on understanding people by doing things together with them or, in other words, learning from doing what others do. We're going to explore how we, as social researchers, might draw on 'taking part' as a technique for both asking questions about, and developing understandings of, both what people do and who they are. 'Taking part' can take a range of forms, which vary enormously in intensity and commitment and might involve all sorts of surprising interactions. Think of the difference between the commitment to some sort of spoken exchange as was required in the Algerian shop, compared to the carefully structured impersonality of the national supermarket chain. Both involved 'taking part'. If we were really committed to exploring the social life of convenience stores, we might get behind the cash register to experience what it is like to sell things as the sociologist In-Jin Yoon (1997) did in their study of Korean shopkeepers in Los Angeles. Taking part might also mean going to other places that might not initially feel particularly social. To find out how to navigate that new store required Alan to find it on the internet – 'Amazon Fresh' – and then watch a video explaining how things worked there. Taking part in this case involved digital, as much as direct human, interaction.

WHAT DO WE MEAN BY TAKING PART?

In our thinking, one of the many delights of doing social research is that, as a starting point, we often tap into some of our existing social competencies. The idea that we might learn from taking part in the life of a social group we are interested in is age-old. As Confucius had it: 'I hear and I forget. I see and I remember. I do and I understand.' In that respect, what we're doing when we 'take part' as social researchers is nothing new to us, though we're doing things slightly differently (as we'll discuss). One of the most common ways of learning to become competent – in tailoring, building, plumbing, painting, repairing, sculpting, video editing, or whatever – is to do an apprenticeship. By following, watching, and copying the actions of skilled practitioners, over time, the apprentice gradually develops the skills themselves. One way to think about taking part is simply as a form of learning by doing.

This definition of 'taking part' as a kind of learning by doing, however, leads to two questions about social research. The first question is this: What are we doing that's different to those who surround us that we hope to understand? When normal people – by which we mean non-social researchers – engage in the process of learning by doing they usually have a straightforward sense of the reason why they are there; they are training to be a competent tailor, builder, plumber, painter, mechanic, sculptor, video editor, and so on. In other words, they're interested primarily in *what* they are learning not *how* they are learning. The social researcher, by contrast, is interested not only in what they are learning, but also in how they are learning, because often it is by thinking about the *how* that they begin to understand how a social setting or activity operates. There is a kind of doubleness involved in their way of taking part. The researcher is constantly switching between observing what others are doing and what they themselves are doing along with details about the wider setting. And that's not always easy.

The second related question is: What are we seeking to understand when we 'take part' in this way? In this case, the social researcher is usually using their participation as a way into exploring some broader process of interest to them. The researcher is participating in a social setting because they have an inkling that doing so will tell them something novel about how the world works more broadly. They learn about how ageing Swedish cars are fixed by a mechanic in a small rural workshop because they want to understand broader cultures of repair (as Douglas Harper did by helping a local mechanic out in order to write *Working knowledge* (1987)), or how sub-cultures work more broadly (as Pavlidis and Fullagar (2015) did in their study of female roller derby competitors), or to understand how working-class jobs are changing in post-industrial cities (as Richard Ocejo (2007) did by becoming a bartender in New York City in order to write *Master's of craft*). The idea is that by 'taking part' we'll be able to draw out wider lessons of some kind or another about society and not just get good at repairing cars or roller-skating or making cocktails, although these can sometimes be happy byproducts too.

If we return to the shopping example from the start, we might ask what makes Alan's project on North London convenience stores more than just hearsay – or, perhaps better, more than a straightforward account of (variously successful) attempts at shopping The answer might again be broken down into two parts. Firstly, there's an intellectual curiosity about the role of stores in urban life. Alan had started to organise this curiosity through a basic comparison of how life went on in both an independent and a chain store. Secondly, there's a commitment to taking detailed fieldnotes about what he encountered that would allow him afterwards to reflect upon his experiences in each store. We might at this point step back and offer a simple rule of thumb about how to define 'taking part' as a research technique. The distinctive thing about how a social researcher takes part is that they're taking notes about what's happening to and around them whilst participating, and that those notes are oriented to addressing some wider problem or topic that reaches beyond the world of the immediate participants.

AN EXAMPLE TO CONVINCE YOU

Let's work through an example to highlight the value of this approach. In Chapter 1, we mentioned our field class on everyday life in cities. One year, when we went to Stockholm, Sweden, we asked our students to spend an afternoon exploring the city on hired e-scooters. The idea was to get them thinking about how they navigate a new place, and how that experience is shaped by how they got around.

Learning to Scooter Together in Stockholm

In many ways, a new place can be ideal for some 'taking part' research because one of the things that we must do – just like inside a new convenience store – is to 'learn the ropes' of how things seem to work there. Our students have a lot of fun doing this exercise. But the notes they initially produce rarely include very much detail about the nitty-gritty of what they did: how they interacted with other road users, how they found their way, how they learnt how to use the scooters, and so on. Their initial notes were often full of general observations about how they felt – they were 'nervous', 'scared', 'uncertain' – and how these feelings usually (though not always!) changed over the course of the exercise – how they grew more 'confident' and 'relaxed', and slowly began to 'enjoy' themselves. Noting how you feel is certainly often part of doing 'taking part' research. But there's more to it than just noticing and then writing down how you feel about activities. One trick to being a good 'taking part' researcher is both to notice how you feel and to connect that to the detail of what's happening.

Figure 4.1 'Taking part' in Stockholm by trying out the scooters
Source: Stockholm students

In response to their reticence about attending to that detail, when we all got together in the evening, we asked them to say more about how they became so 'confident' and 'relaxed': how did their afternoon of scootering gradually get them to that point, and what were the physical and social circumstances that served to produce their confidence or relaxation? Slowly, they'd start to identify, and then share with us, all sorts of processes that we found fascinating. Some of them had eventually developed a certain division of labour as they became a kind of 'group scooter convoy' with some of the bolder students at the front, taking charge by choosing the route for those behind to follow. Alongside navigation, they'd sometimes even develop a series of strategies to help them function more effectively as a group. For example, if the scooter leader was approaching a red traffic light, it made sense to call to all those immediately behind, and who couldn't therefore see the lights, so they'd also slow down to avoid colliding with those stopping upfront. Some of them spoke about how, partly because they wanted to enjoy the experience of a new city together, they often ended up scootering alongside one other – instead of always slotting into the linear 'convoy' format that others went with. That way they could enjoy talking together as they went about all the new things they were seeing around them.

There are clearly certain tricks to becoming a 'confident' member of a city scooter group in Stockholm. And there were different ways in which it could be, gradually over time, practically made 'enjoyable'. Their strategies were fascinating to us partly because we know it can be good to attend to these details. Next, we pushed our students to think harder about the implications. We asked them to use this detail to identify some way of potentially changing things in Stockholm – perhaps in cities more generally – to promote safe and satisfying group scooter rides for visitors like them. The point, after all, as we've discussed, is to reach beyond the detail to address some wider issue. And hire scooters are increasingly found in many other cities too. Some of them suggested wider 'scooter lanes' for tourists who'd want to talk to their peers as they went, when the locals were presumably more focused on getting where they needed to go and less often out scootering together in groups. Some of them wondered whether the Stockholm Tourist Board might want to devise a tourist hire scooter manual so others could immediately adopt some of the formats our students had learnt 'the hard way' that afternoon.

Either way, we say to them that they'd never have come up with these ideas were they not to have done some scootering together themselves. If they'd just observed people going past whilst they sat a bench – like some of the 'observing' researchers we discussed in Chapter 3 – they'd never have known the processes by which 'confidence' was built and how group scooter rides could be made 'enjoyable'. Hopefully, this has helped you to see the value of this method too. You'll also get a sense of an important motivation for doing this kind of work for many: it can often turn out to be fun.

SOME TIPS BEFORE WE GET MORE STUCK INTO IT

Having now hopefully persuaded you about the value of this approach, let's think about how to make it work. A strength of 'taking part' as a research technique is that it can be used in many contexts, to study all sorts of people, and to understand a massive range of activities. This means that any tips for getting going will need to be treated as useful 'rules of thumb' rather than as iron clad requirements. That said, here are some tips for taking part that, together with our master's students, we've cooked up:

- You need to be open minded about what you are going to experience because you'll need to go with the flow of things rather than stick to any fixed sort of plan.
- You need to think about how you enter the social contexts you take part in because how we introduce ourselves to the context can have significant impacts on how people respond to us.
- It helps to think about what your relationship is to those you are taking part with. That can make a big difference, especially if you already have an established relationship with them.

- Making notes whilst you're doing things can be very challenging! Have a note-taking strategy in mind before you start but be ready to change and improvise if it doesn't work.
- It's more fun to be involved rather than just watching people (which can sometimes feel a bit weird). It can also be quite exciting to try so go for it.

A RECIPE FOR SUCCESS?

There's potentially a lot to think about when we do this kind of research. One way of helping ourselves to explore which elements are (or are becoming) most interesting to us when we get involved in some 'taking part research' would be to break things down into categories of things we might take notes on. We've explored this with our master's students by setting them the following task:

Cook a meal with someone of a different background to you. Feel free to define background in terms of nationality, hometown, generation, or something else that you think might be interesting. Tell them that you'd like to make one of their favourite everyday meals or a meal that links them in some way to where they are from. Whilst cooking, ask the person you are cooking with about the meal, and about their relationship to the food they are cooking. You should do the exercise with friends or new colleagues on the course since they'll be easy to recruit and hopefully happy to help out when you say this is a coursework exercise that your lecturers have forced you to do.

As always, we think you could usefully try this too, though you don't necessarily have to.

If you did, and you're anything like the students we teach, you'd probably be surprised at how difficult some parts of the exercise were. And, if you're anything like our students, the difficulty wasn't so much about taking part as developing a sense of what to notice. When we talk with them about what they've learnt from this exercise, one of the first things that comes up is that there are, in fact, many permutations, even though we thought we'd given them a fairly fixed brief. For some students, taking part meant watching whilst someone else explained what they were doing as they made the meal. Though they were quite willing to get more involved, these chefs didn't let them. For some of the more 'control freak' chefs, cooking really wasn't something you do with someone so much as for them. For other students, taking part ended up meaning getting so absorbed in the task they couldn't easily take notes anymore – in some cases people even forgot about this part of the plan because the activity turned out to be so demanding. They wanted to be a genuine help, and they wanted to enjoy a nice meal afterwards, so the research part rather fell away. Neither role, we tell them, is necessarily better – this is more about reflecting, as you go, on what different roles mean for what you end up exploring (and being sure that the one you end up assuming gives you the most useful insights).

When we 'take part' as social researchers we're effectively learning about two dimensions of the social world – we're learning about the activity in which we take part, but also about those we're doing it with. We asked our students what they learnt about these two dimensions. Here are some of the aspects they learnt about (along with some statements about their experience related to each). In this case, 'taking part' clearly told us something about both cooking and the cook.

Cooking

- Understanding the nitty-gritty detail involved in how a particular practice or setting functions
  ('There are lots of tools involved in making a curry that I never knew about before'; 'It's easier to chop vegetables when I'm given a better knife to mine at home')

- Understanding the informal and unspoken rules that define a practice
  ('A lot of what she's doing with the sauce seemed automatic – she's just doing it'; 'It's amazing how he can talk to me whilst doing something so skilled at the same time')

- Gaining a sense of how practices fit into wider contexts and cultural/social norms
  ('I never really thought about how I prepare things differently to others before'; 'Cooking a stir fry in this way requires lots of spices that I've no idea how to get')

- Developing an appreciation of how long things take to do and whether that can be enjoyable
  ('My arm really hurt by the end of it – I don't think I'm a natural chopper yet!'; 'It was really absorbing to do the task – I almost forgot to ask my questions')

The Cook

- Understanding how they feel about doing certain activities
  ('She seemed so much happier to talk when she was relaxed and doing her thing'; 'I was surprised at how it seemed like a chore even though he was excited by the result')

- Identifying good questions to ask given the context being studied
  ('Whilst we were chopping, I had more time to think about how to ask about their background'; 'It just felt natural to move from discussing the meal to where they came from')

- Getting a sense of how people might be socialised into, and invested in, particular ways of doing things
  ('We laughed a lot about our different ideas about the "right" way to make a pasta dinner!'; 'She said she'd never cook the sauce differently because the point was to feel like home')

The key take-home message from their experiences is that in this kind of 'taking part' we are both learning through doing and through talking as we go. Also, that there's a lot going on – so we might want to think sooner rather than later about our focus. Going beyond the kinds of things that our scootering students learnt about effective tourist transport in Sweden, in many settings the advantage of taking part as a social researcher is not just about what is learnt from doing an activity ourselves. Rather taking part's advantage lies in the possibilities it presents for conversation. Taking part ourselves can help us to spot more acute and informed questions, and indeed often give us the time to ask them – you've got space to identify good questions as, for example, when you are cracking on with chopping those vegetables: it's OK to not speak for a while because, unlike in an interview, you're superficially busy with something else. Many of our student helpers were also struck by how taking part gave them a new sense of how doing an activity felt physically and emotionally, something that would be impossible to know from merely watching. But equally, they also spoke about taking part in an activity as a productive 'ticket to talk' (Sacks, 1992): a socially acceptable route into potentially more revealing forms of discussion about both about the activity itself and its significance for the participant.

Something you might have noticed from this exercise is that we didn't say what concept or hypothesis our students should be exploring. That is because one of the key things we are doing when we take part in a social setting for the first time is trying to work out how the setting works and, from that, what might be interesting. As we'll discuss when we consider how 'research questions' animate our studies (Chapter 7), for many researchers, it's unhelpful for these questions to be too fixed at the start because that undermines the whole point. Having said that, we seldom go blindly into these settings. We chose this exercise for our students because it spoke to a particular issue, namely the relationship between food choices, domestic routines, and self-identity. It was actually inspired by Longhurst and colleagues' (2009) study that used cooking with migrant women in Kirikiriroa (Hamilton), New Zealand, to see how familiar meals helped them feel at home. But we also need to put some of our intuitions about what will be important to the back of our minds and stick with the nitty-gritty of what's going on. We're, at least partly, working 'inductively' here, finding new patterns in what people say and do that are more easily spotted through the immediacy of taking part. We're developing our ideas about how things work in context before considering their broader implications (Becker, 2009; Tavory and Timmermans, 2014).

So, is there a trick to doing this well? Well, we'd need to have an intuition that it might work, a sense that you'll enjoy examining how taking part is done, and an interest in the kinds of superficially 'idle' talk that can circulate around the activity. In some respects, and like many of the methods we talk about in this book, it's rather like learning to cook – recipes can help but, as they say, practice makes perfect.

WHO ARE WE WHEN WE'RE 'TAKING PART'?

We hinted earlier that one way to think about taking part is as an apprenticeship, which hints, in turn, at how things are experienced differently as you move through different stages – from the confused 'newbie' to the seasoned 'old hand' who may soon be ready to take on some apprentices themselves. Reflecting on the role that you, as a researcher, take on – and how that positioning might evolve over time – is an important aspect of doing effective taking-part research. Here it's useful to return to the distinction between participation and observation that we introduced earlier. We could draw a line with, at one end, pure 'observation' and, at the other end, pure 'participation' as seen in Figure 4.2.

Observation ◄─────────────► Participation

Figure 4.2 Between participation and observation

In such a schema, pure observation would involve sticking to the techniques we talked about in Chapter 3, whilst pure participation would involve the researcher being fully involved in the activity or the life of the group being studied. This schema works mostly as a reminder that when we're taking part we're often switching between active absorption and stepping back to think about what's happening.

On top of this first distinction, we can overlay another – that between whether the researcher who is taking part is a member of the group involved or not (in some of the above cases, the groups would be expert city scooterers or those who can make certain delicious meals). Again, we might draw a line that runs from being a 'non-member' to being a 'full member' of the group being studied, as in Figure 4.3.

Non-member
↕
Member

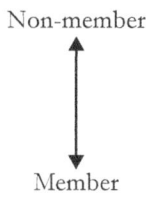

Figure 4.3 Between member and non-member

It might seem odd to put membership and non-membership on a continuum. But it's worth reflecting on how membership of a group, organisation, or practice can have multiple formal and informal dimensions. There are many situations and activities for which membership is very loose. In some social settings the idea of membership doesn't really make sense. Sometimes 'membership' means simply doing an activity. Transit riders, for example, become 'commuters' just by regularly being transit riders – so, in principle, we can take part simply by getting on the train. For other activities, the nature and dynamics of group membership may only become apparent gradually through the act of taking part. If we thought of something like basketball playing, the situation there is clearly quite different. Here, just as with transit riding, membership could, in the first instance, be defined by the simple act of taking part – on most public basketball courts people can simply pitch up and play if they've a ball. But as Michael DeLand (2012) has shown in his study of 'pick-up' basketball games – games in which you superficially can do exactly that, namely just turn up and play – gaining group 'membership' can be complicated. It depended on the skill of the individual, their connection with the other players, and how long the individual had been playing on that particular court. In fact, only by taking part could a researcher like DeLand begin to understand how membership comes about. In other cases, people's background might automatically mark someone out as a member of a group.

Social researchers find themselves taking on a range of roles as they take part. For some, a key issue is about how we think of our fixed 'positionality' as researchers – how our existing social attributes (our gender, age, socio-economic status, education level, and so on) play into the relationships we build with those who we're hoping to understand. We'll talk more about that in Chapter 6. But, for now, what we'd like to highlight is how the role you take on can have implications for the kind and quality of material your study ends up producing. This, of course, was one of the points that our students had already astutely made in our cooking discussions. Taking on the role of apprentice and helper sets up a relationship in which the person being studied has an obvious reason to offer explanations of what they are doing. Douglas Harper (1987) in the study of a rural mechanic in up-state New York we mentioned earlier was treated as such by his key informant Willie – that is to say that Willie showed Harper how to do a range of repairs as

Harper helped him in his shop. And Willie's descriptions of how to repair different kinds of equipment meant that, over time, Harper also became a friend and a kind of confidant. Through these means, Harper trod a careful, and eventually very revealing, line between the participant (who is accepted there and has built trust through their work) and the observer (who needs to think hard about what is being done and said around them in order to write an insightful report).

So, our students in the cookery exercise were right – it pays to think about what role you assume since what you learn can depend on where you're sat on the above continuum. You'll naturally move from one to another as your exposure deepens, but how fast you'd want to get there, and what, as a researcher, you gain or lose along the way is another matter. So, how would you want to present yourself and where might you want to stay on the second continuum?

Novice or non-member:

- More natural to get people to explain how things work
- A stronger sense of how challenging the activity is at the start
- People might feel less judged because you're clearly incapable
- But that could also make you quite annoying to have around

Expert or member:

- You can write with authority about their experience because you know too
- Might get people to open-up more fully because they see you as a peer
- Insider chat is more available because of your hard-won status

WHEN TO TAKE PART? SOME EXPERT EXAMPLES OF WHAT IT GIVES US

Because taking part can involve us so fully – body, mind, emotion – it's tempting to view it as the most authentic social research method. We're enthusiasts of taking part. But it isn't helpful to think of any one research technique as being in some fundamental way better than another. In our thinking, it's more helpful to acknowledge how different research techniques offer different kinds of possibilities and give different sorts of insights. The skill is to know when to use what. So, let's look at a few excellent examples of social researchers taking part so we can learn from the experts.

How Do Societies Manage Exotic Mushrooms Today?

The first case is about taking part – simply to understand what's going on – and comes from a study that uses how people gather and sell a particular kind of exotic mushroom to think about our broader relationships with the 'natural' world. Here's an example from Anna Lowenhaupt Tsing's (2015) account of hunting for matsutake mushrooms in the pine forests of Oregon:

> It was dusk when Kao came back with the water. But he beckoned me to go picking with him. There were mushrooms nearby. In the gathering dark, we scrambled up a rocky hillside not far from his camp. I saw nothing but dirt and some scrawny pine trees. But here was Kao with his bucket and stick, poking deep into clearly empty ground and pulling up a fat button. How could this be possible? There had been nothing there – and then there was. (p. 14)

By being in the Oregon wilderness, accompanying someone who makes a living harvesting matsutake mushrooms, she gains a sense of the work of looking for and digging up mushrooms. She's more broadly interested in what the way in which we harvest these mushrooms tells us about how people live with 'nature' these days. We can see here how this kind of 'taking part' allows a sense of surprise about how things hang together, a surprise that might lead us in all sorts of interesting directions. Indeed, if we're being surprised by what happens, then we are making the most of the methods since the idea is often to allow ourselves to learn from things playing out differently to how we might have expected. Lowenhaupt Tsing's not really doing it to know how it feels. Neither is she doing it in preparation for formal interviews with the mushroom hunters afterwards. She went along to see how it works. Having done so, she can then bear witness to these practices and consider what they say about societies today.

What's It Like to Be a Professional Embroiderer?

Our second case is about taking part to understand the corporeal experience and skills. Clare Wilkinson-Weber (1999), in her study of the working lives of women in the embroidery industry in northern India, spent significant amounts of time working alongside some of them. Through this, she gained an intimate sense of how it felt to spend long days embroidering:

> Chikan embroidery is not a dangerous job, and it does not require strength. It is, however, demanding in other ways. Eye-strain, backache, and muscle cramps are common complaints. The embroiderer must maintain a high degree of precision and coordination in order to produce satisfactory embroidery. The thread is inclined to twist, and the increasing slipperiness of the needle as it is moistened by sweat is a nuisance. These difficulties, on top of the mental and physical concentration required to make acceptable stitches, made my own embroidery efforts proceed extremely slowly. (p. 154)

Wilkinson-Weber might have simply sat and observed the work of the women she was studying, and she did, in fact, spend time doing that. But through learning to embroider herself – even if she attained nothing like the level of skill of those she studied – she gained the visceral feel of what it was like to labour in this way. And that made for more effective writing and a stronger sense of how particular groups of workers cope with certain conditions. So, in that sense, her example was a bit like our scooter riding students in Stockholm, though she was interested in foregrounding and understanding how people handled the arduous work involved. She also thought that learning how to do it would give her more authority to represent them afterwards. She wasn't just flying in to quickly collect some material – she was going the extra mile by learning to embroider herself.

What Are Soccer Field Skirmishes Really Doing?

Our last example is about taking part to appreciate the informal norms and conventions through which a social setting, group, or organisation operates. These norms and conventions are often tacit – that is to say unwritten, usually unstated, and sometimes challenging to discuss for those involved. This means that, in some cases, the only way a researcher can gain a sense of them is by spending significant time with those being studied to experience first-hand how these conventions play out. Consider David Trouille's (2021) work on soccer and social ties that we've already encountered in Chapter 2:

> Cabalo (horse) – a sturdy, aptly named Honduran – begins to question whether Palo had ever really scored those golazos [spectacular goals] when the men's attention abruptly shifts to a small skirmish in midfield. As two men battle over the ball, one player takes offence to his opponent's aggressive tactics. Play stops as the two men argue nose to nose, but they relent when their team mates gently pull them apart. A few men whistle from the side lines to make light of the confrontation. One man shouts out '!Arriba los novios!' (Long live the boyfriends!) As the match resumes, the men on the bleachers return to dating their legacies as players. (p. 2)

Trouille develops a believable account of how players regulate conflict and ensure order because he has spent many months, years in fact, observing dozens of instances of conflict management on the soccer field. Likewise, he has experienced first-hand the processes through which newcomers become familiar with this particular conflict management culture. We see parallels here with the findings of some of our cooking apprentice students who highlighted the many ways in which we can start to develop a focus when we are taking part. Through these means he was able to develop an especially sensitive account of how Latino migrants gradually became a part of the public culture of a place – in this case how their soccer games slotted into the wider life of the park. This was especially sensitive because he'd got involved in the soccer himself and thereby showed himself to be 'making an effort' – even demonstrating that he'd learnt to handle some of these skirmishes himself.

We imagine that all three of the experts had a background sense of why they wanted to take part. And that will have shaped how they did it. Lowenhaupt Tsing tagged along for enough time to know how the mushroom harvest worked, but she didn't need to stay longer. Wilkinson-Weber felt she needed to learn herself because she wanted to really appreciate the trials of doing the embroidery work, but she also felt it important to speak with the workers about this too. Trouille was taking part to become an accepted part of the local soccer scene, but he didn't always play because he knew that he could gather together some very revealing notebook material more effectively from the sidelines.

So once again we're telling you that there are many ways of doing this – even after having tried to divide things up so that we can get a better sense of how things can be made to work. In one sense, that might seem frustrating: 'What exactly do you want me to do!?' In this book, we see it differently. This is all about thinking upfront about what you might achieve when you take part in various ways. And it's actually quite exciting to know you've lots of options. We're giving you some tricks and suggestions here – but how you put things into practice is, at the end of the day, up to you.

TAKING NOTES WHILST TAKING PART

Having said that, we can still try to give you some tips about notetaking. Taking part as a method can be done more or less anywhere. We are all doing activities all the time and, though social researchers often like to do them with others as a way of learning about their lives, we can also learn from just doing something (riding a bike, going out for a walk, trying a new recipe, when that could still tell you something even if you did that alone). That said, for all its apparent simplicity, it can be particularly challenging for new researchers. Howard Becker (1998) advises apprentice social researchers to get into the habit of always taking a notebook with them and taking notes about everything they do each day. The aim isn't to develop a project from the notes. It's to get into the habit of taking notes about what you're doing. But, as we saw in Chapter 3, it's hard sometimes to know what exactly that means.

When we talked about notetaking in Chapter 3, we examined some of the techniques you might adopt to spot and then explore previously overlooked issues when observing a social scene. Arguably we were in a better position then to test out all these different approaches because you can do that so much more easily when you are doing observation alone. You are often sat there undisturbed, so the main challenge is to identify what you want to take notes on and then find effective ways of taking them.

However, when we're taking notes as we take part, there are some additional obstacles to overcome. The main one is about juggling the various activities we're involved in and finding a way of getting the most interesting detail down. All the students we've talked about so far in this chapter have often been at pains to emphasise this when they wanted to let us know that we'd given them a difficult task (especially when they were tired after a long afternoon out on their scooters)! In the scootering example, they'd occasionally expressed mock outrage at how we were apparently putting them in grave danger – 'You wanted us to note everything down, but how could we if we weren't to crash?!'

It's true that we need to think quite hard about when we'll write our notes with 'taking part'. This might be because the activity itself is so absorbing, so demanding of our attention, that we cannot write notes. Some researchers worry about this idea in terms of 'going native' by getting to a point when you are so involved in what you are doing, so fully immersed in the social context, that you forget that you've also got a job to do in terms of building an academic understanding of some aspect of that context. More prosaically, it may also be because taking notes can come across as intrusive to those you're studying. If you are right there with them, and you are stopping to write things down about what you're all doing all the time, they might understandably find this off-putting. Finally, there are some even more practical matters. In the above cooking-with-a-friend exercise, some students found themselves with food on their hands, and that meant they couldn't very easily hold a pen.

Taking-part researchers have found many ways over these barriers. They take notes on any piece of paper they have to hand, they record voice notes for themselves, or write quick notes into their mobile phones. Still, often the notes that are recorded directly when taking part are short, chaotic, and incomplete. To deal with the difficulties of taking reliable notes in the moment, many of these researchers would keep not one but often several notebooks. The first set includes the spontaneous jottings, quotes, sketches, and observations they might quickly note down at opportune moments when they are right in the middle of taking part. A second notebook would then contain more detailed, worked up, accounts based on those initial notes and usually written up at some point soon afterwards.

A good example of these secondary notes is provided by this excerpt from the notebooks of Tara, a friend of ours who did her PhD research on tourist workers in a Canadian ski resort (yes, we were envious!). She was interested in how different forms of 'self-identity' shaped social life in these resorts and, more specifically, the extent to which 'working tourists', who were there for the full ski season, saw themselves differently to those just holidaying there for a week or two (see Duncan, 2007):

'Was talking to my flat mate this morning and we were laughing at how last night we were sort of disparaging tourists in Merlin's and then ended up talking to them all night. In Merlin's we were all trying to guess who the tourists were – or, more likely, where they were from. It was as though being "local" gave us a reason to put down the fact they were drunk and acting out. Veronica said she didn't think they behaved like this at home, it was only when they were away. We were talking, for example, about how people behave and wondering, for example, if the two girls kissing on stage regretted that today. Sandra figured this was an escape, that these tourists didn't know any one and could go back to their normal lives afterwards with no one the wiser.'

This notebook entry is interesting in the way it mixes up temporalities – things that happened that morning (the talk at breakfast) and the previous night (drinking at a bar) – as well as mixing descriptions of what happened at the time with speculations about how to make sense of those events. In that respect, what's particularly interesting here is how Tara is both providing a neat account of a conversation and its context, but also starting to develop some preliminary ideas about how the social settings she's studying seem to work. These hunches are important for researchers in developing their ideas. To be fair, she was always interested in looking at these distinctions. So, this wasn't entirely the product of being totally open-minded about what she'd find at the resort. At a practical level, however, perhaps the most important thing to stress is that, for this kind of more thoughtful (or 'self-reflexive') notetaking to work, it should be done soon after initial notes – otherwise you probably won't remember what those symbols, marks, or half-formed sentences (sometimes called 'scratch notes') mean, and you'll not be able to fill in the gaps with the details you can more easily recall just afterwards.

Tara did her 'second level' notetaking in the evenings, as a kind of academic diary before she went to bed. How and when you do yours will depend on how your life is organised around taking part, how people might react, and when you've the energy to do it. For our students on the scooters, some of them would stop every 15 minutes to record the details when they were fresh in their mind. Then they developed those into something that was both more analytical (in terms of testing out hunches) and fleshed out (adding the details to help them remember the moment and make for a more interesting read) later in the evening. For our apprentice chefs, we effectively did some of this 'second level' work together with them in class when we developed those themes about cooking and cooks. When, and for how long, you do this will depend on you and your project. But force yourself to do it soon. That could give you a keener sense of what you are looking to explore further when you start your next session. Partly because she'd written her diary in the evenings, Tara was primed to test out some of her initial hunches when she began her next bout of working and skiing with breakfast the following day.

Finally, and developing some of the suggestions we presented in Chapter 3, it's also worth noting that your approach to notetaking will very likely evolve when you're taking part. At the start, you'll probably be doing plenty of experimentation as you begin to get a sense of the most interesting aspects of what is happening around you. Much of this chapter has been about giving you some ideas about what you might attend to there. Then, as your project develops, you'll likely be spending increasing amounts of time waiting for things to happen that help you to more fully understand the aspects on which you've decided to focus – instances or interactions that either corroborate or challenge some of your early hunches about how the activity works and what you've been thinking 'for the time being' that you might end up concluding in your study. So, things will likely feel less fraught in terms of notetaking as the project moves along. You're no longer 'freaking out' about how to handle all that's happening, and you're more calmly working towards a fuller appreciation of some process or another.

CONCLUSION

Considering what they liked about taking part, a student on our master's course said it was simply 'much more fun than just watching'. It can also be a highly effective way of getting a sense of how a social setting or activity functions and plays a part in the lives of those involved. The fact that taking part puts us right in the middle – or as near to the middle as we can get – of the group or activity we're aiming to understand forces us into a direct embodied engagement with it, and that gives the experience of taking part an emotional intimacy. Taking part can be used as a technique for entering a social world and generating research topics and questions that are grounded in the nitty-gritty texture of that setting. It can also be extended into a long-term commitment to studying a social world. That links us finally to a question that we haven't yet discussed here – how long should you do it for? We'll say more about this kind of thing when we get to Chapter 10. But, as a headline response, just as with observation, the longer the better. The more time you've spent on the activity, the more authority will be granted to you in terms of representing the group or activity later because your audiences will feel reassured that you've made enough effort to get stuck in. Though this will vary depending on the intensity of the activity and how much of what is happening turns out to be relevant to the focus that you end up having in your project, ideally, you'll be doing it for a while. But hopefully that shouldn't be too off-putting for you. After all, and as that student emphasised, taking part can often be quite fun.

5
STAGING TALK: HOW TO DO AND IMAGINE INTERVIEWS

WHAT'S HAPPENING WHEN WE TALK TO PEOPLE?

We sometimes ask our undergraduates to talk together about what living in London is like. We say we're interested in whether they think moving there for their studies has, in some way or another, changed them. Many of them come from all over the world and London can be an intimidating place. So, we figured we could learn something from their adaptation experiences. Sometimes we even pitch it as a topic our university wants to explore so as to help our new recruits in settling in.

This usually happens in a large common room with banks of wooden tables surrounded by bookcases housing a fairly random selection of geography classics our department has amassed over the years. We start by asking them to brainstorm a set of open-ended questions that could help them explore this topic with their peers. Then we work together to arrange their questions into a sensible order. After that, once their 'interview schedules' are in reasonably good shape – or we'd run out of time, or the students have started to get a bit bored and distracted – we'd settle into small groups. Each group would then embark on a short 'interview' of about minutes or so. The settling down could sometimes be difficult due to the mixture of excitement and anxiety involved. Still, with some careful cajoling, we'd eventually reach a point in which pairs of students were talking quietly, with one using their schedule to consider what a classmate who'd moved there felt London had done to them.

Here's a statement they might typically make:

> *I mean, there's lots of restaurants in London and it's great to try some of those when you can. And I do talk about that when I go home to my*

family. And I do think that I've developed my sense of food a bit and I tell them all about how I want to make the most of it here.

It sounds like they've been enjoying themselves. It also sounds like the interviewer is succeeding in doing what is hoped for from a social research interview, namely starting to develop an appreciation of how someone else relates to the topic that interests you. Part of the point of this chapter, however, is to encourage you to think a bit more about what's happening when we encourage people to talk to us in social research. So, let's reconsider the context:

- *Self-presentation.* It's reasonable to ask whether the student involved is telling the truth. Though the distinction between truth and lies is often too stark to capture the subtleties of what is happening when we talk with people in a project, we've sometimes found ourselves with a lingering suspicion that the student interviewee might be 'just saying things' by discussing only the comparatively comfortable aspects of their London life. In this case, it's worth noting how it's probably easier for them to talk about how they've been enjoying the restaurants than how lonely they felt at the start.
- *Social context.* Then there's the matter of who we're talking to. Over the years, we've noticed how our students tend to talk in these sessions. They like to present themselves as busy. Elsewhere on campus, as keen social researchers ourselves, we've observed how many of them are master's of the apparently rushed, up-beat pleasantry as they check-in quickly with one another as they seemingly dash between lectures, sports, and various social engagements. We've no doubt that many of them are indeed busy. But this way of interacting also taps into and reproduces an idea about what our students should be – they're making the most of their time with us by filling it with lots of enriching experiences. This pattern, we think, can also colour our interview interactions in this class. There are certainly ways in which they tend to talk, especially when paired with peers they don't yet know well.
- *Physical context.* It's also worth thinking about how physical context kicks in. We've said a little already about where we do these interviews. We like teaching in this particular room. The bookcases and the wooden tables made it feel like a library and, in our country at least, we know we should talk quietly in libraries. So that adds to the atmosphere. Having said that, we've often ended up fairly crammed together in this class. Plus, the room can be echoey. All that, we think, shapes how some of our students talk about their new lives in London too. It's easy to imagine how, despite our cajoling and the contemplative library vibes, you'd not want to say very much about how hard it was to adjust if you had to almost shout in so doing. Certainly, you might be less likely to 'open up' in this way if you were always in

danger of the adjacent group coming to a lull in their conversation, meaning they'd easily catch certain potentially incriminating snippets from your own confessional account.

This chapter considers the idea of talking to people in social research. Interviewing is one of the most common approaches to exploring the lives and perspectives of others. But that popularity can sometimes mean that important aspects of the experience fade into the background of the accounts that we read afterwards. We know interviews work, so why discuss them? The point of our opening example is to bring some of them back to the fore. Our students did slowly build a sense of whether those who had moved here felt they had, in effect, started to become 'Londoners' after coming to university. But there could have been many social research projects happening here – one about how people present themselves, one about how students talk together, and one about how different physical and social contexts can produce particular ways of speaking. It's partly as a means of emphasising these dimensions that we've called this chapter 'staging talk'. With interviews we're never straightforwardly collecting people's accounts, much as we might sometimes like to think of it that way. We're actively curating a very specific sort of situation, and we should think about that since that situation shapes the accounts that are offered up to us, and indeed whether we get them at all.

Having whetted your appetite by highlighting how all sorts of things are going on when we talk with people in a social research project, this chapter now considers the ways in which you might do it. We'll start with the basic idea of why we might want to talk to people in a social research project, then we'll consider where you might want to do it and offer you some tips about how you can put yourself in a position to do a decent job. Finally, given that we also want to be creative about how we do social research in this book, we'll consider the right kind of talk for us in our interviews. There are many types, after all, just as there are many formats for talking to people elsewhere in society.

WHY DO WE DO IT?

Firstly, it's worth thinking about our essential purpose (as it always is – see Chapter 2). Different purposes can sometimes get confused or, perhaps more correctly, lumped together when we think about talking with people in our social research projects. So, what are we trying to do here? Here's an attempt at breaking things down:

1. *To understand how something works.* This is rather like some of the talk associated with taking part. The idea here is relatively straightforward – you want to understand how something works and the most efficient way of finding out about that is to ask someone. This kind of researcher is

understandably less interested in the subtleties of how people react. They want to know facts and details and people will, if we treat them right, hopefully share those with us.
2 *To get someone's perspective.* If you're going to talk to someone about a topic and you're a thoughtful and sensitive listener, often you'll soon get a sense that they might be looking at things in a particular way. Many interviewers focus on exactly that suggestion. For them, the essential idea is that, by spending some time talking with a person, they'll gradually reveal to you how they see things in ways you couldn't have entirely anticipated beforehand. For them, that's the whole point of doing it, and a sense of learning something new is often what you are after.
3 *To learn from their reactions.* This is a less common focus, but the insights that come from taking it can feed productively into both the above undertakings. People don't just offer up information and thoughts in an entirely unguarded way, even if we've done our best to put them at ease. There are ways in which they'll be managing the encounter – emphasising some things instead of others, even dodging questions entirely for various reasons that can be usefully analysed.

These three ways of defining our objective don't necessarily translate into different ways of staging talk. It's more that they focus to different degrees on the experience of the interview, with the first being relatively indifferent, the second hoping that if we treat people right, they'll eventually 'open up', and the third keen on the idea of an 'active interview' (Holstein and Gubrium, 1995), namely one with a particular interest in how people are managing the exchange in the moment. Still, as is always the case, it's worth being clear about what we think we are doing and what we're hoping to achieve at the start. When it gets to the writing stage, how we see our interviews will shape how we present this material; with the first type of interviewer using the knowledge they've gained to describe things, the second being more likely to present quotes that help us see where the person is coming from, and the third often saying even more about the situation in which people were speaking together.

IS IT HARD?

This is all starting to sound like something more than a friendly chat. It's true that research interviews can sometimes seem daunting. Interviewing is, after all, more interventionist than the two methods we've considered so far. When we're 'observing' or 'taking part', that's all about getting closer to how things are already happening. If we're staging an interview, we're asking people to step out of this flow of everyday activity. We're taking charge a bit more. And we'll be wanting to do that well since we're asking them to help us out. Still, as attentive social researchers, we've also noticed that talking is a common occurrence. And the chances are you've already developed a whole bunch of skills that could help in your social research interviewing. One of the things we often tell our students is that this could be a good method for you if you think of yourself as a 'people person', namely someone who's naturally interested in the perspectives of others. On that positive note, let's consider some of the issues involved in talking with people in research. Giving some thought to each of them can help us to cook up creative projects that fully deliver on our objectives, whatever they may be.

WHERE TO TALK?

The other day Russell was watching a daytime TV talk show. They were discussing how best to embark on conversations about potentially awkward topics with teenage children. In many modern contexts, so the expert on the sofa was saying at least, talking about tricky issues like sex and drugs has become especially difficult. Apparently, part of the problem is that the whole family now seems so busy and, when they are together at home, the kids often went immediately into their rooms in ways that made a family culture of regular conversation pretty difficult to develop. Then, when the family eventually assembled, there'd likely be plenty of devices around to stop them from even looking at one another. If we accept that it could be a good idea to share thoughts across generations, what should be done? Where can you have a serious talk about life with your teenager these days?

Figure 5.1 Talking across generations in the car
Source: Kay Hitchings

Their answer was in the car. Perhaps on the way to one of the many 'after school' activities associated with childhood these days. Why? Firstly, the kids couldn't get away then. Secondly, there was time to think. They were already collaborating to go somewhere and so this comparatively 'dead time' could more easily be filled with seemingly 'casual' conversation. This also meant there was less incentive to rush things along. The driver was partly occupied, and that gave them more time to compose the next question – they could identify the most sensitive thing to say next as they negotiated the traffic. Finally, everyone was facing forward. This meant that any uncomfortable feelings of being interrogated through direct eye-contact were also avoided. All this made sense to Russell. Some of his most thoughtful conversations have happened in cars. He'd not given too much thought to it at the time, but it was probably because of this combination of reasons.

Good social researchers think about these issues. Though as described just a moment ago, how much they do so depends on what they want from their interviews. Where you talk matters for what gets said. When social researchers report on interview projects, where they spoke with the people involved is a detail often squeezed out of their accounts. The background assumption seems to be that you'd do your interview somewhere quiet and easy for both parties to get to. That way you can encourage a more contemplative conversation and record what they say. A quiet corner in a coffee shop is often recommended. This is partly because there's a sense of how long a 'social coffee' lasts, which often matches up with our desired interview length. If we suggest 'going for a coffee', perhaps we don't have to go into any off-putting details about how long we want to talk. Equally, since your interviewee has made the time to help you out, it can be nice to buy them a drink to say thanks. Small gestures matter in social research. Talking somewhere slightly apart from their everyday lives can also minimise stress about being disturbed or eavesdropped by known others, around whom they'd want to censor their comments. But, as with our car example, and as we'd generally say when taking about project design, we can often reap rewards if we consider whether these 'rules of thumb' are right for us. Here are two UK studies hoping to understand what people get out of 'nature', both of which benefitted from noticing how physical environments discouraged certain kinds of talk and encouraged others. Both were therefore tinkering with the implied 'rule of thumb' about a quiet place to talk indoors:

1. *Learning from silence in the domestic garden.* Our first example comes from some of Russell's own research exploring what Londoners got out of growing plants in private gardens (Hitchings, 2021). Russell knew that gardening wasn't necessarily easy. And that this might be especially the case for those Londoners who could afford a garden but didn't have much time to learn gardening – because they had demanding jobs, or were raising children, and so forth. He asked some of those with designed gardens to

take him on a garden tour. What would they say about their plants when directly confronted by them? Though others in his study had become really animated when he asked them to show him around, he was met with silence in the same situation with some members of this particular group. Why? This was because they didn't really know what to say about individual specimens and were, compared to commenting on the view from the lounge or kitchen, much less interested in thinking about the soil, the pests, and the growing. This situation was, on occasion, a little stressful for Russell – 'Oh my God, what should I say next to get them to talk!?' Still, taking his interviews outside provided insights into why some people who wanted a beautiful garden, but were less confident about learning gardening, sometimes found themselves 'lost for words'. Though he had to hold his nerve, he'd probably do it again because it immediately gave him a sense of how this particular group could be more inclined to look at their gardens more than lovingly tend to the specimens within them.

2 *Learning from silence on the countryside path.* In another green environment, Doughty (2013) spent time with another social group whose members also seemed reticent about the idea of constant chatter. Her project was interested in how the interactions typical of countryside walking groups were an important part of what made walking together enjoyable and attractive. Going along on some of their trips, and talking to some of them as she went, she looked out for when exactly they were more or less amenable to different forms of talk during the walk. One finding, not unlike the justification for having difficult conversations in the car, was that part of the pleasure of walking groups related to how there was less of an expectation to be always reproducing the constant back and forth of conversation. When the path narrowed, for example, that could provide a valued conversational break. It's harder to keep going when you're forced into single file and can no longer hear what your partner is saying. Equally, sometimes a stronger sense of connection came from silently enjoying a view together – a deeper companionship that was partly linked to removing the unnecessary chatter. The physical environment itself was promoting certain patterns and rhythms of talk in her interviews – from pausing when required to quietly taking in the views. Taking her outside told her something about why those who can feel overburdened by the pressure to speak when in the company of others enjoyed this pastime. They liked the group walks partly because they didn't always have to talk.

So, before we really dig into the nitty-gritty of social research interviews, we can benefit from thinking about how where we talk shapes what people say. And, whilst we should stay mindful of whether people will be willing to go to certain places with us, there's scope for harnessing this insight. Perhaps they'll be excited by the idea of talking in an unusual environment or feel that the quiet meeting room you've unthinkingly booked makes things feel a bit pressurised. You'd need to be careful about recording when there's background noise. But the above two studies suggest that being creative with the context can help. That's not to say you should do something other than the 'standard' seated interview in a quiet place that's easy for everyone to get to. You probably wouldn't ask a businessperson to go for a walk because your assumption is that they're too busy – though, who knows, they might appreciate the break if the weather's good! It's more that there are opportunities here.

PIECES OF PAPER AND GETTING PEOPLE GOING

So, context matters. But how to do the actual talking? One of the most common ways in which social researchers divide up interviewing approaches is with regard to the extent to which they devise a plan for that and stick to it. Some say that, if you're a reasonably skilled interviewer, you might be happy to embark on your conversations with little more than a general sense of what you want to discuss. These interviewers are confident they'll be able to control the flow of the discussion in ways that allow them to stay on track with their topic whilst also, given part of the point is often to appreciate where people are coming from, identify the right questions to explore their perspectives on the hoof. The trouble, however, is then you run the risk of 'drying up'. In other words, you could easily find yourself stranded with nothing further to say when you came with the hopeful expectation of talking for an hour or so. Furthermore, if you're not fully on the ball in your interview, and primed to intervene quickly and diplomatically, your conversations can go off on irrelevant tangents. If that happens, once you've gone back to your recordings, you'll discover that, despite all your efforts, you've not learnt all that much about the topic you wanted to understand. We've certainly experienced this.

At the other end of the spectrum, there's an interviewer who'd rather impose a framework. For them, whilst they want to encourage people to talk fairly freely, they don't want to deviate too far from the list of questions they've spent time preparing. This certainly makes the experience a lot less intimidating. But the worry here is whether we're really getting their perspectives. What if our questions don't match up with their experiences and ways of looking at things? Are we really learning from them then? Also, with this approach, the people being interviewed can easily start to react as if they're doing a survey. You can imagine how this might happen if you end up rattling through your list of pre-prepared questions. The interview gathers speed, and this change of pace can mean that it's over in a matter of minutes. Again, you suddenly find yourself left nursing a still hot coffee because it's ended too soon. You might also have told them the conversation would last much longer. Embarrassing!

People call these two approaches 'unstructured' and 'structured' interviewing (Nathan et al., 2019). Many researchers, certainly at the start of their interviewing careers, go for something in the middle. They call this the 'semi-structured' approach. Their hope is that it will give them 'the best of both worlds' – keeping the conversation on track whilst allowing plenty of time to explore their perspectives.

We'd recommend having a piece of paper in front of you with a list of topics questions typed out on that – what's often called an *interview schedule* or *aide-mémoire*. Why the paper? Well, if you think back to what we said about how physical context impacts on the social experience, how would you react if you were sat opposite someone peering at you intermittently over the top of a laptop? You'd probably feel like the subject of an experiment. If part of the objective, at least in the moment, is to make the person feel that you're really engaging with them, that you want to understand where exactly they're coming from, then the barrier of the laptop screen is unlikely to help you in creating the, albeit temporary, intimacy you're after. A piece of paper feels less threatening. We've certainly seen students respond better to a piece of paper and a person – rather than a voice coming over the top of a laptop – in that commonroom exercise about moving to London we discussed at the start. Another way to avoid this issue could be to talk to people through the laptop itself – this is increasingly common and changes the social situation in a number of interesting ways (Adams-Hutcheson and Longhurst, 2017). And, of course, sometimes you might want to sacrifice your piece of paper, if you feel it's more important to talk in certain places where they'd be hard to have around, as with our two examples of talking outside. The point again is about considering whether the 'rules of thumb' are right for you in your study.

Figure 5.2 is an example of an 'interview schedule' on a piece of paper – taken from a study in which Russell looked at how different social groups in Qatar felt about air-conditioning in their everyday lives. This one was designed to explore how those who moved to the country in recent years had adapted to the local way of living with summer, when, despite the desert heat outdoors, people were sometimes kept uncomfortably cold inside (Hitchings, 2022).

We don't think this is an especially exemplary schedule – though it's not bad! But there are three features that we'd like to highlight to you.

1. *The preamble*. The first is the paragraph at the top. It reads rather like a script. There are words here that the interviewer will presumably say out loud to the person. It can be useful to have something like a script at the start. You'll likely be most nervous then so having this kind of conversational crutch can give you the confidence to focus on establishing the right tone by slowly going through your points. In the air-conditioning study, Russell often hadn't met the people before and wanted some 'light chat' with them before they settled into the interview. They often met in different public spaces so

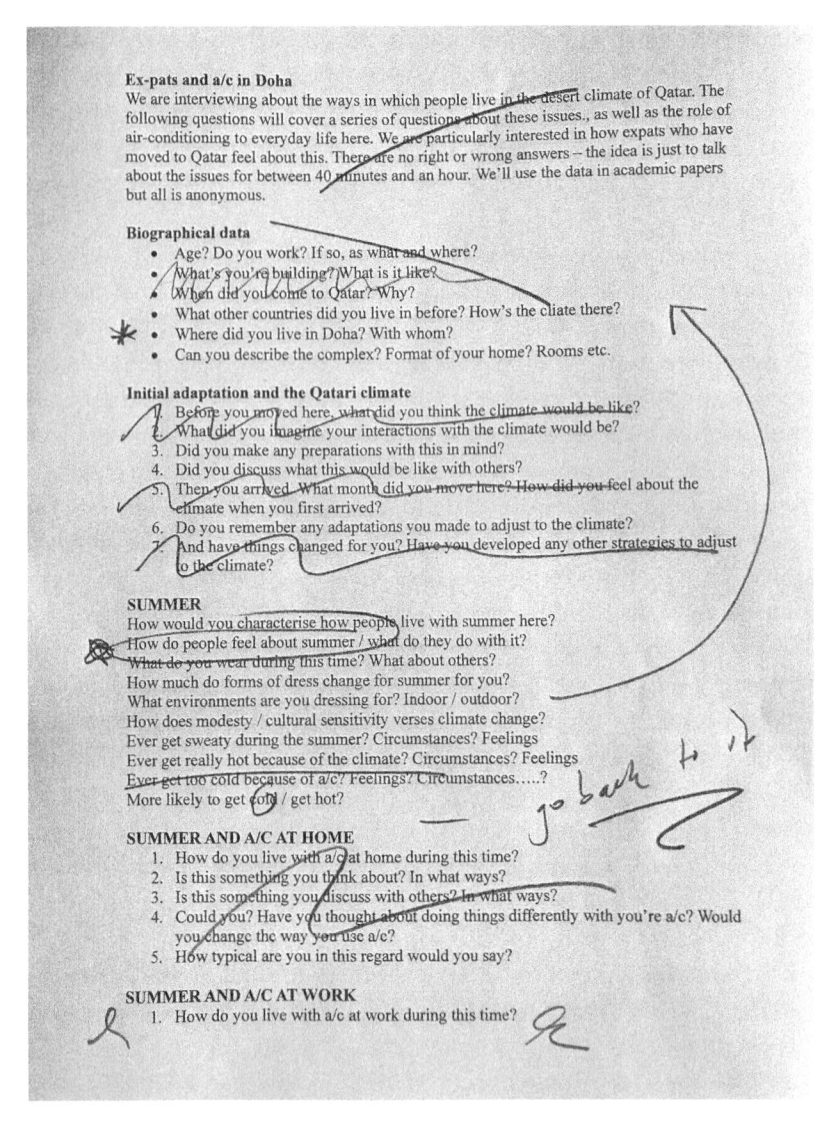

> **Ex-pats and a/c in Doha**
> We are interviewing about the ways in which people live in the desert climate of Qatar. The following questions will cover a series of questions about these issues, as well as the role of air-conditioning to everyday life here. We are particularly interested in how expats who have moved to Qatar feel about this. There are no right or wrong answers – the idea is just to talk about the issues for between 40 minutes and an hour. We'll use the data in academic papers but all is anonymous.
>
> **Biographical data**
> - Age? Do you work? If so, as what and where?
> - What's you're building? What is it like?
> - When did you come to Qatar? Why?
> - What other countries did you live in before? How's the cliate there?
> - Where did you live in Doha? With whom?
> - Can you describe the complex? Format of your home? Rooms etc.
>
> **Initial adaptation and the Qatari climate**
> 1. Before you moved here, what did you think the climate would be like?
> 2. What did you imagine your interactions with the climate would be?
> 3. Did you make any preparations with this in mind?
> 4. Did you discuss what this would be like with others?
> 5. Then you arrived. What month did you move here? How did you feel about the climate when you first arrived?
> 6. Do you remember any adaptations you made to adjust to the climate?
> 7. And have things changed for you? Have you developed any other strategies to adjust to the climate?
>
> **SUMMER**
> How would you characterise how people live with summer here?
> How do people feel about summer / what do they do with it?
> What do you wear during this time? What about others?
> How much do forms of dress change for summer for you?
> What environments are you dressing for? Indoor / outdoor?
> How does modesty / cultural sensitivity verses climate change?
> Ever get sweaty during the summer? Circumstances? Feelings
> Ever get really hot because of the climate? Circumstances? Feelings
> Ever get too cold because of a/c? Feelings? Circumstances.....?
> More likely to get cold / get hot?
>
> **SUMMER AND A/C AT HOME**
> 1. How do you live with a/c at home during this time?
> 2. Is this something you think about? In what ways?
> 3. Is this something you discuss with others? In what ways?
> 4. Could you? Have you thought about doing things differently with you're a/c? Would you change the way you use a/c?
> 5. How typical are you in this regard would you say?
>
> **SUMMER AND A/C AT WORK**
> 1. How do you live with a/c at work during this time?

Figure 5.2 Russell's interview schedule about air-conditioning
Source: Russell Hitchings

that chat naturally happened: a few words about how, say, that shopping mall coffee shop was heavily air-conditioned in ways could be both good and bad. In this context, going through the preamble marked the official start – slowly working through his script at the start allowed Russell to reset the tone and move from upbeat chatter about managing the cold in the mall to a more focused reflection on life in Qatar. It also meant he didn't forget to say various important things to reassure them about how there were no right

or wrong answers, how this was about them saying as much as they wanted to, and how we were going to handle his recordings afterwards.
2. *The sequence.* You can see there are sections here. We'll talk more about what is happening when we pose questions to people in our projects in Chapter 7. For now, we'll just say that it's worth thinking about the order in which you ask them. It can be quite good to clump them together under headings. Why? That way you'll get to cover different facets of the topic fairly fully before you move to the next one. That should make it easier for the person you are speaking with too. Imagine if you jumped around in a seemingly haphazard way between topics. That would be disconcerting. It might make them less confident that you were taking your project – and them – seriously. Unless you wanted to stage something more like a court room cross-examination in which you wrongfoot people with sudden changes of tack, it's often good to let people 'warm up' into discussing each aspect of your topic fairly fully.
3. *The scribbles.* Finally, you'll notice all the scribbles and marks on the sheet. This is partly because sometimes people say things you'll want to explore later – in which case it can be helpful to make a note so that you remember to do that. Another thing is that, despite what we've said about exploring aspects of the topic sequentially, sometimes people take our questions in very different directions. And that's often partly the point (this is only 'semi-structured', after all). This can mean they jump to topics we'd been planning to cover later in the interview. If you strike out those topics as you go along, you can quickly check which topics haven't yet been covered towards the end. Then you can ensure you discuss those too before the interview is over. Basic things like this can really matter. Especially when you're new to all this.

MORE TIPS BEFORE WE CONSIDER SOME DIFFERENT WAYS OF SEEING INTERVIEWS

Building on that last point, and before we consider different ways of imagining interviews, we want to offer a few more tips about ensuring a decent job gets done. We think that any 'standard' model of interviewing can be limiting when there are so many ways of looking at them. But we'd also acknowledge that our students can sometimes, when they return from their interviews, be a bit sheepish about how they'd gone. They'd hoped to speak to people for something like an hour, but they'd ended up coming back with much shorter recordings. This has sometimes surprised us. The students involved have been very focused elsewhere in their studies and we've always enjoyed talking with them. So, we've tried to identify some of the most common reasons why they didn't get as much from people as they'd imagined. Here are some hopefully handy tips about ensuring that you do:

1. *Show an interest.* This sounds obvious – of course, you're interested! You've likely done lots of reading about the topic you want to talk about before. You've possibly made a case for why this is exactly the sort of person likely to tell you some very interesting things about it. But sometimes that's the problem – it's sometimes precisely because of this level of personal investment that you forget about the basic skills of social interaction. Because so much rests on us doing a successful interview, it can be hard to relax into the situation. That can mean we forget we're speaking with a person who, just like anyone would, needs to be encouraged to open up to a relative stranger. We know how to show an interest when we talk with people. So, this is just a question of remembering to do the things that you'd usually do. Prompts to show we're listening, like saying 'interesting!' or 'really?', help. It's also good to punctuate the interaction with 'uh-huh's that confirm that you've understood what was just said and you're still listening. That way the person you are speaking with will be reassured that you value their efforts and feel encouraged to say a little more about their perspective. Going back to that interview exercise with our students from the start of the chapter, we've often seen our student interviewers looking blankly just as their peer was coming towards the end of something quite personal. It can be pretty excruciating to watch their revelations about the challenges they faced in London being met with such flat responses. Put yourself in their shoes. Why would you share this stuff if your questioner seems uninterested? We know the student interviewer was probably thinking about their next question, but it still pays to be encouraging.

2. *Pauses are often positive.* Another tip is to remember that pauses can often 'be your friends' in interviews. This is for a series of reasons. Whilst this depends on what you are trying to achieve, being confident enough to let a pause hang in the air emphasises that this is a thoughtful interaction. If you're comfortable with pauses, it also implicitly signals that you're comfortable with them and that can make your interviewee more inclined to say a bit more in response to the next question. More than that, it also gives them time to reflect. When these are topics you've been thinking hard about already, it's easy to lose sight of the fact that the person we're speaking with might not have them at the forefront of their minds. So, it's unsurprising that they might need a moment to compose their answer, or to add some additional detail. We should let them do that rather than freaking out about 'filling the silence' and rushing to the next question. Finally, pauses also give you extra time to decide whether and how you want to handle what they've just said, which takes us nicely to the next tip.

3   *Depth means digging.* One of the claims researchers often make about interviews is that they give you a 'depth' of insight. Compared to other methods, because you're spending some time with people in your interviews, you'll hopefully end up with a much better sense of where they are coming from. In other words, you are understanding their perspectives in more 'depth' than you would with a survey, for example, that some worry can 'put words in their mouths'. Well, that depth doesn't come effortlessly. It requires you to dig into their responses when the time is right. So, a further tip is to keep your wits about you in your interview and be ready to dig into their answers when necessary. You won't know when that will be beforehand but when people say something that is particularly relevant, hold your nerve, perhaps take advantage of a pause, and find some way of 'probing' them on what they've just said.

4   *Stay on track.* The flip side to 'getting people going' by showing your interest in them is about shutting them up. Perhaps that's putting things too bluntly. But it's true that sometimes, perhaps especially if you've done a good job of deploying some of the above strategies, people can often veer off towards topics that might not be relevant to your study. If we remember that we've probably worked hard to make this feel like a relaxed interaction for them, why wouldn't they? The whole pleasure of talking about life with friends and family, for example, can be about developing amusing asides, setting off on a relatively random journey of conversational discovery. So, what if people 'go off on a tangent' in a research interview? Firstly, we should be mindful of how they could be planning on circling back to our topic. So, what might have seemed like a tangent could eventually swing back to provide us with some of that all-important depth. But, if it's clear that the talk has drifted from your focus, don't be shy to use a gentle nudge to get things back on track. Done diplomatically, saying that their current reflections are interesting but that you'd like to get back to some of your key questions shouldn't be so hard to take. They know you're there for a reason after all.

CUTTING INTO THE FRUITCAKE: INTERVIEWS AREN'T JUST RICH

There are many ways of describing how people talk together:

- A chat
- A confessional
- A confrontation
- A debate

- A diatribe
- A gossip
- A grilling
- A spiel
- A story
- A speech

And whilst so far, we've given you some general tips and advice about pulling off an effective interview, the truth is that the spoken exchanges you might end up having with people in your studies can sometimes adopt each of the above formats. Sometimes you'd want them to, in which case feel free to ignore some of those tips we've just given you! There are also lots of interview variants around in our societies – from counselling sessions to police interviews – and those who interview in particular contexts often find themselves borrowing styles and strategies from other domains (Gubrium and Holstein, 2001). Going back to the common room exercise that started this chapter, when it went well our students sometimes talked excitedly afterwards about how fun it had been and how they felt like the presenter of a talk show or podcast. We tell them we're happy it went well. Then we ask whether that is the right format for getting what they wanted. There are certainly things that we would, and wouldn't, say about our lives on a podcast!

So, What Variety of Talk Do We Want to Stage?

Working through this issue is less common than it might be. This is partly because, as we've said, it's tempting to buy into the idea that interviews generally work so we don't need to say much more about them. Another reason relates to the common idea that an interview is a 'conversation with a purpose'. The idea here is that we're simply talking in a way that will hopefully tell us something useful about our topic. But there are many types of conversation. It's also common to hear people say that interviewing is an excellent method because of all the 'rich' material that results. We think this makes it sound like we're making a fruitcake – naturally full of delicious morsels of insight for us and our audiences to subsequently savour. But what's the recipe? How do we ensure our interview fruitcake is rich with juicy insights rather than bland and tasteless? We could think more about interviewing as a collective craft in which the interviewer responds to the situation to get the richness or, to run with the above metaphor about depth, they dig in at the right points to get the right kind of richness for them.

A different approach is to think more about how we're picturing what will happen when we speak to people. We could, we think, come up with some nicely creative ways of staging talk by considering some of the words on the above list and then asking ourselves which format might be most useful in our particular study. Let's look at some examples of how social researchers are effectively 'imagining the interview' to make for more insightful analysis. In what follows next, we've got some interviewers asking challenging questions about politics in America, some asking people to think harder than they usually do about their everyday lives in the UK, and some collecting stories from different groups of women in Southern Africa.

Ways of Imagining the Interview

The Interview as a Challenge

Imagine a stranger asked you to talk about your political beliefs. That's the sort of topic we'd imagine researchers might want to explore. It feels sufficiently serious to warrant a study. Given many of us are quite passionate about the political topics that made us want to study them in the first place, why wouldn't we ask others about their views on these topics? Thinking forward to some of the issues we'll discuss in Chapter 6, arguably that would be easier with a stranger. There's more at stake in opening up about these topics with someone you already know. With them, you'd need to maintain your relationship afterwards and so you might not want to risk disagreement. Perhaps that's especially challenging nowadays, with all the online political discussion turning us into 'keyboard warriors' who have learnt to belittle others instead of exploring their perspectives. We've certainly found that, when we talk politics with friends and family, even if we started off hoping to appreciate their views, talk soon veered towards something like a TV debate. So, speaking about particular topics can be a challenge and we'd need certain skills to emerge intact.

A good example comes from the work of Nina Eliasoph (1998) who spent a lot of time looking for the situations in which working-class Americans were happy to reveal their 'views' to one another (if we assume they'd already developed them). She found them to be surprisingly skilled in terms of dodging the confrontations they presumed would follow in a way that perhaps helps us to understand why so much political talk happens online nowadays. Arlie Hochschild (2016) did something similar when she set out to explore how some other Americans felt like 'strangers in their own land' – committed to supporting certain political parties whilst also being disadvantaged by the policies of those same parties. To do that, she got to know some of them first before asking some quite challenging questions in her interviews. In order to understand how they lived with and rationalised this apparent contradiction, she felt that she had to.

These examples speak to a particular way of thinking about what is happening when we talk together. Talk is often a skilled undertaking; there are tricks and strategies involved in getting through the experience so as to present yourself in the way you'd most desire. This applies in a particular way to political discussion.

But it will apply to plenty of other topics too. Perhaps these skills should be exactly the things to study and test out in an interview? Why shouldn't we stage something like a debate in our interviews, challenging people's stances to see how they marshal evidence in support of their views? If, for example, we'd like people to talk more openly about these topics with one another, first we might want to notice what we are up against in terms of how they already handle these obstacles.

KEY POINTS

- Talk is often a skilled activity
- This means exploring how these skills are deployed
- That could mean staging interviews to test out these skills

The Interview as Shared Discovery

Imagine a stranger asked you to account for all the details of what you do in everyday life. We can picture this interviewer as like a toddler who repeatedly asks 'why?' when you tell them something that is so self-evident to you that you've long forgotten the reasons why things are done in particular ways. How would you react? One way would be to get annoyed – 'This is just the way it is, stop bothering me with these questions!' Another way would be to see this as an opportunity for collective learning. You're figuring yourself out just as you are educating the toddler about why you, for example, tend to brush your teeth in particular ways, collect certain things first in the supermarket, or seemingly prefer to drink your coffee from a particular mug. It's easy, and certainly commonplace, to imagine that part of what we are doing when we do a social research interview is to collect people's 'opinions'. To think in this way is to reproduce the idea that we have an inner core of active thought that shapes our actions. One way of challenging this idea is to be open to the extent to which people are actively thinking about what they're doing when they live their lives.

A good example would be the work of Alison (2016), who asked small groups of people in the UK to tell her about how and why they did their laundry at home in the ways that they did. She was keen to understand how wedded they were to using water in certain ways and what that said about the potential for encouraging them to use less. She found they often had quite fixed ways of doing the laundry. Yet they didn't always know why. This made for a fun experience as the group gradually figured out how they had come to develop their idiosyncrasies – an enjoyable journey of self-discovery. A different reaction to the idea of interrogating everyday practices in conversation comes from one of our own studies. At the end of an interview in which he'd been asking a casual runner about her running, Russell vividly remembers a rather strident respondent flatly telling him that she 'never wants to think about her running ever again!' (Hitchings, 2021). This was a little difficult to take in the moment. She was thinking of him a bit like that annoying toddler! Still, however they do it, the ways in which people react to the idea of speaking about our topics is always interesting, we think. In this case, we think it told us something important about how attached she was to her current running practice. She felt it was good for her, so she didn't want to trouble it with any critical evaluation.

Here we have a rather different way of imagining things. This interview is more like a journey of discovery in which the interviewer gently pokes and prods at the practices that people carry in ways that help both the interviewer and the interviewee to develop an appreciation of how they live. One of the justifications for observing people, as discussed in Chapter 3, is that people can't always talk about their everyday actions. Our second interviewer would finesse this argument by saying that the extent to which they can, or want to, talk about certain aspects of their lives is exactly what could be interesting for us to research through interviews. And that opens up all sorts of exciting possibilities in terms of attending to how they dodge certain lines of questioning or flatly admit their ignorance about certain topics, not because they are too shy to tell us what they really think but rather because they have good reason to be more or less inclined to consider certain actions in the first place.

KEY POINTS

- Talk can be a way of understanding everyday actions
- This means not assuming that people necessarily 'know' why they do things
- That could mean interviews in which we surface these understandings together

The Interview as Storytelling

Imagine a stranger asked you about how it was to grow up in the place where you are from. You'd probably be flattered that they are taking such an interest in you. We often like to mull over how these sorts of details have influenced us too. This is perhaps that sort of thing that you might have discussed already with friends. In contemporary societies many people increasingly like to dwell on their biographies and we, understandably enough, sometimes curate the accounts that we present to others. Still, this sounds like an easier interview to embark upon – we are just collecting the accounts that are ready and waiting to be shared. Though we might need to be careful to get beyond the curated version, perhaps the apparent truth is less powerful than the stories people live by.

An example would be the work of Floretta Boonzaier and Cheryl de la Rey (2003) who were interested in how South African women rationalised abuse from their partners. By allowing women to tell stories of what they had lived through, their aim was to understand the power of 'cultural narratives'. This was in terms of both broader ideas about the qualities of men and women and how the men involved with them could sometimes act as, but not really be in their minds, monsters. This meant allowing them to tell their stories with minimal nudging back to particular themes or ideas the researchers had beforehand. The result was a focus on the stories these women told themselves which, irrespective of whether they were true or whether some actions didn't quite fit, kept them in these relationships. Malvern Chiweshe and colleagues (2017) similarly compared South African and Zimbabwean women's narratives of abortion to reveal how, though ideas about difficult partner relationships shaped termination decisions in both contexts, a narrative of shame had largely disappeared from the former. In this way, we see how personal narratives are also collective in the sense that the ways in which we justify our actions to ourselves can, whether we think about this or not, draw on locally shared stories.

This third style of interviewing is essentially about listening to the ways in which people naturally speak about their experiences. You can see how this approach might be particularly suited to the sensitive exploration of personal challenges. It would be wrong and insensitive to subject these women to a grilling about any inconsistencies in their thinking. Though this way of thinking about the interview requires more time together because we are allowing people the space to talk in the ways that make sense for them, rather than repeatedly pulling them back to our developing hunches with probing questions, the idea here is that the narratives they naturally reach for are those that are most powerful in their lives. So, the insights that follow from listening to them will hopefully be worth the wait. This is quite different to our last picture of the interview because we are encouraging and collecting their stories now rather than exploring the extent to which they think about certain things.

KEY POINTS

- Talk can be a way of tapping into existing stories
- This means letting people tell these stories in their own terms
- That could mean letting them go and only nudging them back when we need to

As a way of exemplifying how each way of 'imagining the interview' might take us down some interesting analytical paths, here's how our three sets of interviewers might think about the same immediate response from an interviewee:

A Pause

What might it mean when the interviewee stops for a second?

- *Challenger:* Perhaps the person is collecting their thoughts before presenting an argument or point. We should notice how marshalling an argument leads to particular ways of seeing things.
- *Discoverer:* Give them time and look out for how often pauses happen. This could be telling us something about the extent to which practices have become unthinkingly automatic.
- *Listener:* This is part and parcel of telling a story and a key part of remembering. We should consider which reasonings are more or less readily called upon.

A Monologue

What might it mean when the interviewee takes control with an extended account?

- *Challenger:* Possibly a way of sidestepping the back and forth of conversation by taking control. What is this doing to our relative standing in terms of being understood as knowledgeable about topics?
- *Discoverer:* They may be getting lost in a process of figuring out how and why they do what they do. I'll not disturb them too much because it will help me to understand their actions in context.
- *Listener:* A valuable window into how people rationalise the events of their lives. I'm happy this is happening because this is what I wanted, and I'll nudge them back onto topic only when I need to.

A Push Back

What might it mean when an interviewee rejects the question?

- *Challenger:* This helps me to understand the ways in which people deal with being challenged. Why have they decided to push back here and how are they framing topics (and themselves) when they do?
- *Discoverer:* This can show how amenable people are to inspecting, and potentially altering, their practices. It says something about how different groups may be willing to change their ways.
- *Listener:* This is really not what I'd want because I've tried really hard to encourage their own accounts and narratives. I'll listen sensitively to these and hope that helps me explore my topic.

There are many ways of imagining interviews. Our point is more that it's good to think about the possibilities in terms of seeing and staging things. When we work through these three options with our master's students, we ask them to tell us how they might approach the topics they're passionate about researching in each of these ways. What would that do to how they'd tackle their topics? The results are often some rather neat project ideas that they'd never have come up with if we'd stopped at the fruitcake metaphor. What about the everyday practices of the urban policymaker and how their policies reflect their work habits? Could we think about staging debate-like discussions with some climate change deniers? Going back to the example that started this chapter, some of them even say they'd like to listen to the migration stories of others in the class. These are some suggestions. We could also go back to that list at the start of this section. When might we want to encourage a confessional? And when could gossip be something we'd learn a lot from? There are lots of options here.

CONCLUSION

Talk is a fundamental part of social life. But how should we organise our experience of talking with people in a social research project? In this chapter, we've provided an account of some of the things to think about in order to do effective research interviews and some tips about how to ensure you do a decent job. We've done that because plenty of our students have faced challenges even though they've sometimes assumed that interviews would be straightforward. We then thought a bit harder about how we're imagining our interviews so as to identify strategies that could be all the more effective for questioning the standard model. Are people managing their encounters with others, drawing on various interactional skills and strategies in so doing? Are they embarking on a journey of self-discovery in which they come to understand themselves just as we come to understand them? Or are they telling their stories by narrating how they came to live and think in particular ways? As we've emphasised, interviews are sometimes framed as providing 'rich' research material. We're big fans of the interview because we learn so much and so quickly with them. But there are different kinds of richness and different ways of getting it, and we could be quite creative about what we're trying to do with our interviews.

6

ENGAGING PEOPLE: SEEING SOCIAL RESEARCH AS A RELATIONSHIP

WHAT TO DO IN AUCKLAND?

Fresh out from his PhD Alan went to study the social life of an inner-city neighbourhood in Auckland, New Zealand. The funding proposal set out where the project was going to take place and what it was trying to discover. On the face of it, this should have been a straightforward case of finding some locals, talking to them about what it was like to live where they did, and ¡Basta! project done. He began by renting an apartment in the neighbourhood, with the idea that living there would help him to connect with those he wanted to research. Then he started hanging out; shopping in local stores, spending time in the cafés, visiting restaurants as much as his salary allowed, going for walks around the area, talking to people while waiting for the bus. The inspiration for this approach came from various studies of city life where researchers, through spending time in neighbourhoods, gradually gain the trust of the local community, and are eventually offered insights into how that community works.

A few months in, it was starting to become clear that his strategy wasn't working. Sure, Alan now knew quite a bit about the neighbourhood, which stores were popular, where some people liked to brunch on weekends, and where different social groups were found: the cheap Middle-Eastern restaurant that let you bring your own wine was popular with students; media people frequented a flamboyant bar-restaurant called SPQR; and KFC was where the disaffected teenagers went. But he hadn't really got to know anyone. In a way, this was itself revealing. Alan was interested in how people used the neighbourhood's cafés, restaurants, and bars, and one of the defining features of these spaces was that people didn't expect to talk very much to strangers within them. Still, even though Alan, as a young, university educated, professionally employed, Kiwi accented, Pākehā (white) man, more or less fitted the demographics of the neighbourhood, he wasn't getting anywhere. Perhaps that was the problem – maybe he blended in so well that no-one felt especially minded to take an interest in him.

The dilemma of how to engage with those we wish to study is the focus of this chapter. In many cases they initially seem readily available – we know who they are, where they live, the places where they congregate. But gaining 'access', as social researchers call it, in terms of persuading people to take part in our studies can be tricky. In some cases, we may only be able to gain access to the desired social setting with the support of a 'gatekeeper': someone in authority who controls who may enter and spend time with people in a setting. In others, potential respondents might understandably have relatively little interest in helping a more or less random social researcher. For methods like observation, part of the appeal can be that we often don't need to trouble people. But, especially for those approaches that require us to interact for some time with a selection of people, such as interviewing or taking part in activities, this is an important consideration. And it's about more than just getting people to help or convincing them to allow us to become part of their worlds. We are proposing a variety of relationships with people in research. In that sense, our chapter title is apposite – we should consider how we make ourselves and our studies 'engaging' to them and the implications of different strategies.

Alan ended up 'engaging' those who used his neighbourhood's cafés, restaurants, and bars – those who were part of Auckland's emerging urban public culture (the focus of his study) – through various strategies. He asked people he met if they knew others who regularly used those spaces. To get beyond the young professionals he found easier to approach, he put up posters in the cafés with bulletin boards. He even taped notices to traffic lights at the major crossings in the neighbourhood with tear-off slips at the bottom with his phone number on – a trick he'd learnt from living in Berlin. He ran ads in the two local free newspapers (this was before the internet had taken off). He'd probably be thinking about social media groups and online discussions about the locality nowadays. Because he'd discovered the main commercial strip was the heart of gay and lesbian Auckland, he put an ad in *Pink News* – a free newspaper for the local LGBTQ community. He even got himself onto the local radio station to drum up a little extra interest. Alan eventually managed to get 50 participants from a variety of backgrounds to speak with him about public life. But there was more to it than just going somewhere and effortlessly starting to learn from the locals.

We don't always hear so much about these faltering attempts at 'recruitment' because, in social research, it's understandably often more appealing to present yourself as someone who can easily charm their way into their chosen community instead of someone who might be dismissed as a possible weirdo at bus stops. But thinking about these issues is crucial to making a project work. More than that, it's important because we should treat people appropriately and respectfully and in ways that show sufficient gratitude. This chapter explores a range of strategies for engaging those we wish to research. We'll examine some of the ways in which people generally talk about this topic, how you can use this issue to come up with original project ideas, and how different approaches to engaging people in research can end up shaping the accounts of their lives you eventually produce.

A SHORT EXERCISE TO GET US GOING

As Alan's Auckland experience suggests, persuading people to get involved in a research project can be challenging. Still, like so much of social research, these challenges are not all that distinct from many of those that we face elsewhere in our lives. You'll have had experiences where you've wanted to convince people that you're the right person for a particular role or to accept you into their lives. You might have joined a new sports team and needed to demonstrate to others that you'll be a useful addition. Those of you who are at university may have moved into a hall of residence where you didn't know anyone, and you've suddenly had to hustle to make a new circle of friends.

What did you do to help people welcome you into these groups? Here's an exercise that it would be good for you to do now, if you are up for it. Think back to when you've been interviewed for some kind of job. Grab a piece of paper or open up your note-taking app on your phone. Now take two minutes (set a timer!) to draw up a list of all the things you did to prepare. Now write another list of all the things you needed to remind yourself to do in the interview to make sure you came over well (set another timer!). If you did our exercise, your lists probably look something like this…

Before the interview:
  Research what the job involved
  Research the company you're applying to
  Choose what clothes to wear (thinking about the kind of job you'll be doing)
  Think of how you'd explain why you wanted the job
  Come up with some snappy answers for why you'd be a good hire
  Make sure you're on time

During the interview:
  Make eye contact
  Shake people's hands (firmly?) at the start, don't leave anyone out
  Introduce yourself clearly and confidently

Control your language (don't use too much vernacular, don't curse)
Remember to ask questions at the end (even if you don't care about the answers)

If we asked you to write up a list for the other social situations we mentioned – joining a sports club, moving into shared accommodation – you'd probably have come up with a somewhat similar collection of suggestions. But the advice would also be a little different for each case; shaking everyone's hand in a new dorm might come across as strange, whilst making eye contact and introducing yourself to everyone you meet could be just the ticket.

The point of this exercise is to get you thinking about how we present ourselves to others. That this work, what the sociologist Erving Goffman (1959) called the 'presentation of self', is a fundamental aspect of our everyday interactions with others has important implications for how we organise our interactions with those we're hoping to research. How we present ourselves, consciously or not, can often have a profound impact on whether people will want to get involved in our studies and how open they'll be if they do. This feels like quite basic stuff, but, as we discussed in the last chapter, sometimes we've found our students – including some of those doing PhDs – don't think about these matters that much when they are starting out with their projects. That's, we think, understandable because they've many other things going through their minds already – What are the right questions to ask? Have I got all the equipment I need? How and when will I record things? All this can make it easy to forget about the obvious stuff, namely how others will react to them as people. The trouble is that, if we don't think about this obvious stuff, we'll never get to ask our questions, however beautifully composed.

HOW TO WORK WITH OUR EXISTING CHARACTERISTICS: ON BIG 'P' POSITIONALITY

Of course, we can't know with certainty how specific individuals will react to any given situation. Nor do we have unlimited capacity or licence to alter how we present ourselves to others. We carry all sorts of ascribed aspects of who we are into any encounter with other people: our sex and gender, our body, our voice, our skin colour, our accent, to name just a few aspects that might very well play into how these encounters unfold. Still, thinking hard about how others might react to us, and considering carefully about how we might influence that reaction, are an important part of being a good social researcher. It's also a useful reminder that the research encounter isn't about 'us' so much as about the 'we' that, as social researchers, we're trying to fashion with those we're enrolling into our research projects.

Let's start with how to think about some of the comparatively fixed characteristics we possess as individuals. There are some who argue that if you're from a privileged section of society, you should be especially wary of studying marginalised groups because of the inherent 'power imbalances'. Their argument is that, as social researchers, we're already and always caught up in society's hierarchies and systems of power. When we think about things in this way, what people call our 'positionality', namely the social characteristics that we carry with us when we start out on our projects, cannot help but shape what happens afterwards. We might call this big 'P' positionality, partly because these are, without doubt, important issues that deserve our attention. Researchers such as Kim England (1994) and Robyn Dowling (2000) who have considered the role of positionality in research outline a series of reasons why it matters: it affects the questions you are likely to ask, the way respondents are likely to reply, and even whether those you wish to study will let you spend time with them at all.

To illustrate why positionality matters, England tells a nicely candid story of a failed research project. As part of some of her research on vulnerable women, she came across a range of organisations that supported women with marginalised sexual identities. The lack of social research into such institutions, so she reasoned, represented a compelling case for studying such spaces. There were also a number of prominent organisations in Toronto, where she lived, which seemed ideal for her to examine. As England developed her project, however, she ran into a number of roadblocks. These roadblocks were all about her positionality as a researcher. As a heterosexual woman, she knew little about the culture of Lesbian and Queer women. And she didn't have any insight into the challenges of living with a marginal sexual identity, or the very intricate politics of LGBTQ organisations in Toronto. All that made it difficult to build relationships with those she planned to study. Indeed, it eventually led her to question whether she was the right person to be doing this research. Ultimately her research project, for all its laudable ambitions, failed to get off the ground. This was partly because those groups she was hoping to work with couldn't see the value of her proposed research, but mostly because after much self-reflection, England decided that she had better leave this topic for someone else to study.

What typifies big 'P' approaches to positionality is that the dilemmas of the research encounter are framed as inherent to the existing characteristics of the researcher and the researched. And that means thinking hard about who you are as a researcher and what that means for the potential for forging relationships in your studies. Big 'P' positionality also alerts us to the broad ethical challenges and dilemmas of doing social research – who should really be doing particular studies and in what ways. Ann Oakley (1981) has famously discussed how the very idea of women interviewing women might not make sense in view of these positionality matters. Why? Well, as a feminist, she argues it's almost impossible in this situation to be neutral and 'objective' by following established protocols to build some kind of rigorous appreciation of how others live and think. Women can't really 'interview' one another because that kind of more formalised encounter is not what they should want or what would naturally happen anyway. Better, she says, to acknowledge that you're working towards a shared sisterly understanding since you'd naturally do that anyway because of your common characteristics. Whether intentionally or not, with big 'P' positionality the social identity of the researcher often comes in effect to be either a barrier or an opening that defines what you can and cannot research, and with whom – women will do better studying women, ethnic minorities other ethnic minorities, people from the same place or class would find it easier to talk together, and so on.

We might summarise the key points around big 'P' positionality as:

- People will respond to us differently depending on who we are
- This means thinking about how to work with our fixed attributes
- Often this amounts to the suggestion that sharing characteristics is helpful
- This often connects to the idea of helping (as much as studying) people

In terms of what that means for how you'd engage people in your studies, you'd need to think through these matters. What challenges would you face in speaking to and interacting with particular social groups? How would things go if you were to engage with some of those with similar characteristics to you – age, gender identity, sexuality, ethnicity, class – and how might this help you to identify on what terms you'd want to engage with people in your project?

Having said all that, there are other aspects we could consider, and the 'big ticket' issues of race, gender, class, sexuality, and so forth may not always turn out to be the most important ones (see Chapter 10 on how we reproduce certain 'images' when we design our research projects). Furthermore, shared characteristics don't always guarantee immediate rapport and better insights. Sometimes we might want to challenge and question as much as build strong connections with people. To give you a very short example, we've mentioned in Chapter 5 how we did a project on what runners in London felt about the different environments in which they ran (Hitchings and Latham, 2017). As runners ourselves, part of the challenge for us was about not rehearsing the things we'd naturally say to other runners and instead staging some more reflective discussions about where and how they ran. We needed to turn away from the usual 'running chat' about injuries, how training was going, whether they've done races, and so on. Being the same isn't always helpful.

REFRAMING THIS AS SELF-AWARENESS: ON SMALL 'P' POSITIONALITY

Good social research is founded on a basic ethic of empathy – that it's possible through careful work for people with different backgrounds and life experiences to gain an understanding of one another. That being so, we might reframe the positionality question in terms of how we go about presenting ourselves to, and engaging with, people, along with what that means for how they subsequently interact with us. The fixed characteristics that we possess as individuals play a part in this work of self-presentation and inter-personal engagement. But assuming that we can only research those who share our characteristics, or to whom we feel we can more instinctively relate, is a bit self-defeating. One of the most exciting things about being a social researcher, after all, is about knowing that, if you do your work well, you'll soon get a sense of how another group of people – about whom you might not have known very much before – sees things. What about the journey of discovery and the social research adventure that we made so much of at the start of this book? With that in mind, we'd also do well to think about what we'd call the small 'p' positionality issues of how we present ourselves and manage our relationships with other people in our studies – we can, after all, do something about those, whereas the die often seems already cast if we linger for too long over the big 'P' issues.

In this reframing of ours (Hitchings and Latham, 2020a) our research positionality is as much about how we handle people as it is about what we do with our fixed characteristics. These personal strategies of approaching and building relationships – however short-lived – with other people in research might be called small 'p' positionality. We call it that because it's about the subtle ways in which we establish the relationship we want, and more generally present ourselves to those involved in our research. This is about the little things that we do to make our projects work for us more than the weightier issues to do with identity and the rights and wrongs of researching certain groups.

Mario Luis Small and Jessica McCrory Calarco (2022) encourage us to think of our relationships with those we research as an outcome of our 'self-awareness' as researchers. As they put it:

> [A] good interviewer can talk to anyone about any topic and elicit
> empirically rich and accurate information, even about difficult or sensitive
> parts of participants' lives. (p. 124)

They'd also say the same for other methods such as taking part. The thinking here is that this doesn't give us a licence to study anything – the big 'P' issues still matter. However, having worked through the question of the appropriateness or otherwise of our research, we can then think about how we present ourselves to those we are studying. Cultivating a sense of self-awareness about how we currently do, and potentially could, build the right sorts of relationships in this respect is a skill that social researchers can cultivate. That's what Small and Calarco mean when they talk about being a 'good' interviewer in the above quote someone who has cultivated these skills.

What does this self-awareness mean in practice? We'll explore that in more detail in the following sections. But an illustration from Alan's Auckland project can help us to get going. To remind you, Alan's project was focused on the changing urban public culture of an inner-city neighbourhood – how and when people came together in public spaces there, and what that said about effective and enjoyable ways of sharing cities. When he applied for his funding, he knew only the basic demographic facts about the neighbourhood. It was only after spending time in the neighbourhood that he discovered how important it was for Auckland's LGBTQ community.

As coincidence would have it, just when he was starting to recruit people Alan read England's positionality paper and so was mindful of the dilemmas of studying sexual minorities. Still, if gay women and men were an important part of the neighbourhood then the project clearly needed to include their experience in some way. Yet as a straight(ish) man in a long-term relationship with a woman he didn't have much direct insight into what it was like to be gay or lesbian. This is what he sometimes ended up leading with: that he was researching the neighbourhood, but as a straight man he needed the help of gay and lesbian locals to understand how the neighbourhood worked for them. He also started reading the weekly *Pink News* and read as much LGBTQ history as he could.

Fronting with this naivety proved surprisingly effective for him, both in recruiting interviewees and in generating fine-grained accounts of how exactly these interviewees related to the neighbourhood. Interviewees were happy to be placed in the role of teachers leading Alan through the intricacies of gay and lesbian life in Auckland (Latham 2003a, 2003b). Being straight-up about his straight-ness helped build trust with respondents – so being different was a good thing here. It also opened up a whole range of useful conversations about the differing experiences of how – and when – they managed the presentation of their sexual identity in the different spaces of the city he had come to examine.

We might summarise the key points around small 'p' positionality as:

- Being a self-aware researcher involves being attentive to how you present yourself to others
- A skilled researcher can build relationships with people very different to themselves
- Sometimes being from a different background can be exactly what you'd want

We'll talk more about how others have done this work later on in this chapter since there are different relationships to cultivate, depending on the warrants of your work.

WAYS OF GETTING PEOPLE TO HELP US OUT

Now that we've thought a little about how who we are plays into our research, how others might respond to that, and how we should work at being self-aware about this throughout our projects, let's look at some of the ways we can convince people to participate in the first place. The above issues can lead us down particular paths in terms of thinking about what we are doing and towards certain concerns about ethical treatment, whether we are studying people or advocating for them, and who has the right to represent particular groups. But the truth of the matter is that the more essential task is often a bit more prosaic – we want them to be willing to help us. We've already mentioned how Alan used advertisements, flyers, and posters, as well as a process of participant 'snowballing' (getting people to recommend others who might also be willing to help) to recruit people.

In his flyer Alan was trying to connect with people's enthusiasm for the hospitality spaces of the neighbourhoods he was studying. As part of the project, participants were asked to produce a one-week diary, as well as taking part in an interview so the 'honorarium' indicates that the project takes people's time seriously. Emphasising that the honorarium was small simultaneously discouraged

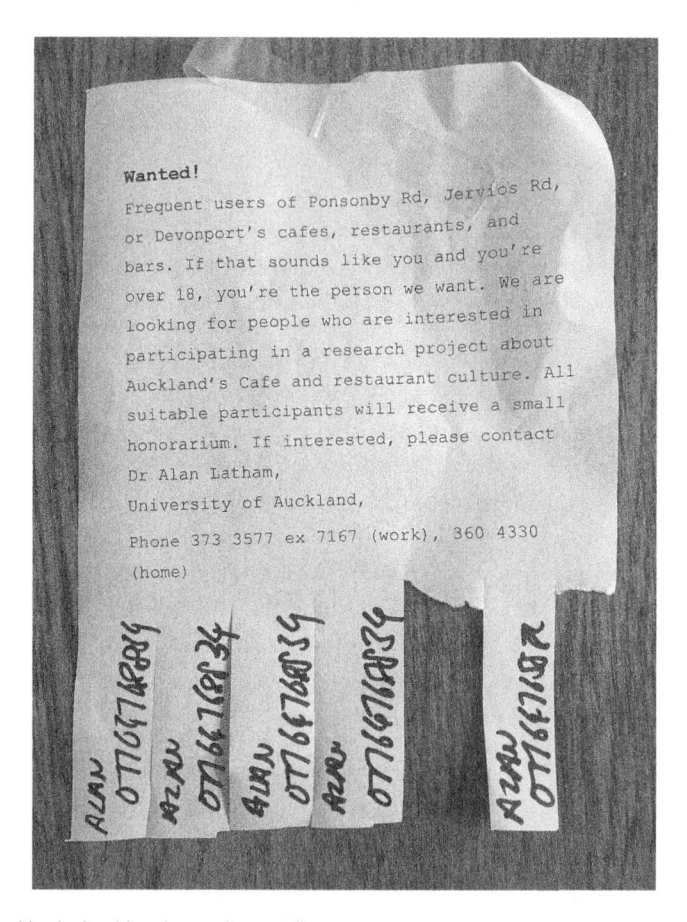

Figure 6.1 Alan's Auckland recruitment flyer
Source: Alan Latham

people only motivated by money. This was a sensible approach but, in retrospect, it might have been better to have used more everyday language in the pitch for respondents! Once people contacted him, Alan explained how the project was interested in as diverse a range of people as possible. His pitch was that the neighbourhoods he was studying – and the hospitality spaces within them – were interesting to him because this was where new ways of living together in cities might be forming. In that respect, he was flattering people that they were part of something important and exciting. He also stressed that his was non-commercial, university funded, research and he sometimes said he was writing a book on these neighbourhoods (though that never happened in the end). Looking back, Alan thinks this was partly to emphasise the seriousness of his work. He was, after all, only a young man then – fresh out from his PhD as we've said – and he worried that people might need persuading about the seriousness of the project, though they might have helped because he looked young and eager. You'll also see he used 'we' in his flyer when it was actually only him doing the study. That too was, looking back on things, an attempt to emphasise seriousness by emphasising that the study was under the umbrella of a prestigious institution, the University of Auckland. Either way, Alan was marshalling a serious of implied claims – your neighbourhood is exciting, my study is serious, we're a team – to get the project off the ground.

There are many reasons why people become part of a social research project. Reflecting on how we present our projects to potential participants is worth doing in terms of both getting them involved and what happens afterwards. A list of the key reasons why people might agree would include:

- We convince them it will produce useful knowledge
- We offer to tell their stories to the wider world or particular audiences
- We position ourselves as an ally in a bigger conflict or debate
- We show an interest in them and they reciprocate
- We flatter them that their accounts are important
- They do it because others they know have and they feel they should too
- They do it because they want to help us out because they like us
- They do it because they like talking about the topic or are invested in it
- They do it because it takes little effort and they don't want to seem mean
- They do it because their professional or public roles mean they must
- We pay them (an 'honorarium' or otherwise)!

The right way to recruit, and the right strategy for convincing people of the value of helping out, will depend (as it always does) on the warrants of our research (Chapter 2). If we're interested in witnessing people's lives or in persuading outside audiences they should care about these lives, then we need to explain to those involved how we wish to use our research skills to help tell their stories and present them to the wider world. Still in all likelihood people are participating in our projects because they want to help us out as much as anything else. Equally they might have some spare time and just feel flattered that you're taking an interest in them. There's nothing wrong with any of that of course. But it's useful to be realistic about why people are letting you work with them. If you think they're doing it because they like you and they've a little spare time, you might want to get down to business and not talk too much about any wider ambitions before they change their minds! Either way, by putting yourself in their shoes at this point, you'll have a better sense of how you'll want to work with both your big 'P' and small 'p' positionality in the most productive ways for you.

TWO EXAMPLES OF ENGAGING OTHERS IN RESEARCH

One of the challenges we've faced in teaching about this sort of self-awareness – and, as part of that, the process of engaging those we hope to study – is that researchers don't always talk explicitly and honestly about how exactly they've harnessed it. It's easy to recognise high quality social research; we can tell from the subtlety of the presented accounts and analysis when they've done a good job in terms of, for example, coming to really understand the group they've studied. But the interpersonal strategies and decisions behind the production of such work is less often talked about – the proof of the pudding is in the presented analysis (to add another cooking metaphor to those of Chapter 4).

Still, sometimes we do get a sense of the engagement journeys involved in the studies that we read. Let's examine two examples of exemplary social research, focusing on how the researchers involved went about engaging those they researched. Both are drawing on projects that were largely based on interviews since, we suppose, given the amount of time you spend with someone when you do interviews with them, it's especially important to think about how you get, and keep, people engaged with your project for that length of time. Still, these issues are always there.

Example One: Life as a Migrant Domestic Worker in Hong Kong

'And everything is very strange, just like, things that you're not seeing at home. And then thinking, yeah, and crying all the time: I can't do this I can't manage. I don't know how to do this, iron bedsheets, shirts, so I call my Aunty, I said, "Aunty, I can't do this." And she said, "You're stupid, you are already here, you must do it." So, I'm going to ask.... And I said, "I don't know how to do this." She shows me how to do it, iron those sheets her way. And then little by little I'm learning ... but the thing is all the family members would come over for dinner almost every night, you know, thousands of families, you know, you have to cook, you have to do all the laundry and everything.... And then again I think I found a job with an Australian family which is quite demanding. And then she expects you to be perfect with everything you do. Everything, everything, and once you do something wrong she say ... she's going to tell you, it doesn't suit her. People have different way, of housekeeping, and so on. ... It's like when you're preparing food for Chinese you just have to, OK, bring all the plates, cutleries and the chopsticks and that's all.... And soup, you know first, but in a Western family, no. You have to serve wine glasses first or cocktails and bring everything; after that the main course, the soup and there's a mat. So there is really a big difference. Yes. When it comes to household, really, Chinese is simpler, but you learn. They are going to teach you the way they want.' (p. 163)

This is a quote from Janine, a Hong-Kong-based, Filipina domestic worker, from Caroline Knowles and Douglas Harper's book, *Hong Kong: Migrant lives, landscapes, and journeys* (2009). It's part of an extended discussion of the experience of living and working 'inside other lives' (p. 157). In the interview, Janine gives a detailed account of her experience working for a range of families across her 20 years in Hong Kong. This interview is notable for the sustained narrative about her circumstances that Janine develops, and also for the space that Caroline Knowles, the interviewer, allows for it. The interview is conversational, and Janine is being allowed to work through her answer at her own pace. Through the interview – and the careful presentation of extended excerpts from it – the reader gains a nuanced sense of what it is like to work as a migrant domestic worker in Hong Kong.

Thinking about how social researchers engage with those they wish to research and how this shapes the responses they receive, there are three important elements here. Firstly, Janine is skilled and experienced at domestic work: she understands the intricate differences between the demands of Chinese compared to Western households; she knows how to cook, clean, and organise her workload; and she is skilled at navigating the emotional labour of living within the life of a family. In her world, she's evidently an expert. However, in much of her everyday life, she's positioned as subordinate, someone who takes rather than gives instructions. In her interview and her wider study, Knowles self-consciously positions herself as the non-expert who needs Janine's guidance. Secondly, this carefully crafted inversion of the role we might have expected Janine to take – given that the interviewer, Knowles, is a professional British woman, not dissimilar in many ways from Janine's employers – was partly a product of Knowles' self-awareness as an interviewer and the personal trust that she had developed with Janine from spending extended periods with her. The interview quoted above was a result of having already spent time hanging out with Janine on Sundays, when she didn't have to do any work, as well at at her place of work – it wasn't just a one-off encounter. This interview happened in a place where Janine was comfortable, the apartment of her long-term employer. The exchange between Janine and Knowles has the feel of an intimate conversation and its context, together with the work Knowles had put into spending time with her there, helped with that. Thirdly, Janine's enrolment into the study was the result of an introduction from her employer, a woman who had taken the role of mentor and friend to her, so this was a particular kind of introduction – she wasn't just doing it because a comparatively distant boss had demanded that she did.

Example Two: The Life of a Long-Distance Commuter

'I'm glad that you've come here to see this, because people do not have any conception. If you say to people, "I do a laborious job, where I sit at a computer all day; I hardly get up, except to have a pee; I don't talk to anyone" – you know. There is no fun in my job. It's laborious, it's intensive, it requires concentration and there's a lot of it; it never ends. It is like pushing – it's like the labour of Hercules: you are just pushing a stone uphill all day long.'

I feel a lump in my throat and swallow. There is a brief silence and I nod, lips pursed. Her lips are downturned. My eyes are watering a little. She continues:

'So maybe, if I had the kind of job where I had a secretary bring me nice cups of tea and had a long lunch, you know, and I went to meetings and I strutted about and I was an important, you know, chap on, you know, megabucks, the commute wouldn't be a problem, would it? And, as an important chap, I could probably work from home two or three days a week and ....' (Bissell, 2014: 195)

This is an excerpt from an interview with Alice, an office worker, who commutes daily from a small rural town on New South Wales' Central Coast into downtown Sydney, Australia. The interviewer, David Bissell, was interested in the life of commuters there and how people managed the stress associated with commuting. Wary of imposing his own view on how his commuters might experience that, he started his interviews by asking those he spoke with to describe their travel to and from work. The above discussion happened at Alice's workplace – a small, dispiriting, room 'painted monotone grey' where 'on one side black boxes of paper files fill floor to ceiling' (p. 194). Amongst the 50 people that Bissell spoke with in his study, Alice's commute was one of the longest. It took more than three hours each way, meaning she left her house at 5.40 a.m. and often didn't return home until 7.45 p.m. The excerpt comes towards the end of a long, detailed description of the logistics of her journey from the Central Coast involving two trains and two buses, along with the main 'beefs' she had about her commute. It's only after that account is presented that she starts to talk about the cumulative strain of both her long commute and her mundane office job. This excerpt comes from Bissell's paper *Encountering stressed bodies: Slow creep transformations and tipping points of commuting mobilities* (2014).

Here Alice introduces the experience of working day-in-day-out in a demanding, but mundane office job. That Bissell has taken the effort to come to her work is interpreted by Alice as a marker of his commitment to understanding what it feels like to experience a commute like hers. That partly gives her the confidence to start by getting a few gripes off her chest. This sense of wanting to put them in charge somewhat was also amplified by Bissell's decision to open his interview with a question that offered Alice the licence to talk at length – immediately displacing the suggestion that the interviewer is the expert scientist who will set the tone of the interview, emphasising instead that he is there to listen. He's also clearly working hard to empathise, whilst also giving her plenty of space to talk – note the pause and the 'pursed lips'. Janine's interview with Knowles has the feel of friends talking together. This conversation feels more therapeutic. The interview is a space for Alice to explain her everyday life without judgement about whether that life has worth. The role of the interviewer is to listen non-judgementally to the themes that the interviewee wishes to develop. Of course, there's a risk in such an approach that the interviewee will take the conversation in directions that have little to do with the research project (it would be interesting to know whether Bissell had an interview schedule on a sheet of paper similar to those we discussed in Chapter 5). He'd also recruited people who were already keen to discuss the topic, having found interviewees through recruitment adverts with the headline 'Commuting Stress' (p. 194) in a free daily city newspaper. This can be a good way to recruit, but it might also give you a certain type of person and that might mean a certain type of interview. You'd expect people to have things to say if they came through this route. It's probably no surprise that Janine had things to get off her chest – she'd responded to an advert that assumed she might. Recruiting in this way established the focus ahead of the interview, along with the kind of the conversation they'd have.

The two examples demonstrate how different research contexts and different research aims will ask different things of the researcher and those being researched alike. Whilst Knowles as an interviewer and participant observer took on the role of empathetic friend, as an interviewer Bissell adopted the role of something closer to a confidential therapist, providing a holding space for the interviewee to slowly explore their relationship with work and commuting. Both cases demonstrate the importance of fostering a sense of self-awareness as a social researcher about how they should present themselves at the start and interact afterwards to get the most useful material. Both took time to do this – Knowles investing in people like Janine through a variety of gestures because she wanted to understand the detail of where she was coming from; Bissell giving Alice plenty of space for her rant whilst also showing that he felt for the challenges she was facing because he wanted to get a handle on how she coped with stress. This probably came naturally to both of them as people who were interested in the perspectives of others, but they still harnessed their skills to make their projects work.

WHAT OTHER ROLES MIGHT WE ASSUME?

There are many roles we might assume as social researchers beyond those of friend or confidant(e). The point is to think about how others respond to them. In our master's methods class, we sometimes organise an exercise that encourages our students to start to reflect on – that is to say to be self-aware about – the roles they might adopt in a semi-structured interview. We ask them to interview a friend, relative, or other student on the course, about the topics we know they are passionate about (climate change, migration across Europe, or neighbourhood change in cities). Then, once they've done their short interviews, we ask them to swap their recordings with another student and listen to their friend's interview carefully – three times over. We then ask them to note down the ways in which they encouraged their 'respondent' to open up about the topic. Finally, we ask them to decide how they would characterise the interviewer's way of interacting with their respondent: were they seemingly talking as friends, as a scientist with her subject, or was this in some other kind of way?

It's fun to discuss this in class and many of the interviewers are (comically?) shocked by some of the terms their (former?) friends chose. Here's a list of some roles they came up with:

Catalyst	Investigator
Listener	Controller
Expert	Mirror
Guider	Arbitrator
Moderator	Therapist
An equal	Friend

If we also thought about taking part, we could lengthen this list even further:

Apprentice	Chronicler
Helper	Sounding board
Annoyance	Observer
Confidant(e)	Ally

Each of these possible roles is associated with different tactics for engaging with people. We could draw up a list of the conversational tricks associated with assuming each of them. Everyday conversation is surprisingly complex when we dig into it (Stokoe, 2018) and the roles we assume in social research clearly shape the responses that we get. Going back to the methods class, we then – in the spirit of openness and mutual support – force ourselves as their teachers to think through the roles we've tended to assume in the past too. Here's one that has worked for us.

Appreciative Stranger to Relative Robot

Often you are different things at different stages. We've definitely started off some of our research encounters with an emphasis on being interested and appreciative in the past. Who wouldn't at the start? Then, as time passed together, we've been emboldened to float out some of the more analytical questions about people's lives that we've been developing. In normal conversation, as (we like to think) fairly friendly and supportive people, we'd have been tempted to 'fill the conversational space' if they took some time to answer. We've sometimes channelled the idea of being a kind of 'research robot' to overcome this (the robot being oblivious to such conversational conventions). People need space to work through their ideas, just like we do – so we'd float out the challenging analytical 'robot question' and then force ourselves to wait. For some respondents they've appreciated the chance to take stock of their lives (so, we think they liked the robot in the end!).

THE ANALYTICAL EXCITEMENT OF RESEARCH RELATIONSHIPS

Growing up in Northeast London, one of our undergraduate students wanted to study the impacts of the nearby Olympic Park redevelopment. As her research plans progressed, Ayesha reflected on how she and her high school friends had used the Park and its commercial developments – most notably a large shopping mall – as teenagers. Looking through the literature on urban regeneration, she saw that little attention had been paid to how local teenagers were impacted. So, Ayesha recruited some of her local friends to explore their relationship to the Olympic Park. Questioning their common experience allowed Ayesha to move from a generic study of urban regeneration to a much more original project on how young ethnic minority women relate to a major urban regeneration project. And it turned out to be a very effective one too, partly because her existing relationship with those she was studying meant they were happy to help her, and she could immediately ask more informed questions.

Ayesha's project shows the analytical potential of starting with existing relationships. The project was effective partly because she didn't end up attempting to present herself as a sort of neutral, somewhat 'objective' scientist character. Rather Ayesha allowed herself to lean into the potential of a fairly obvious fact – that in social research we're often talking about two or more people building an (often albeit temporary) relationship in which both parties are getting something out of that experience, even if it's just a matter of something a bit different to do (as was the case for Ayesha's friends).

Returning to the short interviews we asked our master class students to undertake, after we had reflected on the roles they'd assumed in their interviews, we then considered what might happen next. Could thinking a bit more about the relationships – both implicit and explicit – inevitably involved in social research suggest some interesting future projects?

Many students interviewed their parents. This naturally led to some fascinating conversations about how different generations relate to global warming or migration or urban change. Working with this observation, perhaps there's a study here on how grown children speak to their parents about the environment, rather than just a general harvesting of apparent views on climate change? Plenty also talked with friends who also cared about the issues they discussed. We heard about some very interesting conversations in which friends supported, but sometimes challenged, each other when discussing 'difficult' or 'contentious' topics such as these. So, perhaps there's a study here on how friends who care about a particular topic talk together about their shared commitments?

The point is there's an opportunity to think about how our research relationships could become the focus for our projects. These relationship issues are always there anyway, so perhaps we could make them our focus. Our relationship with others is now more than a problem or an issue to reflect on; it could feasibly become the study itself! And, if we're interested in friends or peers or those with whom we have existing relationships, then we could put that feature front and centre and examine what that does to how we interact. This is, of course, not to say that we should always be researching friends and family: it's more that our positionality can sometimes become an opportunity.

Here's a list of ideas of possible research topics that came out of this exercise:

- How do different generations talk about climate change?
- How does friendship affect how and when we talk about difficult topics?
- How do families who disagree politically negotiate that disagreement?
- How do our peers deal with speaking to us about topics they know we really care about?

As discussed in Chapter 5, the ways in which people deal with political topics can make for an interesting subject to study. Now we spotted a way of harnessing how that is likely to kick into the discussions and encounters we'd have with certain people because of who we are. As our students sometimes say, we've 'flipped the script' by making a possible problem a project. So maybe we should start with the relationships that you already have, or could have, with those you might want to study and turn that to your advantage. Lots of discussion has been had about the implications of being an 'insider' or an 'outsider' in research. For the self-aware researcher, how people react to you is something to learn from as much as an obstacle to overcome.

THE BREAK-UP!

At some point our research must finish. We need to take what we've collected from all our engagements with people – our conversations, our interviews, our notes from taking part – and start to write whatever it was we set out to produce when we began our relationship with them, the dissertation, thesis, research article, or report. This doesn't necessarily mean the straightforward end of the relationships we've built. But it does transform them.

Some researchers maintain the relationships they've developed 'in the field' long after the initial research project that brought them together ends. Some of them return to the communities they're studying repeatedly over very long periods of time (DeWalt and DeWalt, 2011). And given that most of the analysis of the material we've gathered from people happens well after we've interacted with them (done well, social research is often quite a slow process) our relationships with those we've studied live on within the work of analysing and assembling our research material into some kind of coherent account. This includes considering the ethical responsibilities and ambitions baked into our research relationships – that we would tell people's stories, witness their way of life, or so on.

But let's be clear. Many researchers don't maintain personal relationships with those they are studying. For many doing interview research, recognising that the relationship between the interviewer and interviewee is going to be a one-off meeting encourages the focused conversation that the interviewer needs. David Bissell, for example, only met his interviewees once. He organised his interviews such that the conversation had a clear end and the interviewee had sufficient time to disengage and decompress after the interview finished. Caroline Knowles' relationship with her domestic workers was more complicated as her research methods also involved hanging out with them. But her relationships with those she was researching were also defined by the fact that she was in Hong Kong specifically to carry out a research project and, when this was done, she was returning to London. Many social relationships are temporary, and we shouldn't feel bad that some – or indeed many – of our research relationships take that form too. Of course, if you're researching your friends, your family, or some institution you already have a role in, you'll need to think about how you're going to return to the role of non-researcher afterwards. This might be quite straightforward. Friends, family, and colleagues will most likely be keen to have 'the usual you' back – as opposed to the pesky, slightly challenging, researcher with all their tricky questions. Still, it's important to remember that going back to that normality doesn't mean you can forget the parameters of your research relationship – would your report be anonymous? where would your findings end up? – that you promised earlier in the process.

SOME FINAL RELATIONSHIP ADVICE

We've covered a lot of ground in this chapter. Some of the key points we've made are, on the surface at least, quite simple:

- Engaging those we might want to study isn't always straightforward
- How those being researched react to being approached, along with what they might tell and show us, depend on who we are and how we present ourselves
- Different reactions are an inevitability in social research though they're particularly apparent when we spend more time with those we're studying
- Good social research emerges out of the researcher's self-awareness of, and thoughtfulness about, how all this might affect the material they produce in their studies
- Self-awareness is crucial all the way through the social research process: in research design, in gathering research material, and in thinking about how to analyse it

Perhaps the central idea that runs through the above list is this: rather than thinking about our presence as a social researcher as something that brings bias into the process – and is therefore something that needs to be countered in pursuit of a certain idea about scientific neutrality – we should reflect on our research relationships, partly because that can often make for better work. And, since social research always involves relationships, we should think about how they evolve – how we present ourselves, how we adapt as we become more familiar, and how generally we say goodbye at some point.

PROJECT PLANNING	DURING THE PROJECT	AFTER THE PROJECT
What do I know about the people I'm studying?	Are they saying or doing things that change our relationship?	How should I organise my exit from this social context/encounter?
How should I present myself to them?	Do I need to assume a different relationship (based on how things are going)?	Should I or might we want it to continue in some way?
How might they react to me and how should I handle that?		What does the relationship that developed between us mean for how I should write about them and how they might be involved in that?
What kind of relationship am I proposing exactly?		

Figure 6.2 Working towards happy relationships in social research
Source: Alan Latham

CONCLUSION

In social research we are often building relationships with others. We need to be self-aware about this. We've tended to focus on certain methods in this chapter (observers aren't really 'building' relationships with those they observe and those who do surveys like to stick with the idea of being a more neutral, appropriately scientific figure). This is partly because methods like interviewing and taking part mean we must think more about these matters. We also haven't talked a great deal about the ethics of all this. That's because there are plenty of books out there already that you could consult on that (try Israel and Hay, 2006) and the universities or other institutions to which you're linked will often think differently about these important matters. Rather we wanted to run with the essential idea of how we handle 'people as people' when doing social research, which can, we think, often leave us with a thoughtful position on ethical matters. For sure, thinking about our relationships with those we're researching is challenging. But it's also a skill that can be learned and developed. You can learn from looking at what other researchers have done. You can also learn from some of the ideas we've covered in this chapter. If you do that, the result should be sensitive and exciting projects that are all the more effective for being alive to how social research can be usefully seen as a relationship.

7
ASKING QUESTIONS: EXPLORING A BASIC ACT THAT FEATURES IN MANY METHODS

A FAILED OPINION POLL

Let's start with a short example of the perils of asking questions. In our master's class, we like to know how people are getting on. So, about halfway through the course, we take a quick poll. Firstly, we put up a question on the screen behind us that asks our students to raise their hands if: 'You think this course looks like it will be one of the best courses you will take this year.' After a few moments, we add the next – put your hand up if: 'You are wondering why you ever decided to do a master's course.' Some look confused. Others laugh. Most avoid eye contact if we make a direct plea to individuals. Hardly anyone – in some years, no-one – puts up their hand for either question.

As an opinion poll, our survey is a failure. We haven't found out anything about what these students think about the class. Our quiz does, however, point to some interesting aspects of how social researchers ask questions. Firstly, it matters who is asking and answering. In our case, we – a couple of professors – are asking a group of students to make a judgement about the quality of our teaching. Secondly, the context matters. We're in a lecture hall where any responses are being made in front of the whole group. In such situations, who wants to be the first or only person to respond? The teacher might then ask you more questions and you'd have to answer in front of your peers, and who wants to do that? If we asked these questions somewhere else, say in the privacy of one of our offices or informally over coffee, we would get not just a simple answer but potentially quite a detailed one. Thirdly, it matters how we ask the question. Our questions were binary. Either you thought this was the best course or not. Either you were having doubts about your MSc or not. And we only gave students one way to answer – raising their hands. Faced with the dilemma of making such a stark choice, quickly, publicly, and directly to us, our students refused to answer.

So how do you avoid situations in which people just won't answer your questions? Better yet, how do you go about getting responses that are really useful? Here's this chapter's key idea, one that clearly made a difference with our failed classroom poll: asking and responding to questions is a social interaction. If that's the case, it follows that as social researchers we need to think carefully about how we ask our questions because that will in all sorts of ways shape the responses we potentially get. In this chapter, we'll firstly look at some of the main reasons why social researchers ask questions. Then we'll turn to questionnaires and surveys. This is partly because they represent one of the most common methods for asking questions in social research that we haven't yet discussed. But it's also because this way of asking questions highlights some broader issues. We'll think about how the 'images' we inevitably have in surveys can lead to questions that keep our images intact. Then we'll emphasise the importance of not ignoring the social contexts in which we ask survey questions. After that, we'll consider how and when we'll allow our questions to evolve as our projects continue to roll on, before ending by challenging a couple of common questioning conventions.

Asking questions is so ubiquitous in social research, such a fundamental part of what we are doing, that how we work with questions doesn't always get the attention it deserves. Many research papers present quotes without any sense of the questions that came just before (Hitchings and Latham, 2020a; Staller, 2022). That's a shame when sharing tips and ideas about different ways of asking questions can lead to original and effective projects. This, at least, is what we tell everyone in our methods class when we eventually reveal to all that our poll wasn't 'real'. We say we're sure they're loving our work, but we wanted to do an exercise in which our way of questioning was clearly wrong. We're secretly hoping they are, but our chosen approach means we don't know.

WHAT DO SOCIAL RESEARCHERS USE QUESTIONS FOR?

Different questions set up and organise the research encounters we have with people in different ways. So, to get the ball rolling, it's useful to consider, at a general level, the different aims that we have for our questions. Thinking about all the reasons why we might ask questions in a research project, we think our questions can be summarised as usually acting in one of four ways:

- As a prompt for conversation
- As a means of drawing out a worldview

- As a route into finding out what happened
- As a way of collecting facts and opinions

As with the warrants we discussed in Chapter 2, researchers are often juggling a number of purposes, which makes it all the more important to stop for a moment and acknowledge what we are trying to do with our questions.

Let's go through each of the four in turn.

1. As a Prompt for Conversation

One thing that questions can do is act as a door into a conversation that explores a topic or theme. This is the kind of questioning that we most often associate with open-ended interviewing. Here the questions we ask are an invitation for people to tell us about themselves or their thoughts on a topic. Like any good conversationalist, we ask people questions because we're interested in what they'll say, and we don't have any strong sense of what the shape of their answer will be. The specific questions we might pose here are comparatively unimportant because the idea is just to get people going on a topic and then to see where that leads. When Richard Sennett (2006) examines the changing nature of work in America, for example, in *The culture of the new capitalism*, he began his interviews by simply asking people to tell him about their careers. He had an intuition that something had changed in how middle-class professional Americans experienced work, and to find out about that he embarked upon some very open-ended conversations with his interviewees. Moreover, the interviews that form the basis of his project took place in a wide variety of settings. As a privileged academic, he started conversations with the people he met as he went about his life. He talked to the people sitting next to him on flights, the people he came across at conferences, and so on. Sennett uses these conversations to discover what it is like to try and build a career – and a life – as a professional in contemporary America. He asks about the common dilemmas and challenges people faced – he's a tenured professor so his own experience is quite different – and how those he was talking with made sense of their lives. By thinking hard about what follows after he set off with some of his open-ended questions, Sennett eventually developed an argument about the wider society to which those he'd spoken with belonged.

2. As a Means of Drawing Out a Worldview

A second way questions are used is to understand the 'worldview' of the person or group being studied. Used in this way, the researcher is asking questions to understand how people make sense of the world around them. Often the reason why we're studying a specific group is because we find their way of understanding the world puzzling. A great example of research that uses questions in this way is Katherine Cramer's (2016) *The politics of resentment*, a study of the values of a rural American state. Cramer met with groups of Wisconsin residents and asked them questions about what mattered to them. She would start her conversations with, 'What do you think are the main issues facing people [in your town/county] these days?' She'd follow up with: 'What do you think should be done about this? Why do you think this has been overlooked? Whom does the current policy benefit?' (p. 233). Her questions opened up conversations about what these groups thought about how the state of Wisconsin worked, how rural Wisconsinites saw themselves within this, and about commonly held ideas around how urban dwellers thought about those living in rural areas. This led her to distinguish a distinctive 'rural consciousness' – a collectively held way of looking at the world – possessed by many non-urban Wisconsinites. So, whilst Sennett was merely striking up a conversation, Cramer was trying to join in and make sense of a set of conversations people were already having.

3. As a Route into Finding out What Happened

A third way questions are used by social researchers is to try and find out what happened in a particular case or instance – why did people do what they did? Often as social researchers we're working a bit like detectives. There are a number of ways that social researchers might do this. They might be able to look at official documents, media reports, and so on. Still, often the quickest and most effective way of finding out what has happened in a given situation or place is simply to ask the key actors involved. A nice example is Anique Hommels' (2008) *Unbuilding cities*, a study of how the Maastricht expressway was buried so that a linear park could be added in the Netherlands. Hommels had a lot of official material to work through. But these documents could only tell her so much about how the project had developed. To help make sense of what was being said in the official documents, Hommels also talked to those who had been involved – architects, planners, engineers, community representatives, local and national politicians – and grilled them a little on whether the documents she'd read matched the experiences they'd had. These interviews did not provide an account that overrode the official one. And like the official documents, the interview accounts were patchy and, in places, contradictory (people's memories are never perfect). But questioning these key actors in this way allowed her to make sense of what she'd read in the documents and to write a much more nuanced story about what happened.

4. As a Way of Collecting Facts and Opinions

Often social researchers just want to find the facts. They want to know certain characteristics about a person, or activity, or organisation, or institution. Or they might want to find out someone's immediate opinion about something. We might, for example, want to know how much someone earns. If they have a job or not. What that job is. How many hours they work per week. Whether they're married, divorced, cohabiting. Do they have children? We might like to connect all that to what they're going to do in the future. We might want to know who they'll vote for in the next election. Whether they'll replace their petrol-fuelled car with an electric one. And we might like to know people's opinions on important topics too: Do they think human driven climate change exists? Different ways of organising local healthcare? What would a fair retirement age be? Social researchers often work with data from official survey sources, but many also produce their own when official sources do not provide what they need. For example, community health activists in Brooklyn, New York, surveyed the fishing practices of residents in a neighbourhood with many economically marginalised, immigrant households (Corburn, 2002). They were aware that many low-income families were reliant on fish caught by hobby fishermen from the polluted East River, and that this wouldn't be captured in standard urban food consumption surveys (which assume that urban households buy it all from stores and markets). This was potentially an environmental risk – depending on the amounts of fish consumed. To reliably calculate the extent of this risk, the survey needed to understand as precisely as possible a range of facts about hobby fishing in the East River:

- Who was doing the fishing?
- How often were people fishing?
- What kinds of fish were being caught?
- How many were caught per week?
- The number of fish eaten per week by the family of fishermen alone
- The size of the fisherman's family
- Whether fishermen were sharing their catch with others

The results were striking: 'local anglers were catching between 40 and 75 fish per week, and each family member of an angler was eating approximately 9.5 fish per week' (Corburn, 2002: 245). These results made it possible for environmental scientists to calculate the individual risks faced.

It's tempting to plot these four options onto a hierarchy of effectiveness. The more 'interpretative' researcher – those who like the idea of gradually getting to grips with other people's perspectives – would put 'Opening up a conversation' at the top. A more statistically inclined one would see 'Collecting facts and opinions' as the most efficient route to understanding. In truth, many research projects question in ways that involve – at least to some degree – all four of the above ambitions. We might be asking questions to open up a conversation because we simply want to see where it goes, but we will likely also be trying to find out something about people's worldviews as part of it. We'll probably want to nail down certain facts about that person too – how old they are, their education level, occupation, income, and so on. What's important, however, is that we're aware of what our questions are doing and how we're using them to get what we need. So, which do we want to prioritise – is this about getting information or opening things up? If we want facts and opinions, perhaps we can just ask for them. If we want a worldview, then something a bit more sensitive might be in order. If we want to get people going on a topic, perhaps we just need to appear interested and then ask the questions that reassure them we still are.

It's also about what we are looking for and how we imagine people will respond to us. We've talked about a few methods now. One of the ways in which we could compare them is to consider how they think about questions. For some of those who buy into the argument for 'naturalistic research' (Chapter 3) – the notion that the social world should ideally be studied in a way that minimises or removes the potential for things being disturbed by us – we'd probably work with questions in a particular way. Working in this way, we'd likely let the questions we'd ask slowly emerge out of the ways in which people already spoke and did things, as shown in Figure 7.1. Others who are more hopeful about people being straightforwardly able to tell them what they want to know – or, at least, feel positive about being able to minimise these effects – feel happier about sticking with their own questions.

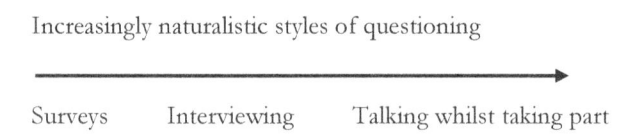

Increasingly naturalistic styles of questioning
⟶

Surveys   Interviewing   Talking whilst taking part

Figure 7.1 Different styles of questioning

Either way, as we've said, this is not often an explicit topic of discussion. People often do the method they like the sound of and then fall into line with the way of thinking about and asking questions that comes along with it. The point we'd like to make is that it's good to think through what way of working with questions will take us where we want to go – in terms of enjoying spending time with people, embodying the persona that we think is right for us, and also in terms of delivering on those all-important warrants we discussed at the start (Chapter 2).

WHAT'S YOUR IMAGE?

So, let's talk surveys. For the survey researcher, we need to either make it snappy or get people to care about what we're doing, since we are pulling them out of the current of their everyday lives in order to help us. And that means asking the right questions so as not to waste their time. How do we know they are right though? When we do social research, whether we acknowledge it or not, we always have an 'image' of what we're studying at the start. In other words, we have certain ideas about how people relate to our topics, what motivates them or what drives them to do things. These images might be implicit and never stated, or explicit and placed front and centre. In either case, the questions that we pose are shaped in fundamental ways by this inescapable 'imagery'.

When researchers consider researching a social setting they often do so as relative outsiders, which is to say they know little about how that setting actually works. That's often exactly why they're interested of course. This is what Henry Blumer (in Becker, 1998) had to say about that (with apologies for the gendered assumptions of the late 1960s):

> '[D]espite this lack of first-hand acquaintance the research scholar will unwittingly form some kind of picture of the area of life he proposes to study. He will bring into play the beliefs and images that he already has to fashion a more or less intelligible view of the area of life. In this respect he is like all human beings. Whether we be laymen or scholars, we necessarily view any unfamiliar area of group life through images we already possess. We may have no first-hand acquaintance with life among delinquent groups, or in labour unions, or in legislative committees, or among bank executives, or in a religious cult, yet given a few cues we readily form serviceable pictures of such life. This, as we all know, is the point at which stereotyped images enter and take control. All of us, as scholars, have a share of common stereotypes that we use to see a sphere of empirical social life that we do not know.' (p. 12)

The fact that these images exist isn't a problem – one of Blumer's points (and one that Becker emphasises as important) is that imagery is unavoidable. The problem comes when we don't reflect on them or take them for granted. Rather than being the puppets of our unexamined assumptions about the people and places we research, we might instead use our images as a tool to help us develop more astute research questions. We might, for example, be ready to flip our intuitions about what we think is going on. A nice example of this is Philippe Bourgois' (2003) study of the lives of Latino drug dealers in New York City. Far from being the moral deviants they are often portrayed as, the young men he spent time with were notably hard working and entrepreneurial. Marginalised as they were from mainstream American culture, they nonetheless shared many of its core values. So, rather than working with the image of outsiders resistant to mainstream culture, Bourgois' analysis is animated by the counter-intuitive image of socially ambitious individualists thwarted by that mainstream. The question is no longer about how to deal with deviants but has instead become one of how they might find more acceptable ways of channelling their entrepreneurialism.

So, we need to think about how the life of images in our work – whether some are transformed and when others stay in place. Back to our master's class. We usually ask our students to devise a short questionnaire. We haven't talked about questionnaires much yet, but they are a common research tool in which a precise list of questions is drawn up by the researcher. Their 'respondents' (which is how these researchers would often see their relationship with those they are studying – see Chapter 11) are then asked to work through the questionnaire filling out their answers as they go, or to listen to a researcher who reads them out and records the response. It's a little like the interview schedules – the 'pieces of paper' – we talked about in Chapter 5. But the idea is not to deviate from the script here. Questionnaires are, after all, a central part of survey research where the aim is to get lots of responses that can be more quickly analysed because we've imposed a structure.[1]

Coming back to our students and their questionnaires, we ask them to devise a short series of questions related to the topic they're studying with us. At this point, we always find it interesting how, compared to some of the other methods we experiment with together, they don't ask us too many questions about what a 'questionnaire' is or what they should do. We suppose that's partly because surveys are so embedded in contemporary life – it seems, for example, that every time we buy something online, we get an upbeat request for feedback immediately afterwards. In any case, having designed their questionnaires, we ask them to get five family members or friends to complete it. Finally, we ask our students to talk to these respondents about their experience of 'filling in the questionnaire': Was it easy? Was it hard? What did they feel about the questions?

Let's look at sections from two of their questionnaires.

We treat this as a fun exhibition as we present some of them to the class; the student involved is sometimes a bit sheepish, but we're all there to learn! What did the others in the class think was good and bad about this first one? They liked the mix of questions. Indeed, many say it's good to have a mix of closed questions – ticking boxes or providing one-word answers in a questionnaire – and open ones where you write something in. This is because it apparently gives you a bit of variety – you feel like you are making progress with the closed questions, and you also get the chance to communicate your personal views with the more open-ended ones. Makes sense. Good start!

But, after reminding them about Becker and Blumer's ideas, we ask 'What is the image?' How is climate change being defined here? Well clearly, it's something it is assumed that the person answering the question should know about. Another thing we note is that climate change is seen as an issue that should probably be 'tackled' according to the researcher. Fair enough. Many people share this

---

1 What's the difference between a questionnaire and a survey? A questionnaire is a research tool used to gather information from people (a list of structured questions), whilst a survey is a research method that involves using questionnaires but also includes the sampling and analytical techniques to produce statistically robust results about a population of people (Fowler, 2013).

17. Do you think climate change is something that is affecting or is going to affect you, personally? ☐ Yes ☐ No ☐ Don't know

18. If yes, in what way(s) is it affecting you, or is it going to affect you? _____

_____

_____

19. Do you think anything can be done to tackle climate change? ☐ Yes ☐ No ☐ Don't know

20. If yes, what do you think can be done to tackle climate change? _____

_____

_____

21. Who do you think should have the **main** responsibility for tackling climate change? *Please tick one box only:*
   ☐ International organisations (e.g. the UN)
   ☐ The national government
   ☐ Local government
   ☐ Business and industry
   ☐ Environmental organisations/ lobby groups (e.g. Worldwide Fund for Nature)
   ☐ Individuals
   ☐ Other (*please write in:* _____)

Figure 7.2 A student questionnaire
Source: Russell Hitchings

view but, the group wonders, there are also things like seasonal changes or the weather that could be a kind of 'climate change'. So, on a shorter time-scale, it can be good, no?

The image is that climate change is a political issue to be tackled and one people are assumed to have opinions on. We'll come back to 'opinions', as an idea in this chapter, but the most interesting thing that we learn in the discussion, we think, is about how the people they asked to complete their questionnaire all found it fairly straightforward. A lot of them answered in ways that showed how worried they were, and how they agreed about the importance of 'tackling' it. We ask the student whether their respondents – their friends and family – were thinking about these issues all that much in their everyday lives. The answer then is that it hadn't come up so much, but the student didn't really think so. So, the student had translated their way of thinking about the topic (from their readings and their own political commitments) into a survey that reproduced that idea. Then their family members dutifully replied in that register. Here we have a story of our social research images being maintained (as in lots of areas of life, the people involved got a sense of what the researcher wanted from them and then dutifully provided it; see Schaeffer and Presser (2003).

Our second exhibit is a questionnaire about refugees in the UK. In discussion, our students liked the straightforward design – though they generally say something nice when they are talking about the work of their friends. Certainly, it looks easy to answer. And that is something that can help when you are doing this kind of work because people only expect to give you a few minutes of their time when they're doing a survey. The boxes are commented upon positively too. They seem clear, and the impression is good. And that can also really matter if we're asking people to help us out as they'll expect to see a well-designed questionnaire that shows we know what we are doing.

But as we naggingly ask them once more: 'What's the image?' Well, again there is something here about politics and about political decision making. No surprises there. We are, after all, used to thinking that surveys are about accessing 'views' in this way. Again, the people they asked found it quite easy to respond, so the student who administered the questionnaire told us. They told them that it was nice to be able to rattle through and tick the boxes when they didn't have all that much time to spare. We asked them whether that meant they'd ticked 'neutral' for everything so as to avoid giving it any thought. Apparently not, but they could have done.

What can we take away from these two examples? Firstly, that it pays to reflect on how we're inclined to compose our questions. Our students rarely explore their

Q1: Women with children, Unaccompanied Minors and LGBTQI+ applicants should be prioritized in the UK asylum system as they are particularly vulnerable to persecution

Strongly Disagree	Disagree	Neutral	Agree	Strongly Agree

Q2: Asylum seekers pose a security threat to the UK

Strongly Disagree	Disagree	Neutral	Agree	Strongly Agree

Q3: The UK asylum system is being exploited by economic migrants

Strongly Disagree	Disagree	Neutral	Agree	Strongly Agree

Q4: Refugees should be deported if they commit a criminal offence in the UK

Strongly Disagree	Disagree	Neutral	Agree	Strongly Agree

Figure 7.3 Another student questionnaire
Source: Russell Hitchings

topics in terms of warmer weather around our university or whether respondents have ever met refugees. Instead, they tend to dive in with questions that feel appropriately 'political'. Secondly, that there are particular types of question that we naturally associate with a survey – things to do with opinions. We could ask about other things. Our students say they would have done if they pictured themselves interviewing about these topics. Thirdly, that those who answer their questionnaires can be quite compliant, and they will often do their best to help us out. This can help our images remain intact, because respondents don't (or cannot) challenge how we've framed things. Here our students had assumed that those they were researching had opinions ready and waiting to be aired. In fact, their respondents might well have produced them in the moment, or they were only half-formed beforehand.

None of these 'image issues' are exclusive to questionnaires. It's more that our exercise brings them nicely to the fore. Often when we design questionnaires, we send them out through the internet or go up to people and ask them to answer directly. Either way, we don't spend too much time with the individuals involved. So, we never get a feel for how they are responding to the task: whether they just want to get it over with or whether they think the questions really fit with how they see things.

To deal with this, what is generally recommended with this approach – and what we effectively did with our students – is to do a 'pilot study'. That involves asking a small number of people to respond to a draft questionnaire and tell you about it: Did they understand all the question? Did they have views that didn't fit with the choices they were offered? Was it easy to do? Did they get bored and start reaching for the same sort of encouraging response without really thinking? Given how compliant many of the parents and friends who acted as respondents for our students turned out to be, you'd want to really push people to think through, and talk to you about, all these issues in your pilot study. If you don't, they might just say it looks very nice to get you off their back.

TWO SURVEY SITUATIONS

The point about reflecting on how people react to us in social research runs throughout this book. But it is especially worth thinking about when you're creating questionnaire questions because you can't really change them once the design stage is over. It also means we should think hard about the situation in which we ask our questions. We've talked about this for interviews in Chapter 5, but where and how should we pose our survey questions? Here are another two examples:

Figure 7.4 How do you feel about showering at summer music festivals?
Source: Russell Hitchings

Showering at Summer Music Festivals

The first example comes from a project about water consumption that Russell was involved in (see Hitchings et al., 2018). In the UK, young people are quite keen on using water that, thanks to climate change, we don't have so much of anymore. So, together with some colleagues, he wanted to know how young people at summer music festivals felt about going without showering. They did a survey as a part of this. If you want to get an overview of how a large group of people feel about a topic this makes sense. You can ask a large number of them some questions and then hopefully that's exactly what you'll get. But when to do the survey? The morning seemed like a good choice. There were plenty of people around then and not too much going on. The festival was just warming up – people were going to get coffees and breakfast and they probably had a bit more time spare before the bands started and there was fun to be had. But were they yet ready to answer their questions or will they still be feeling the effects of the night before? And were the early risers a special group? They might have got up early to shower! So, what they said might very well not apply to the rest of them who were happily languishing in their tents with no thought about maintaining their personal hygiene standards when they eventually emerged.

What kind of questions could Russell and his colleagues ask in a context such as this? One decision they made was often to ask the questions directly, rather than giving out their sheets and asking people to fill them in. This wasn't just because they could explain things, if need be. Their presence also encouraged respondents to stay focused and 'take it seriously'. The questionnaire included many closed questions and also used lots of scales – 'How dirty would you say you were on a scale of one to ten?' etc. This was partly because they wanted to get respondents thinking. But this was also because they felt that if they didn't do that, respondents might rush through the questionnaire and leave their 'open-ended' questions blank. The respondents were, after all, at a festival, and they often had better things to do – get breakfast, meet friends, check out a new band, go back to bed.

What Money Do Migrant Family Members Send Back Home?

Our second example comes from a study on a rather different topic. The aim here was to explore whether those who had moved away from home – either to cities or overseas – were likely to send money back to the family in small towns in Cameroon (Mercer et al., 2008). After some training in how to pose the questions, a number of local students went to different houses in these small towns to gauge how often, and in what ways, these 'remittances' featured in the lives of the households – mostly farmers – living there. Rather boldly, they just turned up and presented themselves, hopeful that the kudos attached to being visited

Figure 7.5 'What do family members send back to you on the farm?'
Source: Ben Page

by someone 'from the university' might be enough to secure participation. The aim was to speak with the 'head of the household'. But would those who were suddenly asked to stop what they were doing have the time and energy to give full and accurate answers? Also, if the 'head of the household' was away, would the others know the answers or feel pressured to come up with something when they were flattered by the interest? Though they were reassured about anonymity, it might also have been more appealing to present yourself as someone who was benefitting from money being sent back – especially when the woman from the university with her pen and paper was right there!

The point of both examples is simple – think about the survey situation (see also Ryan and Golden, 2006). With a questionnaire you've got your questions all lined up. So, just ask them! Well, when you ask them (as in the festivals study) and who's around when you do (as with the farmers project) clearly make a difference. To be confident about your conclusions, you can't sweep the situation under the carpet. It's partly because with questionnaires you're spending less time with people that researchers sometimes downplay these issues because they're less confronted by them. We can't predict how this will work for you – the issues on the farm are clearly different to those at the festival, for example – but one thing that we say repeatedly to our students when we turn to this topic is to remember how 'it's always social' – we're always staging a social encounter, irrespective of the method at hand. Put yourself in the shoes of those you hope will answer your questionnaire and then see what that tells you about when and how to engage with them.

WHEN THERE'S NO SECOND CHANCE: 'HOW OFTEN DO YOU EAT OUT?'

Another thing to consider, if the idea is to ensure you get truthful and honest responses that can be used to say something about a broader group, is being careful about ambiguity. This is partly because you're not going to get a second chance. You send out your questionnaire and you hope for the best. Or, when you approach people directly, it can be hard enough to get them to help without going back because you think you should pose some of your questions differently. We sometimes do an exercise with our undergraduates in which we say we want to know how students at London universities relate to food (see Chapter 9 on how we got interested in this). Are they all about the budget because they've little time to work alongside their studies? Or are they all eating out in London because they've already paid a lot to do their degree and hope to land a well-paid job afterwards? We ask them to devise a short questionnaire that explores some aspect of this.

But what does 'eating out' actually mean? The phrase feels self-evident at the start. This means restaurants, right? Perhaps cafés at a push, though maybe there's less of a social occasion to that? But what about buying a sandwich at lunchtime from a supermarket and enjoying it with friends in the local park? They are literally eating out! We start to get tangled up. Should we ask about how often they buy and consume food: Does it have to be a full meal? In places other than their home? But that sounds really weird! Many settle on asking about restaurants instead. Phew ...

Our point is that you've got to get the words right. And, whilst you can explain yourself in an interview, the idea with a questionnaire is to be more standardised – we don't want to risk someone dropping out because they don't know what sorts of meals we mean or giving us different answers because they interpret the question differently. Some come back from their forays into asking others around campus with funny stories about being asked what 'eating out' meant and feeling forced to stay silent and stony faced because they wanted to appear appropriately scientific so as not to 'corrupt' things. As a class we laugh a little about this afterwards. Still, you do want to avoid that reaction. So, it is important to give thought to the many possible ways in which people might interpret the questions you're asking. What's self-evident to you isn't necessarily self-evident to others, and reflecting on that is especially important with this method.

DIFFERENT PURPOSES, DIFFERENT QUESTIONS?

So, questionnaires, and the broad surveys of people's opinions or practices to which they belong, are a bit different to other ways of doing social research – is that what we've been saying so far? Well, yes and no. It's more that different assumptions are baked into them, partly based on the idea that you don't get the chance to amend things and you want answers that are easy to analyse afterwards. Let's compare two series of questions to think a bit more about the difference. Below is an example of a questionnaire developed by the World Bank to study 'social capital' (effectively the amount of mutual support that people can draw upon) in communities in different parts of the world.

This questionnaire is designed to be easily administered by a trained researcher in a wide range of social settings – it aims to be as intelligible to a farmer in Nigeria as to a suburban mother in Canada; they've done a lot of pilot studies to test the questionnaire and they've thought hard about ambiguity. It's also designed to produce numerical data that will be comparable temporally – so we can see how relations might be changing over time – and spatially too, so we can see differences between societies, or parts of a society. The survey follows

1.3 Of all the groups to which members of your household belong, which two are the most important to your household?

[ENUMERATOR: WRITE DOWN NAMES OF GROUPS]

Group 1 _____

Group 2 _____

1.4 How many times in the past 12 months did anyone in this household participate in this group's activities, e.g. by attending meetings or doing group work?

Group 1 [   ]   Group 2 [   ]

1.5 How does one become a member of this group?

1 Born into the group
2 Required to join
3 Invited
4 Voluntary choice
5 Other (specify) _____

Group 1 [   ]   Group 2 [   ]

1.6 How much money or goods did your household contribute to this group in the past 12 months?

Group 1 [   ]   Group 2 [   ]

1.7 How many days of work did your household give to this group in the past 12 months?

Group 1 [   ]   Group 2 [   ]

1.8 What is the main benefit from joining this group?

1 Improves my household's current livelihood or access to services
2 Important in times of emergency/in future
3 Benefits the community
4 Enjoyment/Recreation
5 Spiritual, social status, self-esteem
6 Other (specify) _____

Group 1 [   ]   Group 2 [   ]

Figure 7.6 World Bank social capital survey
Source: Grootaert, 2004: 28

strict procedural conventions: questions are kept as simple as possible, multiple answers to the same question are avoided. For these researchers, open questions are to be avoided because they can produce ambiguous and hard-to-interpret answers. A key ambition for this survey is that, having been developed and tested by researchers at the World Bank, other social researchers interested in social capital could simply take the survey and apply it to other settings. In fact, the design of the survey is based on the idea that a universal or shared model of social capital can be defined by researchers. In this model of research, the specific social context in which the survey is being administered is something to be overcome and controlled for – we need to make sure that the same questions make sense for everyone. Then we'll get them to explore our questions in our terms and then, all being well, we'll start to see how social networks are drawn on by people all over the world. Perhaps that could help us to spot when and where some contexts might learn from others to promote happier communities everywhere.

Now let's look at another study also interested in social relations. A rather different approach to asking questions can be seen in Ann Swidler's (2001) project on what American adults think about love. Here we are starting with the very much less defined topic, that of 'love' – as opposed to the social scientific concept of 'social capital'. So, already a slightly different way of working with questions. Looking at her interview guide, quite a different approach to asking is evident.

The Basic Interview Guide

Introduction

Autobiography–Cultural History

1. Can you tell me something about your background?
     Where you grew up?
     What your family was like?
     Where you lived?
     What your childhood was like? (Was childhood happy/secure? Less happy?)
     [Probe here for anything that seems important to the person.]

2. And now I'm particularly interested in more ideas about love or marriage or personal relationships you might have had when you were young.
     What ideas about love do you think you might have gotten from your family? Were your parents religious?
     Did they have any influence?
     Other relatives?
     Friends?

3. Thinking back now, say to when you were younger, maybe a teenager, do you remember what you thought love was, or what you expected it to be? [Probe]
     Do you know where you got those ideas? Family? Friends? Popular songs, books, TV, movies?
     And did you ever think you were in love?
     How did you know?
     What did it feel like?

4. Was there a first time when you would say you were really in love?
     How was that different?
     What made you think it was love?
     Is there an idea of love you still hold?
     [Here some interviewees may start describing their marriage over most important love relationship. If so, fine. If not, pursue the whole history of their changing beliefs, hopes, and ideas about love for as many steps as they can reconstruct.]

… Continues in similar structure through two further sections …

Figure 7.7 An interview schedule about love
Source: Swidler, 2001: 224–5

Swidler is talking about 'love'. It's easy to imagine this being the sort of subject that fits with an interview – these are personal matters and something about which you'll need to have built at least some degree of rapport to get people to talk about with you. When we think about where and when society talks about love, it's easy to jump to confessional accounts between friends at the end of a night out, or someone on television giving advice about relationships, or asking advice from family members around the kitchen table about how they've handled things. So perhaps we should tap into those sorts of situations and do some of that sort of talking ourselves. But perhaps we should be careful not to think that certain topics map on specific ways of asking questions. Swidler has used open-ended questions to explore middle-class American ideas of love. However, it could be entirely possible to design a survey-based study of love which had at its centre a questionnaire. The questionnaire would ask different kinds of questions – it might ask respondents to rank on a scale how important love is to them, for example – and generate different kinds of answers.

It's tempting to think that certain topics mean certain methods. Remember how our students naturally assumed they should be thinking about opinions when designing a questionnaire. If you want to get things like facts and evidence – as the World Bank did – that will travel and seem like an appropriately sturdy platform for comparison between countries or for new policies, then perhaps a survey is for you. But surveys could be done on many topics and, going back to the value of thinking through how people might respond, we'd be more interested in completing a questionnaire about love than filling one out about political issues that left us disappointed in our limited relevant knowledge. So, choose based on your warrants and perhaps be open minded about what topics go with what methods. The difference between them, as we'll now discuss, is more about how to handle a rather different set of questions, namely our 'research questions'.

THE LIFE OF QUESTIONS OVER A RESEARCH PROJECT

So far, we've been thinking about how social researchers ask people questions. Much of our discussion has understandably focused on the nitty-gritty of doing research: how we pose questions in interviews; how we design questionnaires; how we develop and expand questions during our interactions with people. However, we're usually asking them because we want to address another set of questions: the wider 'research questions' that animate our projects. As well as thinking about posing questions to and about those we hope to understand in our studies, we also need to think about how, and whether, our more fundamental questions about what we want to know should be allowed to evolve over the life of research projects.

Let's return to two earlier examples. In Russell's festival survey (Hitchings et al., 2018), he and his collaborators spent a lot of time defining their key 'research questions' – thinking about the existing literature, reflecting on their own experiences of going to festivals in the past (which acted as a kind of virtual pilot study) – ahead of visiting the festival where they carried out their survey. By the time they were at their festivals all their questions were nailed down. They had to be. Otherwise, they wouldn't be able to reliably compare across their responses. They also didn't have any possibility of printing out another hundred pieces of paper there. Similarly, the analysis and final write up of their questionnaire data was defined by their original research questions; it couldn't be otherwise as this was the data they had. Theirs is a story of research questions not changing after the research design has been settled on. All the effort was in getting them right at the start.

For others, research questions are allowed to evolve. In Katherine Cramer's (2016) interviews about the political opinions of rural Wisconsinites, she started out with a broad concern about the divide in opinion between rural and urban dwellers. Analysing her initial interviews, she began to develop the concept of a 'rural consciousness'. She did this by translating her research questions into ones that were open ended and allowed her to see the extent to which those she was speaking with thought in the terms she had begun with, and whether there was a better way of characterising their thinking. To test and explore this concept, Cramer constructed a new interview schedule for a second round of interviews. She then analysed this material to further test and refine her analysis in a third round. Her interview questions evolved along with her analytical focus as the project developed.

So sometimes our research questions evolve as we work through our research projects. And sometimes they don't. This depends on how we've designed our study. Small and Calarco (2022) argue that in a high-quality in-depth project we should expect our research questions to change as we learn more. But with a questionnaire we must sacrifice that opportunity because we want to see what a lot of people have to say about our topic. Neither is necessarily better (Becker, 2009) but it does mean that you should think about which one appeals. Do you want to do all your thinking upfront or do you like the idea of following your nose as you revisit and potentially refine your questions?

It's tricky for our students sometimes when they are expected to have strong, clear, precise research questions when they are getting ready to do their projects. If they are bold, and they know they want to let things evolve, they might well say that they'll talk to people about their topic and then just take it from there! A few years back an undergraduate student we supervised refused to say what their research questions were ahead of starting their dissertation project. They argued that although they knew what their topic was – they wanted to study how a public square in a small French city was used – without spending time there it made no sense to claim that they knew what the right research questions should be. To find these they needed to see who was in the square, observe its rhythms of use, and so on. This student was taking seriously the claim – following Becker (2009) – that for some types of social research doing it well meant waiting to discover the right questions.

So be mindful of how different methods fit with different level of willingness to let your questions evolve. You might find yourself, like that bold student of ours, being pulled to think in one way. You'll often find that you're asked about your research questions at the start. Sometimes, you'll need to be ready to say something relatively vague, secretly knowing you'll want them to change.

TWO QUESTIONS WE'D BE CAREFUL ABOUT

As this chapter nears its conclusion, we want to finish with some examples to get you thinking about how exactly our questions can work as interventions into particular situations – rather like the lecture hall survey that we did with our students at the start. By thinking hard about some of our conventions, we think we can cook up some innovative projects.

Why Did You Do That?

Why do people act in the ways that they do? An interest in such questions is probably one of the reasons why you decided to have a look at this book. If that's what we're interested in, why don't we just ask them? There's nothing wrong with asking these sorts of 'why' questions – after all, asking for explanations is a fundamental part of being human (Tilly, 2006). But always remember your images. To ask such a question is to position the person you're speaking with as someone who knows – someone who can offer an account of their actions in which these actions are the logical outcome of their intentions. If you did something, you should have a reason why you did it (Becker, 1998: 59)! This, at least, is how people can often experience this line of questioning and it can put you under pressure to offer 'reasons' so as not to seem silly. Perhaps a more productive way of starting off might be to ask: 'How did you end up doing that?' You can see, straight away, that this invites a more open and reflective perspective (if that is what you're after). Certainly, the person is no longer under such pressure to provide a defensible account, as if they were in a courtroom.

What's Your Opinion?

To go back to the short questionnaires that our students designed, what about all these supposed 'opinions'? Much of how we think about social research is founded on the idea that people just 'have' them; that, as individuals, we've clearly held views and are forever poised and ready to present them should the researcher only bother to ask (Osborne and Rose, 1999). In the UK, we often see television presenters pouncing on people in the street and asking them to say what they think of politicians or government policies. These poor people – happily shopping just moments before – manage, just about, to generate an opinion, of sorts, in the moment. We are deeply suspicious of the suggestion that they were already there. Perhaps we should do studies of how 'opinions' come and go in our lives. Perhaps we should ask 'How often do you think about a topic?' instead of assuming people have a view on it. We've certainly found that productive (Hitchings, 2023).

CONCLUSION

Some years ago, on our field class – this time to Berlin – we took our students to a bar to celebrate the end of the teaching. Loosened by a few drinks, a couple of them challenged us on our insistence that they should ask questions about everything. Wasn't it exhausting? Didn't it, eventually, after some time, get tedious for us? Wasn't it annoying for our friends and partners? We don't do it all the time! We're often more than happy to sit brain-dead on the couch after a hard day thinking about research. What we said to them is that, when we're working, we try to ask a lot of questions because doing that can mean we do better projects and feel more confident about our conclusions.

As social researchers we're always asking questions. Some of us respond on our feet to how people react – such as those who do interviews or take part. Others don't have that luxury so must be sure they've crafted the right questions at the start – such as those who work with questionnaires. Either way, we should think about the social contexts in which we pose our questions and what that means for our results. And whilst there are conventions, or received wisdom, about what questions are good and bad in social research, it's definitely useful to think about what will work for you in your projects, attending to the images behind your questions rather than unthinkingly toeing the line.

8

PLAYING WITH WORDS: STRATEGIES FOR SEEING AND EXPLORING PATTERNS

WHAT ARE YOU?

You'll have noticed by now that we like to invent short exercises to exemplify the value of certain activities when studying social life. Another one is to start by flatly asking those in our master's methods class what they are. A little odd, but bear with us. Unsurprisingly enough, one of the most often reached-for collectives is 'students'. OK, we respond, but what are some of the defining characteristics of 'students' and how do different groups tend to think about them? We ask them to come up with a 'taken-for-granted' idea that can be found somewhere about what 'students' are and the qualities they apparently possess. They should know all about this after all, being students themselves!

We find it's not always easy to identify some of these 'taken-for-granted' ideas because, by definition, the people involved don't think so much about them anymore. That's probably why we get quite a lot of blank looks at the start (though they could just be bored). We emphasise to them that it's worth sticking with it. There's more to it, we say, than just flatly saying they're studying. We think about different places where we could look and eventually identify some possibilities:

The student as:

- *Brainbox* – OK, so we know a student studies. But how much of that do they actually do? One of the places that some of them spot relates to a TV show in which students compete in a quick-fire quiz. The students on this show seem able to answer questions about all sorts of esoteric topics – how particles work, the thinking behind different art movements, who composed

a particular piece of music based on the shortest of excerpts. They think fast, they know a lot, and the host is often impressed.
- *Customer* – This is a new idea in the UK, but we see it in emails from our university. Especially when they were deciding on whether to join us, our students were encouraged to look at websites that made university seem like an experience well worth paying for. They're being treated like customers who deserve a decent product in view of the cost. We joke that we hope they're satisfied with our service.
- *Reveller* – In some ways connected to the second framing, and in opposition to our first, is the idea that students come to university for a good time (all that business about particles and art movements is really a smokescreen). We've seen lots of posters around campus about 'student nights'. Apparently, so some of them tell us, there's a big night for sports teams on Wednesdays with cheap drinks.

There are two things we take away from this exercise. The first is there's often an important implied politics – or point of view – when we look closely at some of these representations. For example, some mature applicants who really want to attend university might be put off if they imagine they'll be surrounded by young party animals who might mock them for that. If we were thinking about funding universities, the TV show would suggest there's a lot of knowledge produced there so perhaps that would be a very good idea. But if we turn to those posters, we might see things differently – who'd want to waste public money on helping young people to party on Wednesdays?

The second is that it can be worth spending time thinking over these ideas in order to see and engage with those politics. We hadn't thought about them too much at the start (hence the blank looks) but part of the point of being a social researcher is often to force yourself to spend time in this way. The idea is that, hopefully, we'll come away with stronger and more interesting conclusions in our studies. In this case, we could do that by closely inspecting these student representations (the kind of talk that happens on the TV show, the phrasing of the university emails, the language of the posters).

This chapter considers how to work with words in social research, both those we've generated in our own projects (through interviews, fieldnotes, and so on), and those out there in the world already (in social media, newspapers, films, and elsewhere). In the first half of the chapter, we'll explore how we work with the words produced through interviews, casual talk, and notetaking (methods we've discussed in earlier chapters). Some researchers don't say a great deal about how they do this when they write up their results (Elliott, 2018), and that can make the process intimidating. With that in mind, we'll talk you through a project to give you a feel of how to approach the analysis of these sorts of words. In the second half of the chapter, we'll turn to our 'words in the wild' and explore some of the many ways of finding, and then devising a strategy for examining, material that doesn't require us to go to all the trouble of pestering anyone to show us or speak about how they see things. The 'take home message' for both is the same – it pays to have a procedure that works for you, and you should slow yourself down in order to see the patterns and eventually speak with authority.

ANALYSING THE WORDS WE'VE ALREADY GENERATED, WORKING THROUGH AN EXAMPLE

In Chapter 3, we saw how pushing ourselves to think carefully about particular words associated with our surroundings helped us to start exploring how exactly certain contexts work. Remember, for example, how, when we forced ourselves to stop and think really hard about the social life of 'bags' in different towns and cities, that we started to generate all sorts of new ideas for potential projects. It's not always easy to slow down and do that. We've often got many other things going on in our lives alongside our social research projects. But you'll need to do it, if you want to speak with authority about your topic and to identify the most interesting aspects of what you've collected. And, if you've gone to all that effort of doing a load of interviews or spending a long time in a particular place and making lots of notes about what's happening there, then you'll want to do justice to that too. That means not jumping the gun by grabbing the best bits of your 'results' and then offering them up as hopefully representative morsels from your 'rich' interview or observation sessions.

So, how do we do this? How do we stop ourselves jumping the gun? To show you how to do this we're going to work through an example of analysing some interview material from a project Russell carried out a few years ago. The problem underpinning Russell's project was that many professional people spent long periods of time working in air-conditioned offices, and they spent very little time outdoors in nearby greenspaces – even though doing so had health benefits and air-conditioning uses lots of energy. Russell's study involved interviews with lawyers working in central London: a place with a high density of air-conditioned offices and law firms. Russell chose London because he already knew some likely participants and there were plenty of others around there too. He also thought the behaviour of office workers in London would likely not be so different from cities elsewhere. So far, so good.

The next step was to talk with some of these lawyers about their working lives. You'll remember from Chapter 5 that part of your job when you do interviews is often to turn your 'big academic ideas' into topics that will make for an enjoyable and insightful conversation. And, given that the idea was to step back from the bigger issues and to learn from how these lawyers lived and worked, one of the things Russell asked about was their lunchtimes. It wasn't always easy to turn up and ask a lawyer to stop what they were doing and tell him all about whether they had a sandwich, where they had it, and whether they might go elsewhere – they were often so busy that they gave this little thought! But, once they were persuaded that his project was worthwhile – they saw he was taking it seriously and that it meant something to him from his fumbling nervousness – they seemed to go OK. That was a real relief to him when he hoped to speak with each of them four times over the course of a year.

As he went along, he 'transcribed' his interviews. That meant listening to recordings of the interviews, typing out everything that was said. You do this so that you can then do your analysis thoroughly and effectively, because your research material, the words from the interview, are now more to hand. Most social researchers recommend that we do this. The other option is to listen through the recordings and pick out the interesting parts. But the trouble with that is you probably don't know what's really interesting until you allow – or force! – yourself to spend time considering everything that was said. The key point here is that good analysis is about slowing down. By slowing down you can begin see the patterns in your material – that's why transcription is important. Russell also thought it might be an idea to look at how people reacted to his questions. So, he included notes about pauses and grunts and so forth in his transcription, to help him when he was analysing the material later on.

Let's look at how his relatively detailed transcription helps us analyse interviews. Here's an exchange from about halfway through an interview from his second round of meetings:

> Russell: And have you still been going out for your little walks and things like that?
>
> Sally: Yeah, I've still been refusing to go down to the canteen for lunch. People in Employment, I'm sure you know, go down for lunch. Not every day, but at least a couple of times a week – someone comes round and says 'Are you coming down for lunch?' And I always say 'no' and, in fact, Thomas said 'You are really stubborn, you always say no, you should go sometime' (laughter) ... But I always say 'no' because I always have in my mind that I want to go out – and I could actually potentially do both but there's something about taking time to sit downstairs and have your lunch and going out too that seems a bit excessive – so I get a sandwich outside.

Looking back on it, Russell feels a bit embarrassed about the patronising tone of 'little walks' but he's kindly let it stay here because part of the point of this book is to show how we are all faltering researchers who sometimes make mistakes. He also remembers that she used that phrase earlier on in the interview herself, so it wasn't so much that he was making fun as much as showing he had been listening by 'mirroring' some of her phrases back. In that respect, the 'little' was also interesting in how it positioned the walk ('little' is unimportant?). Either way, the next question was what to do with chunks of text like this. We've worked hard to get them, but what to do next with our new words?

In this excerpt, the interview looks like it was going well enough. He was, broadly speaking, getting Sally to talk relatively freely about aspects of her life that might help him to understand indoor office work in London. But, if he was hoping to look across all his interviews afterwards – he'd done 48 altogether – to see how everyone related to particular topics, he needed a way of exploring them across the whole set of interviews. We'll come back to ways of doing that in a moment. First, we need to tell you about the idea of what is generally called 'coding' in studies of social life involving words.

COMING UP WITH CODES, AND WHAT IS A CODE ACTUALLY?

Coding sounds a bit scientific and intimidating. That is kind of the point. 'Coding' in social research projects of the type Russell was doing is about systematically identifying patterns in the textual material that we've collected in our studies. But it's also about demonstrating that we've done that exercise in an appropriately systematic and rigorous way. The scientific air can help with this. Either way, the idea is that this kind of exercise can help us to find and explore patterns in what we've collected.

A code is more often than not a one- or two-word phrase that encapsulates an idea that you have an inkling could be worth exploring in your analysis, though there are lots of variants if you want to get into this (see Saldana, 2021). It usually has one or two words because you want to make it clear to yourself what you are exploring with each code, so you don't want to make them too long. The idea then is to look through all the transcripts, diary entries, or field notes you've collected and note each time that idea pops up. Then, later on, you'll be able to go through all the material that relates to particular codes and (all being well) eventually reach a reasoned conclusion about how that idea features across all the words you've collected. So, this is about moving from a time when you are fully immersed (Rivas, 2012) in all the material – all the things people say, all the things you've seen – and start to identify and then test out your early ideas about what you've found. You've probably got at least a few ideas about codes already since you've been thinking hard as you went about what you were collecting, sometimes following up with improved questions or more acute observations as you went along.

A useful way of thinking about how you identify codes in the material you've collected is to draw a distinction between what they call 'etic' and 'emic' codes (Olive, 2014). Etic refers to ideas you already had – things you'd imagined you'd wanted to look for – concepts and ideas from your readings that you wanted to test out in terms of how they helped you to make sense of what people said or what you saw. Emic refers to ideas that came from the material itself: things that relate to your wider interests a bit but are also derived from the ways in which people talked to you or things you noticed they were doing or saying. We could think of them as 'outsider' and 'insider' codes too.

More often than not, you'll have a combination of the two; some codes will be etic and some emic. You wouldn't have done the study if you didn't have a sense upfront about what it might help you to explore (etic). But, equally, if part of the point is to be open to learning from the ways in which those you studied talked and did things, you'll want to be relatively open minded about what is interesting there too (emic). So, let's move on and get back to the codes for Russell's office worker study.

A Semi-successful List

Below is an excerpt from the 'code list' Russell created in his project:

Light – 13	Outdoor desire – 3
London – 8	Outdoor need – 19
Making an effort – 16	Presenteeism – 18
Meetings – 4	Purposefulness – 33
Minutes outdoors – 15	Relaxing – 30
Office layout – 32	Resignation – 27
Office location – 9	Routine – 44
Outdoor alibis – 44	Sensitive people – 28
Outdoor annoyance – 30	Shoes – 6

You'll see he had rather a lot. This is only an excerpt; in total, there were 45 codes. This was a fairly sizeable project and he'd allocated quite a bit of time to it. So, he was in a position to work through quite a few codes. But you should always think about the time that coding will take. Coding, and the analysis that follows it, are all about slowing yourself down to see the patterns. But, if you've less time, you'll have to make some difficult calls about the ideas that you think are most useful to you. You'll have to think whether you want to test out those you had already or respond to some of the new patterns you're seeing. For the undergraduate dissertation students we work with, who have about six months for their projects, we tell them that as a rule of thumb about 20 codes to start off with might be an idea – the important thing is to have codes that work, rather than lots of them.

You'll also see there are numbers attached to each one in the above list. These refer to the number of excerpts – like the quote about Sally's sandwich, presented above – he attached to each code in his study. As we've described, Russell had gone systematically through all his interviews. Every time someone seemed to be saying something that related to each code – routines, shoes, people being sensitive about their physical experience – he'd attach that chunk of interview text to the code.

How did he come up with the codes? Well, his was a mixture of both the above approaches, which is a widespread way of doing it. Russell knew from the start of the study that he wanted to explore senses of 'purposefulness', so that was an (etic) code coming from the ideas he already had, whilst the idea to look at office layout was more something that came from them (emic). After having done all his interviews he'd developed a pretty good sense of what people were saying about the topics he'd discussed with them. He'd also made notes of what he thought could become effective codes for him during the interviewing process. Then he read through all the transcripts he'd produced (taking notes of course) to get a final sense of things before putting together his final code list. Sounds easy enough, but, as we'll now discuss, it can pay to play around with how you do that.

BACK TO SALLY'S SANDWICH

Let's go back to the interview excerpt we presented earlier. We use that excerpt in our master's class sometimes. It's a specific example, but the idea is to see the process. Before showing them the above list, but after giving them a short explanation of the project, we show students the excerpt and ask them to sit for a second and reflect on what they think might be a 'good code' for it. What might be an idea that can be seen in this excerpt that could be worth exploring in the wider project? There are often more than one, and the words we've collected can be 'coded' in a variety of ways. Here's the extract again; have a think about what you think the essential or interesting idea might be in here:

Russell: And have you still been going out for your little walks and things like that?

Sally: Yeah, I've still been refusing to go down to the canteen for lunch. People in Employment, I'm sure you know, go down for lunch. Not every day, but at least a couple of times a week – someone comes round and says 'Are you coming down for lunch?' And I always say 'no' and, in fact, Thomas said 'You are really stubborn

> you always say no, you should go sometime' (laughter) … But I always say 'no' because I always have in my mind that I want to go out – and I could actually potentially do both but there's something about taking time to sit downstairs and have your lunch and going out too that seems a bit excessive – so I get a sandwich outside.

Here's what our students have come up with over the years (we've been doing this exercise with them for a while now):

1. *Peer pressure.* This one is clearly there. Sally is resisting for now, but Thomas is definitely encouraging her to go to the canteen. That's where 'everyone else' is perhaps and she wouldn't want to miss out on this chance for team bonding even though it might be good for her to get outside and have a walk around. And, true enough, this was definitely part of his coding in this study – even though it wasn't something that Russell was particularly interested in at the start. One of the reasons why our students pick it, we think, is that it feels appropriately 'academic'; they've a background sense that this is the sort of thing you should analyse to say something that sounds sufficiently clever about how social relationships shape everyday life within, in this case, the professional offices of central London (and sometimes their canteens).
2. *Conventions.* This one comes a close second. It's a bit like peer pressure in the sense that people influencing others is part of how conventions are made. 'Conventions' was one of Russell's codes too. He picked it partly because he had done quite a bit of reading around the idea of people being drawn into patterns of everyday life and he wanted to be sure his results connected to that idea in some way. He didn't want to waste all that reading he'd done about this topic after all, and he had a feeling that there would be something to say here about the times when people reflect on how their lives are going and when they just go with the flow.
3. *Laughter.* This one is often put forward a bit more gingerly. There's often a bit of a gap after we've gone through some of the popular ones and talked about where they might take us in terms of understanding how and why these city workers lived in the ways they did. We think this is partly because it feels inconsequential – Sally is literally 'laughing it off'. Also, for many of our students at least, the idea of analysing our reactions to speaking about particular topics feels quite alien. But, going back to Chapter 5 on different ways of staging talk, this is not to say that we might not want to look at how reactions such as these can tell us something interesting. It's possible that sidestepping any further inspection by the use of strategic laughter is part of how this group coped with their long hours of work inside offices – a quick laugh and a shrug and it's back to work? So, perhaps we could learn something about our topic by looking for all the instances when these lawyers laughed at their situation?

4 *Lunchtimes*. What often surprises us, and what we always present with some degree of mock bemusement, is their reticence about mentioning the most obvious one. The whole excerpt is about lunchtimes! Yet, our students often pull back from saying that could become a code. It's all a bit obvious, no? Well, yes, it is, but if part of the idea is to run with the ways in which the people involved most naturally talk about how they relate to the bigger issue that interests you – in this case how and when they might venture outside their office – then 'lunchtimes' is surely a candidate? In that sense, it's an 'emic' code, which is the kind of code that some would particularly prize because you are starting with how the people you are studying see the issues. We can understand the reticence. We've not seen many 'theories of lunchtimes' in our reading. It's hard to imagine scholarly journals having a lofty debate about the nature of the lunchtime. But perhaps that's exactly what we should be thinking about if we wanted to get people outside. Sure, it's partly about convention. But it's also about the threatened lunch-hour – and whether and when people still talk about having a 'lunch-hour' is very much part of that.

Slow Down to See the Patterns

The point in the above exercise is about recognising the trade-offs you're making when you devise and put into practice a coding procedure. And to sometimes be open-minded about running with ideas that might not have been those you imagined you'd be testing out at the start (see Staller, 2015, for a similar account). Perhaps thinking carefully about lunchtimes could be a very good way to understand how and when indoor workers might connect to outdoor greenspaces and stave off a growing dependence upon cooled indoor spaces. Many of our students (and, to be frank, also some of our peers) talk about analysis and coding as a drudgery (and it certainly can be). But it's also where you really start to figure things out. It's where your conclusions slowly start to take shape. This is all about doing justice to all the words you've got. And that's also, in effect, about slowing down so that you can start to see, and then systematically explore, the patterns. Part of the idea behind this is that, if you don't force yourself to go through this process, it's easy to become too focused on the most exciting responses or experiences that seem to fit really well with what we're trying to do.

Some people call it 'cherry picking' when we stop thinking once we've got some good examples (see, for example, Morse, 2010). That's not to say that you can't make the most of the 'juiciest quote' or the most telling field experience. Depending on your warrants (see Chapter 2), they can be exactly what you'll need to get people interested in your findings or concerned about the people or places that you've studied. It's more that our status as a considered field researcher often rests on us having taken the time to do something a bit more systematic. We used to say to our students that 'cherry picking' is what journalists do, in what we now think was a rather disparaging way. This was partly because we've since been confronted by students who'd been journalists before, and they've forced us to climb down off our high horses. But there's still something to the distinction – a journalist will naturally look for the most engaging case, quote or individual who will best capture the attention and trigger emotions from the reader or viewer. And a social researcher might want to do that too (we'll talk about different ways of writing in Chapter 11) when they present the most engaging quotes and excerpts to their readers. But, if they've done a good job, they should probably only really be presenting them after having done some analysis that was, yes, a lot of work in terms of testing out the potential of certain ideas and then thinking really hard about how they feature amongst all the words they've collected. That's the point! The authority that hopefully gets conferred onto an academic study is fundamentally based on that. This means slowing yourself down to see the patterns. And coding helps with that. You could well discover that what you see as your 'cherry' changes as you get to know the material better.

NOT TOO BIG, NOT TOO SMALL

A quick note on how much text to attach to a code. You'll want each 'chunk' of text to be big enough so that when you look at it in isolation (or alongside all the other chunks that relate to that code) you can still get a sense of what's going on in that chunk. You'll want to remember that part of the interview or the interaction you observed and decided to write down. One or two words attached to a code won't really cut it because you won't remember the context when that's all you see. Having said that, if you've very long chunks, then there's a lot of work ahead of you, if you are going to read through everything you've collected that relates to every code. In our experience, something like a couple of sentences is a good rule of thumb for the chunks that you'd code. The chunk in which we hear about Sally's sandwich isn't too far off the right kind of size. It's perhaps a little long if anything.

A FLOWCHART OF WHAT YOU'RE DOING

We've gone through quite a bit of detail here. So, it might be useful to present what Russell did in the form of a flowchart (Figure 8.1).

Make notes on what you think are the most interesting themes or ideas in these materials

This can relate to etic or emic ideas

↓

Stop and force yourself to come up with a diversity of possible 'codes'

It can slow things down if you come up with new ones later on

↓

How much time do you have and what does this mean for your number of codes?

If it takes a while to follow the process, which ones interest you most?

↓

Work through your material attaching chunks of text to your chosen codes

Usually about one or two sentences so that you've some context when you look at that excerpt on its own later on

Figure 8.1 A flow diagram of analysis

How Long Does It Take?

But how long does all this actually take? Well, as always, it depends. It depends on how many codes you want to have, how closely you are planning on reading through your transcripts, and how much of what was said is really relevant to your study. Still, as another rule of thumb, we'd say that it would likely take you about half a day to go through an interview of about an hour to assign codes to relevant chunks of text so that you're then in a better position to look at what exactly you've learnt about the idea associated with the code by looking at all those chunks together.

And that's what you'd do next if you were doing this process. By looking across all the material you've got about particular ideas, you'll start to see how each idea features in the context you're studying. The key thing is you've got to trust the process. Often the interview material does not seem to 'say' anything. At various points you will feel stupid, overwhelmed, even defeated by the material. But every good researcher has these moments. The point is to go through the process. You'll start to see things and you'll certainly come to a more robust conclusion about the ideas you're exploring because you've gone through this exercise. So, yes, this can be quite time consuming. But you actually want it to be. You'll want to spend time with all the material you've collected. Then you'll be able to see the patterns and speak about them with an authority that largely comes from the time that you've spent on this.

SOFTWARE CAN HELP

It can be hard to find out about the lived experience of social researchers doing this work. Crang and Cook (2007) talk of how one of them cut up pieces of paper to get their chunks and then moved them around on the floor. Belotto (2018) used lots of annotations to mark out his codes in a standard word-processing package. One of us remembers a senior professor telling us how she once found herself covered in Post-it notes as she tried to see the patterns in the interview transcripts she'd printed out and laid on her carpet. Sometimes, when our students come to discuss their projects with us, we eventually get them to show us the bundles of typed-up transcripts or fieldnotes on which they have used different coloured highlighters to indicate sections of text that relate to each of their favourite codes. They'll need an extensive selection of pens if they want to have quite a few codes.

Managing these seemingly little things is where computer software can really help. Some of these issues sound banal but, when you've spent all morning looking repeatedly through your bundles to find the specific sequence of discussion you wanted to think more about, you'd soon see the benefits. There are lots of different software packages around nowadays but what all of them essentially do is allow you to go systematically through your material, applying your codes, and then seeing what you think about each of them. Crucially, they also stop you from losing track of where you are with that. In addition they do things like allowing you to compare how particular types of people talked about particular topics or how particular processes might have worked out differently when you took notes in particular places or at particular times. Basic coding with a computer doesn't take long to learn so it could be worth considering. If you've got a decent amount of material, it can make a lot of sense – it could certainly save you buying lots of highlighters or getting lost in Post-it notes on the carpet.

WHAT HAPPENS NEXT? A TALE OF TWO CODES

As we've said, we can all learn from parts of our projects that haven't gone brilliantly as much as the times when things have really worked out. We don't hear so much about the former, though perhaps we should. Either way, in the spirit of openness, let's go back for one last time to that office worker study of Russell's and, more specifically, back to that list of codes that he had.

You'll also see that these numbers vary quite a bit. When he did his brainstorm at the start to identify all the different themes or ideas he thought it might be worth exploring, he was probably a bit eager. If you're hoping to get a sense of how a particular idea features across all the interviews, you're going to need a decent number of excerpts for each idea. He ended up only 'using' some of his codes in so far as those were the ones that ended up shaping the final reports. This is how that went.

Code 1. 'Going Without Urban Nature'

Here's an excerpt from a 'policy report' that came out of that office workers project. Because Russell wanted to see whether various 'officials' in charge of life in London might respond to his study, he sent a report to a range of people involved in managing life in London.

I don't really think about the outdoor environment around my office. I guess the only thing I think about is whether I can read my book and cross the street at the same time in the morning. And most of the time I can.

Anna: interview 1

Respondents reported how they would often never leave the building until they went home at the end of the day. The majority spent only brief periods outdoors during this period. The average, including travel time, was a total of about 30 minutes. The shortest was estimated at around ten minutes as one respondent described a brief hit of stimulating outdoor conditions during his brisk morning walk from the bus to the foyer. Whilst this was, in itself, unsurprising in view of their hefty workloads, the more interesting finding related to the lack of previous reflection or degree of initial concern. That is to say that, in most cases, this was not something they had thought much about or, during the early stages of the project at least, cared a great deal about. Indeed, it was only through the process of being involved in this study that many described how they gradually came to consider the extent to which they were inclined to remain indoors and the outdoor benefits that were potentially forgone as a result (Hitchings, 2009).

When I am walking into work it is almost like being in a building anyway. It feels like you are inside almost ... because it's just seas of people going across the crossings, and it really doesn't even feel like being outside. It's quite weird.

Samantha: interview 2

What we have here are the results of a code that 'worked'. 'Going without urban nature' was a largely etic code – Russell had done some thinking and reading about this idea already – that always interested Russell in his study. He collected all the quotes that related to that idea and then sat down, made himself a tea, and took a long hard look at them all together. Forcing himself to do this (he'd used software to print out everything related to that code) made him consider everything that was said about this topic: all the different quotes and ideas that were presented by all the people he spoke with that were related to how they felt about potentially missing out on greenspace experiences in their everyday lives. Then, with all that fresh in his mind, he wrote out a summary of what he figured they were saying about that. Using that summary, together with some of the best quotes (we told you it was OK to use them, just not to think about only them), Russell eventually wrote the above report section (see Chapter 11 on how writing things up can take time). He felt confident about what he had produced because he'd followed a carefully thought-out procedure that made him slow down and be systematic.

Code 2. 'Shoes'

There's a rather different story to tell about the second code. You'll have seen in the list above that 'shoes' was a code that didn't attract so many quotes. When he came up with it, he was thinking about the issues that might stop people from going outside and spending time there. He was thinking about issues of self-presentation and of how you might not want to get yourself dirty on the grass if wearing smart attire and you had a meeting that afternoon. One or two of his lawyers had said something that piqued his interest about what they were expected to do with their shoes; he remembers some disdain about those who wore suits and trainers on the underground on their way into work. So, could 'shoes' – rather like lunchtimes – be a good code for him? It probably could have been (if he had asked everyone to speak more about them!), but it didn't come up so much (as it turns out) in his conversations. So, during the weeks that he'd devoted to coding, he'd looked out for everything that was said about shoes that might be interesting. And, in the end, he didn't find a great deal. Not enough to say he was doing a sufficiently thorough analysis of shoes. You'll remember that we said at various points you'll feel stupid, overwhelmed, even defeated by the material. In some respects, he feels a little foolish about his 'shoes' efforts, looking back on them now, but then again, that's the process. You can't expect all the ideas that you think have potential at the start to work out. And following the process in this way helps you to decide which ones you can confidently talk about.

WORDS IN THE WILD

So, what are we effectively looking for when we do a study focused on words? Well, it's often about finding a way into exploring ideas that can often be encapsulated by a word or two, and then finding a way of getting stuck into what they do for certain groups or how and why these ideas might have collected in certain places. Another way of doing this sort of work is to say we're interested in 'discourses', namely representations or simplifications of some topic or another that are partly an outcome of how particular forces in society encourage particular groups to see things in certain ways. This is more common when we are examining the collections of representations that are already available, rather than writing or recording our own words. In the exercise at the start of the chapter, we'd effectively identified three different 'student discourses'.

So how do things work when we are looking at some of these 'already existing' collections of words? Here are three different examples to get you going:

1. Talking About Immigrants on Social Media

A lot of social life now happens online. Many worry that too much mediated interaction, rather than 'in real life' exchanges, can have negative consequences. Does this encourage us to be less friendly, more aggressive in expressing our views because we want to attract attention or don't have to look someone in the eye as we criticise them? Either way, we'd need to think about how interacting online shapes the ways in which different groups talk and think about things. It was with that in mind that, in the context of recent waves of migration, Victoria Yantseva (2023) used a software package to examine over a million Swedish Facebook posts to explore how different immigrant groups were being discussed. She found that, when people talked about 'immigrants', the discussion was more often about the costs and benefits to Swedish society. Yet, when they spoke of 'refugees', the importance of supporting those in need immediately came to the fore. That perhaps is unsurprising. What she felt was more significant was how both ways of talking about things served to downplay the lived experiences of those involved. That, so she worried, made it harder for Swedes to find common cause with this group. They were economically useful (or not) or those needing care (or not) – either way, both ways of talking online crowded out the suggestion that they might essentially be the same as those posting.

2. Government Letters About Covid-19 in China

Some of the favourite places for social researchers to set about looking for how words shape our thinking is to look at newspapers and policy reports. They do that because they've got a sense that this is where the action is – it's here that society is collectively discussing what it should do. But there are many ways in which governments and populations interact. In China, during the Covid-19 pandemic, one way used by Qing Liu (2023) was through official letters that experienced a resurgence as a government communication form at this time. By comparing the words that were used in letters from the central government and the local authorities, this study helped us to see how different arms of government sought to persuade citizens to stay indoors and follow the rules to stop the virus. Reading closely through 84 letters, they saw different strategies in the letters coming from each level, with relatively polite requests sometimes sitting alongside impassioned demands. The local level sought to speak in a way that emphasised common cause and shared experience (let's pull together), whilst both levels spoke of a 'war' on the virus. We don't quite know what people felt when they (potentially) read these letters. But we do gain a sense of how the pandemic shaped persuasion strategies in a country with a particular relation between the state and the citizen. It would be interesting to compare the words used elsewhere.

3. Popular Novels and the Israel–Palestine Conflict

In this work the argument is often that we should look for the assumptions embedded in the ways in which we can unthinkingly describe things – especially when we are probably extra alive to how news reporting and governments can nudge us to see issues in particular ways. If that's the case, we should consider when we are less alert to these manipulations and less likely to subject them to critical inspection. So, perhaps we should look at the times when people want only to be entertained to see how their ways of seeing the world might be unthinkingly influenced at these times. Perhaps novels could be worth a look? Many researchers have looked at social life in this way. For example, Toine van Teeffelen (1994) read around 20 best-selling books from the 1970s and 80s depicting the Palestine–Israel conflict. What metaphors were these books reproducing and how were they encouraging their readers to think about the different groups involved? One thing that he noticed was the way in which family life for Arabs was seldom depicted as harmonious and recognisable. Another was the way in which Arabs were often seen as hot-headed. In this way, certain racist ideas where sustained that were, rather like the Swedish Facebook example, likely to discourage readers from being more empathetic towards others because they were encouraged to see some groups as very different to themselves instead.

There are lots of places where we could explore the words that organise the thinking of different sets of people on all sorts of issues. The trick here is about finding a way of establishing a limit to your study – what can you feasibly do in the time you have and what can you claim to know based on doing that? But what you see here is that this also depends on what you want to do. If you want to really think hard about how books depict things, you'll need to consider how many you can read in the time that you have. In the Middle Eastern example above, 20 novels were deemed enough to get a sense of how things were generally depicted. If you want to deal with a much bigger number of social media posts, then it makes sense to use some software to count how often particular depictions appear. That made it possible for the Swedish study to tackle over a million. If you have a relatively limited number of letters, then read them all very closely because that's all you've got.

The other part is about finding a way of spending time considering the representations that you find in order to notice how things might have been represented otherwise and to think through the implications of current representations. So, once again, it's a matter of slowing yourself down.

Discourse Hunting

As we've discussed already, part of what makes this kind of exercise impressive and enjoyable is about looking out for, and then bringing to the fore, some of the background assumptions that we can see in certain parts of society (like the student as a brainbox on the TV show or the subtle ways in which students were being repositioned as customers). With that in mind, we sometimes dare those taking our master's course to identify unusual places to explore these issues. We tell them 'the more unusual the better'. This is riffing off the idea that discourses can be found everywhere. And that those found in contexts which aren't so overtly political might be those most likely to shape our thinking without us really noticing it. We ask them to do a basic 'discourse analysis activity', which is to note how particular topics, groups, or issues are represented 'as if' they possess particular qualities.

Some examples:

- Climate change as positive in cooking articles
- Cites as complex in academic papers
- Migrants as determined in job interviews
- New Yorkers as sassy in TV series
- The Swedish as eccentric in furniture adverts
- Older people as comical on TikTok
- Geographers as passionate in their lectures
- Shiny hair as empowering in commercials
- Vegans as smug in everyday conversations

One trick to this is about spending time examining the sources and forcing ourselves to think about how any given group, issue, or hair style could be represented otherwise. Some have usefully called this 'listening for silences' (Waitt, 2010). In that respect, like a lot of the methods in this book, this is about spending time with your sources in ways that mean we'll slowly start to see the patterns. Either way (and though there's always a bit of background motivation to getting stuck into this), we'd encourage you to wait a while before you start to engage with the political part. There will always be something political there when we give ourselves the time to reflect on the representations. No need to jump the gun when that can mean you end up collecting examples that prove your point, rather than doing something more systematic. We tell our dissertation students: 'You'll never be able to write 12,000 words on why you were right all along anyway!' Give your material some space to breathe so that you can slowly start to see the nuances of how shiny hair is depicted, or the various qualities that New Yorkers might feasibly possess.

A final trick, we think, is about being sure that your collections have enough relevant words in them. So, how often do cooking articles actually mention things that relate to changing climates, how often do academic articles talk about city complexity, how many words are actually on the back of the hair dye box? You'll need to be sure there's enough of them there to make it worth doing a study. And then you'll need to be sure that you can get hold of the words and come up with a sensible strategy for looking closely at them. So, how many job interview transcripts could you feasibly get hold of and what can you do with them? Are you able to record all your lectures and then look at how the lecturers talk about themselves (gulp)? In that sense, this is essentially about coming up with a plan that works; in which you have enough material to justify spending a good chunk of your time going through things.

How Patterns Were Explored in the Three Earlier Examples

Let's go back to our three examples of 'words in the wild' to see how that's done.

Swedish Refugee Talk on Facebook

Compared to Russell's office worker study, analysis will likely have been a lot quicker here since the idea was to use software to explore the patterns. People can get reticent about using numbers in some of the approaches we talk about in this book. This isn't surprising as the idea is often that we want to gradually explore how others see things, rather than forcing people to choose from a menu of answers. But there is no reason why you shouldn't use numbers to get a sense of things. In this case, the time that you spend on doing so will be a bit more about learning how to do it – how to get your head around the software that can help you categorise over a million Facebook posts, for example. Having said that, once you've done so, the patterns will flow in and then you can think about them. You'll have to recognise that you'll never quite get really close to a sense of where particular groups were coming from (because you are doing relatively quick categorisation rather than spending a lot of time with them in the hope of seeing things as they do) but you'll have a good sense of how much, and how often, they are saying particular things – and numbers can be persuasive.

Chinese Letters During Covid-19

For this second case, the researchers had already done a good job in terms of identifying a manageable amount of material with which they felt confident that they could probably learn something, from looking at the differences in how the issue was presented. If we are going to, for example, 'listen for silences' then picking contrasting sets like this could be a good idea because we'll immediately spot the subtle differences, if we're lucky. So, this was a simple question of reading through them all, possibly subjecting them to that kind of coding process detailed above, and then coming to a reasoned conclusion about how and why the pandemic was spoken about in particular ways, along with how responsibility was constructed and communicated to citizens there. Whilst this approach means you can be exhaustive, the risk you run is about whether you've enough material to write a report – since you can't go back and collect more if there's no more to be had.

Popular Novels and the Israel–Palestine Conflict

Our final researcher was a bit more literary. In fact, some of this work is a lot like the kind of exercise you might do in an English degree. Here we're spending time reading, and re-reading, relevant books and then thinking about how and why groups and issues are presented as they are. What's a bit different about this one, as a social research study, is that we'll always be returning to how the novels are part of a wider conversation about what certain people and places are like; this is about how novels function in society more than about how, say, they might belong to particular stylistic movements. This author presumably read through the relevant passages again and again (and, if they'd wanted a bit more structure to that, they could have thought about coding too) to gradually build up a sense of how the representations worked. Then they'll reach their conclusions through reflection, more than procedure, and use examples and extracts to exemplify this.

WHAT'S THE DIFFERENCE BETWEEN PRODUCED AND FOUND WORDS?

One thing we always discuss when we talk about all these different sources of words with our students is the difference between those we've found and the words we've produced ourselves. Can you do coding when you're looking at magazines instead of interviews or fieldnotes? Should you? We say you probably could (it's just a process for organising your thinking and slowing yourself down, after all), but that you'd need to be sure it's worth your while. It's less certain that there'll be the same concentration of material related to your project when you go through some of these wider sources; they could be discussing all sorts of other things with relevant stuff popping up only every now and again. You did your interviews or observation so that you could get lots of relevant stuff (you asked pertinent things, and you noted down the most related interactions). There is no such agenda with these other sources.

Having said that, you'd still want to be systematic in some sort of way. One of the temptations when we look at wider sets of representations is to skip to the political (see Dittmer, 2009). This is understandable, we think. It's easier to get stuck into representations containing political ideas that we might want to challenge when we are a little bit removed from them, whereas when we are talking about people who've made the time to speak with us it's a bit harder to be too critical of them. But, as we've said, your readers will smell a rat if you only provide evidence which proves your point, and your status as a researcher (rather than social commentator) rests on being a bit careful and open-minded too.

CONCLUSION: DO NOT JUMP!

And so we come to the end of our discussion of 'words'. The point of this chapter has been to consider how social researchers tend to work with words in their project: both the words they have produced themselves in their studies through talking with people or making their notes and the collections they've found out there in the world. We've tried to give you a sense of how you might be creative in doing this sort of work – What are the codes? Where might we find some interesting discourses? – since thinking about those matters can be important too. All this takes time, since taking that time means we are doing a thorough study. When we go on our undergraduate field class looking at what people do in different cities, we tell our students not to jump to conclusions, to 'delay their explanations'. And that's essentially what you'd be doing here, irrespective of the words you've got. The idea is that, if you concentrate on things long enough, you'll start to see something. Maybe that sounds a bit mind-bending! Well, this chapter gives some guidance on not going mad when working with words. It can be dull sometimes. Sometimes it doesn't yield any useful results either (remember those shoes). But when you suddenly see a pattern or feel your understanding really grow, that's exciting because you're bringing new things to the fore that might not have been thought about so much before.

9
LOOKING AT PICTURES: WAYS OF GETTING DRAWN INTO SOCIAL WORLDS

SEEING POTENTIAL IN THE DETAIL

A book of field studies (2004) by photographer Stephen Gill is, we think, a lovely collection. Inside he presents a series of photographs he's taken of the mundane moments and everyday objects currently found in most UK cities – shopping carts, people on commuter trains, road works, cash points. The photographs are initially puzzling. What's interesting about the patterned trolley being pulled along by this older woman? Or the orange plastic barricades that seem to have been drunkenly scattered around a hole in the road? Why on earth has he taken a photo of the spaces behind billboards? On repeated looking and closer scrutiny of Gill's photographs, however, you begin to notice interesting repetitions within the series – in the similar bored expression of the train travellers, in some of the styles in which people are dressed, the slight variations in shopping trolley design – along with noticing all the detail held within the photograph's frame. Gill's photographs are pointing towards something important about the social worlds he is documenting, even if it's not immediately clear what that is exactly.

Gill named his collection 'field studies' after the Observer pocketbooks of illustrated encyclopaedic 'field guides' popular from the 1930s to the 1980s. These guides covered topics as diverse as postage stamps, British birds, common fungi, automobiles, airplanes, lichen, cats, flags, cathedrals, even fossils. Alan and his brother were obsessed with these books when they were boys because of the beguiling way in which they seemed to describe whole worlds within their 3.5-inch-by-5.5-inch covers. They even tried producing their own versions – warplanes of WWII, beer cans of the world, native birds of New Zealand. Starting out as a social researcher, Alan took photographs of things he was studying. He did this with the simple aim of having a physical reminder of the places he had visited, but also of building a photographic archive of those places – a kind of personal Observer Guide. So, when he began studying the inner-city Auckland neighbourhood discussed in Chapter 6, he took a pocket-sized Olympus 35 mm automatic camera with him whenever he went. He took photographs of the shops, cafés, bars, and pubs that he found there. He photographed signs, advertising hoardings, and street furniture. He photographed car parks, people, litter, pavements. He took lots of photographs! Through these means, he gradually amassed a collection that was – not unlike his childhood Observer Guides, but more, like Gill, with an interest in the mundane – a visual record of all the interesting things he saw along the retail strip he was researching.

Of course, photographs – and any illustrations for that matter – never tell the whole truth. Sometimes they barely tell us anything at all. But they can offer an invitation into a much closer examination of things than we might otherwise undertake. They fix our attention. They provide evidence that something exists.

Figure 9.1 Auckland field studies
Source: Alan Latham

In the case of Alan's Auckland collection, at first, he had little sense of why he was photographing the things that he did. However, over time – and as he reviewed his growing collection – he started to notice some interesting patterns: how the bars and cafés blended in with neighbouring stores; the variations in frontage styles; how cars and buses were as much – sometimes even more – a part of the rhythm of the street as the pedestrians, to name just a few examples. Photos can clearly help the social researcher.

Drawing on examples like this, this chapter explores some of the most common ways of using photographs and photography to study and present social life. Like the words discussed in Chapter 8, the value of Alan's photographs in his social research partly stemmed from how their presence pushed him to linger over what they contained – as you might do with your interview transcripts – because, once you've begun doing that, you'll hopefully start to notice, and then potentially begin to explore, how exactly social life works in particular contexts. We might have thought certain details unimportant at the start. But, to return to the Gill example, could there be the makings of a project on facial expressions in different social contexts? Maybe there's a study here on shopping trolleys, where they can be found, and what people do with them? Firstly, we're going to focus on how we can use photography to get to know a new research setting. So, that's about us looking at the pictures we've taken ourselves. Here we're using photography as a form of notetaking and concentrated documentation that helps us to tease out some puzzles to explore further. As part of that, we'll introduce some specific tricks to focus your attention. Secondly, we're going to consider how social researchers use photographs taken by others as a resource in the discussions we subsequently have with them. So, that's about looking at pictures together with people. Thirdly, we'll examine the use of photographs to develop and present our final accounts of the people or sites we've been researching. So, that's about how and why we ask wider audiences to look at our pictures. We end with a few words on the ethics of photography in social research.

With photographs, social researchers can respond to the liveliness and concreteness of social life in ways that are difficult to match. This is because photographs keep pulling us back to the detail of how lives are, or have been, lived. Our account of how you might use them is once again not exhaustive (there are many ways of using photos in social research: see Harper, 2023; Pink, 2021). And we don't cover more formal ways of analysing images in social research (though the process, we think, isn't too dissimilar to that we described in Chapter 8 – you slow yourself down to see the patterns). What this chapter does do is give you some useful tricks and ideas so that you can make the most of photographs in your own social research. And, as with all our chapters, you should end it with a good sense of how you could put some of them into practice.

IMAGES TO DRAW US IN: PHOTOGRAPHY AS FIELDNOTES

When Alan did his Auckland project, taking photographs was expensive and involved both a dedicated device – a camera – and the physical development of photographs (his rolls of film were sent away before prints were eventually returned). Because of smartphones, photography is almost everywhere now. We take photographs to remind us of where we've parked. We take photographs of things we see when we are out and about – cute dogs, beautiful sunsets, weird looking buildings, shop windows, a gnarly tree trunk. We take photographs of things we see in shops that we might want to buy later. We take photographs of friends when we meet them. We take photographs of our food. Some people take photographs of almost everything. Some of them we share with others – over WhatsApp, WeChat, Snapchat, Instagram, Facebook, X (formerly Twitter). Others we keep to ourselves. In turning to photography as a social research tool, we're tapping into what has become an everyday skill for many of us. How can we channel these mundane skills so that we can effectively use photography as part of our research too?

Let's look at an example from our field class. As you know by now, each year we go to a city, where, after we've tested out a range of observational techniques, groups of students are assigned some neighbourhoods in which they're tasked to develop, and then explore, a specific theme using these techniques. We don't tell the students anything about the neighbourhoods – we just dish out maps with locations marked on them and off they go. Their first task is to use observation to start identifying possible research topics. They begin by spending a morning taking notes and, crucially for this chapter, taking photographs to create an initial documentation of these sites. Figure 9.2 shows some of their photos from when we went to Vienna.

As with Alan's Auckland inventory, most of them seem pretty boring at the start. The students are often bemused by their collections. They're of all sorts of prosaic and initially uninspiring things – rubbish bins, signs, streets, pavements, bus stops, deli counters, buildings, corner stores, benches, and so on. Many of them find it hard to do this exercise because they don't know what might be important or worth documenting. But that's the whole point, we say. This kind of photography is meant to be exploratory and generative – a technique for feeling towards what could be interesting, what might be useful to study. After spending two or three hours doing it, they're asked to sit down and look through the results with us in the evening. Slowly they begin to notice all sorts of relationships that, we think, could evolve into research projects – how things are being sold and paid for; how and where people wait; how people eat food on the go; how people are dressed; how spaces are organised (or not), and so on.

Photos, used in this way, allow you to collect material you can then afterwards, at your leisure, use to come up with ideas for things to examine next time you visit – in ways that could mean more photography or another method too. It can be hard to do this in the moment. But, as our students eventually tell us, looking

Figure 9.2 Surveying all sorts of things in Vienna
Source: Vienna students 2023

at photographs afterwards together allowed them to usefully revisit what they saw when they were out. Having the photograph right there helps them to see, and slowly develop hunches about, all the details of everyday life. And you don't have to go to an unfamiliar city to experiment with photography in this way. If you've a spare couple of hours, go out into your neighbourhood and try using your smartphone to document what you see. After you've spent an hour collecting photographs, sit down with a notebook and look through them all – try flicking through them quickly, followed by a slower, more reflective consideration. You might start to notice some of the things our students did. Maybe you've noticed different things. Either way, the point is to give yourself the time to do it and to allow your mind to wander around what photos are really good at – showing us the detail of where people are found, the things they live with, and what they may be doing.

THREE USEFUL TRICKS

The style of initial photographic notetaking introduced above is by its nature not very systematic beyond the injunction to take lots of photographs before mulling them over afterwards. As we've said, in practice, doing that can be hard – in life we're often used to having a bit more purpose and that's difficult to shake off. Our students often want more direction – 'OK, guys ... but what do you want us to actually take photos of?!' Fair enough, we say – we never go out with our cameras and no agenda at all. Especially when many of our students are quite adept at taking photos of city life that will, they hope, be well received on social media; perhaps they need some tricks for getting more fully immersed into the environment, for starting to come up with ideas for studies, for not taking photos of themselves looking wistful in front of a strikingly colourful graffiti arrangement that just seemingly happened to be there. Here are three simple tricks for taking photographs as social research fieldnotes:

1. What Are the Different Kinds?

The first trick involves trying to document (that is to say to find and photograph) as many cases as possible of an object or activity that interests you.

Back to our field class. With some nagging encouragement from us about being willing to dwell on everyday things that don't initially seem worthy of 'academic' study, one year some students decided they wanted their project to explore the theme of 'windows'. They'd noticed the ubiquity of windows in Vienna (perhaps no surprise but trusting the process is key), along with a wide variation in types. We thought it was promising how they were willing to go with the detail – 'what are windows all about?' was a neat question to get going with, we told them. To get a better sense of the variety of windows, next they photographed all the types of window they could find in their allocated neighbourhoods – apartment windows, supermarket windows, café windows, car windows, door windows, bus windows, tram windows, bookstore windows, office windows, fast food kiosk windows, and so on. So far so obvious. But what they started to notice through this audit was the different ways windows were addressing the pavement or the street. Some apartment windows were blank. Others were decorated with pot plants. Some with figurines. Other windows had political messages attached – gay pride flags, national flags, environmental posters, and so on. These were windows to be looked at as much to be looked out from. In commercial premises there was variation too. Some shop windows had been turned into placards advertising what was inside, blocking any actual view. Other windows were set up to highlight the interior within, some as an invitation to enter – in the case of cafés – and others as a projection of wealth and taste – in the case of many office blocks (see Figure 9.3).

Figure 9.3 Surveying the windows of Vienna
Source: Vienna students 2023

The focused attention of a photographic audit gives an expanded sense of what is distinctive about that object or activity. In the window example, the students' efforts began to show the different ways in which ideas about 'public' and 'private' spaces are constructed and managed in Vienna. They also pointed to the systems of visibility and protection through which people are encouraged to interact or stay apart. Indeed, through carrying out an audit you may well begin to ask what should be included. In the window audit, our students found themselves puzzling out whether a frosted window was still a window; whether a boarded up or shuttered window should be part of it; whether a glazed door might count? In a similar audit of 'seats' in public spaces you might end up asking yourself questions like 'Is a step a seat (given that you saw many people sitting on steps)?' One year a group did an audit of rubbish bins. They found trash left in flower planters and bike baskets. Does that transform them into bins? In the windows case, it led them towards an examination of which sorts of window practices were found where in the city. Could the extent to which people adorn their windows or shield themselves from prying eyes tell us something about the character of particular neighbourhoods? Well, yes, actually they could!

2. How Are Things Used?

In our second trick, we start with a determined focus on how a particular practice actually proceeds or how objects are used.

In addition to inventories and audits, there are many other ways of exploring variation through photography. Can we perhaps document all the different ways in which people arrange themselves in particular contexts? Another group of students we've gone away with – this time hoping to understand city life in Stockholm – documented the many ways people sat on crowded subway trains. Through a combination of photographs and observational work they began to explore the tactics transit riders used to make space for themselves whilst not impinging on the personal space of others. They made this space in many ways: they sat sideways on seats, they rotated their legs away from fellow passengers; sometimes they hooked their feet under seats, or they hugged rucksacks to their chest as protection (see Figure 9.4). So, they were looking at all the different ways in which seats were shared – or, perhaps more correctly, how people kept an appropriate distance or tried to – on public transport in Swedish cities. Just like how we live with windows, what you do with your legs on the Underground can easily fade into the background. Your legs are just there but, for these students, legs and feet became especially interesting. The discipline of taking photos to see all the leg and feet arrangements in the metro train got them thinking about the circumstances under which different arrangements formed – Do the men spread their legs? Is it different at different times? What about when it's less crowded?

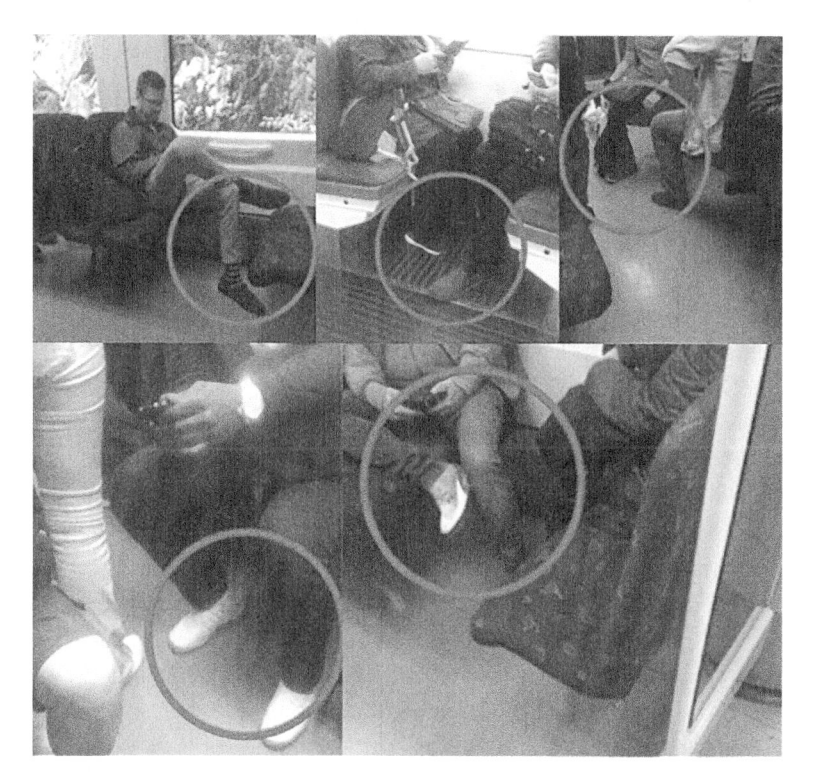

Figure 9.4 How to use a Stockholm subway seat
Source: Stockholm students 2021

Another thing we've done on the field class is to give students a picture of an object found in that city. We ask them to sit and pore over that picture. We've given them pictures of plant pots in the past. Sculptures in parks. Even pictures of lawns. Then we ask them to itemise all the possible things that could be done with that thing. As they look again and again at the image, their lists start to grow and get increasingly eclectic. They say that, maybe you could run around that piece of public art, if you were a child. If you were a dog, it might be a great thing to sniff if you wanted to know what the other dogs of Stockholm had been up to. If you wanted to see a friend, perhaps it's a handy landmark – nothing else looks quite like it which makes it a good place to meet before going for lunch. And of course, some of them could be excellent for social media posts that show you're enjoying yourself in an interesting new place too. Either way, how photos keep you focused on the detail of the brute materiality of the object at hand can draw you productively into the very many ways in which that object is woven into the fabric of everyday life. The things our students were noticing were probably already an issue for local planners and policymakers, but these officials might also learn something from the social researcher. They could tell them all about the detail of how exactly people, children, dogs, and tourists come together – or not – around a public artwork in a city square. Here photography helped us to explore the reality and diversity of how different objects were lived with.

3. How Do Things Change?

In our third trick, photography is used to notice and examine how, over time, the way in which a setting or activity functions can change.

This might be over a relatively short period – an hour, say – or a longer one (a day, week, month, season). Whatever the timescale you choose, taking a series of photographs over a fixed period can give a powerful sense of the temporality of an object, activity, or place. This is akin to the time-lapse photography commonly used in nature documentary films to narrate the passing of the seasons, or the growth and maturing of plants and trees. A 'time series' highlights the rhythms of social life. It trains our attention onto how things are sequential, how one thing follows another. That's often in the natural order of things in particular contexts; what some have rather poetically called a 'place ballet' – see, for example, Seamon (2015). And whilst video can show us this detail too, we've found the discipline of the time series approach can pull us into temporal processes in a very effective way. For example, one group of field class students spent an hour documenting the platform of a suburban subway station with a single wide angle shot, and taking a photograph every 20 seconds. Ending up with a total of 180 images, their series gave a sense of how the activity on the platform shifted as the platform filled up with people and then emptied as trains arrived and departed. This showed how people, once again, created a kind of order out of how they dispersed themselves along the platform in busy times and how, when they had to wait, groups made a kind of temporary home by sitting down and settling into platform life.

That same day, before heading out, we also staged an experiment to show how this technique might work for them. This time we went to our teaching room a little earlier than usual and arranged the chairs into a sort of artwork – stacking them into what we felt at the time was quite a stylish pile in the centre of the room. Then, when they (sluggishly and gradually) joined us, we told them they should sit down when ready (gesturing to the pile of chairs we had carefully assembled just before). Then one of us took a picture every ten seconds. Below is part of the result. What do you see? Well, we firstly see evidence of etiquette and a similar social signalling. In particular, have a look at the student in the middle. She didn't have too much time to wait and wasn't at all bothered about the photographer in the corner. She'd just had her breakfast, and it looks like she really wanted to sit down. But, in doing that comparatively quickly, you'll see how she signalled with her folded arms and her fixed look forward that this was OK – the task was complete. Nothing to see here! The point is quite the opposite – photography is helping us because it is allowing us to see, and then scrutinise, the sequence.

Figure 9.5 A strange arrangement of chairs after breakfast
Source: Russell Hitchings

Each trick trains our attention onto details we might otherwise easily overlook. Our students sometimes feel a bit foolish when we tell them to just 'go and take some photos'. To be fair to them, it's hard to slip immediately into the role of a photographic social researcher, which is why we came up with these tricks. So, whenever you're in a context you think could be interesting in terms of social life, perhaps set yourself some of these mini-tasks – or create some of your own. At the start, you might be thinking it's just a street, a park, a shop, a train carriage. Well, yes and no. If we try some of these tricks, with a bit of luck, we'll soon start to see how a great deal of work goes into making them shareable and functional as places for people.

Though we've focused on public space, these tricks can be put to use in all sorts of settings. You could do an audit of the objects found around office workstations to understand the culture of labour control within a company and how and when people express themselves in terms of 'personalising' these sites. If you're interested in people's everyday material culture, you might do an audit of all the things some of them own at home. Indeed, if you wanted to experiment with photographic auditing, you could try this yourself – take a picture of every object you own, or if that's too strenuous try an audit of everything in your bedroom. Looking through the series of photographs you've produced, what does this suggest about you and the material culture of which you are a part? For inspiration, try comparing yourself with the pictures found in James Mollison's *Where children sleep* (2010), a series of portraits of children's place of sleep from around the world, or Peter Menzel's *Material world: A global family portrait* (1994), a photographic study of family possessions from 30 different countries.

IMAGES TO DRAW THEM OUT: WORKING WITH PHOTO-ELICITATION

In the chapter so far, the focus has been on photographs that researchers can take themselves to see and then examine aspects of social life. Another way of using photography is to ask others to take photos for us. Could that be a better route into understanding their social worlds?

What Were You Doing at 6.30 p.m. Last Night?

Certainly, there are places where the first approach wouldn't work because we can't generally follow people around all day, and they might understandably be unwilling to grant researchers access to certain places. It's for that reason that sometimes we ask the master's students to help us understand their lives a bit better by taking photos of their immediate environments in the evening. Choosing a random weekday (things are likely to be different on weekends) we send a polite message to everyone taking the course, asking them to 'take a quick photo' of their environment at 6.30 p.m. – emphasising how they shouldn't do it if they were doing anything personal and not to take photos they wouldn't be happy to discuss. We ask them to email their photos through to us.

When you're asking people to help you in this way, you'll need to be quite thoughtful about encouraging them (remember the discussion in Chapter 6) so we tried to be as charming as we could. We were also asking them to do us a favour after all; this wasn't a compulsory part of the course. We'd picked 6.30 p.m. because we figured that specifying the time might mean they'd be more likely to remember. We were also thinking that students today are used to taking lots of smartphone photos, so maybe there'd be no problem for them to take a quick one for us. Usually, we receive something like 80 images to consider – not everyone, but enough for us see if we can start seeing patterns, perhaps spotting interesting topics suitable for social research.

Many of the photos don't initially seem especially promising, for example the photos of washing machines or pictures of the pavement. Other than helping us to know these students were doing all sorts of things early on Wednesday evenings, we didn't think we could go much further with those. However, we often get lots of pictures of food. Sometimes this could be an image of a bowl of instant noodle soup nestled against a laptop as the student cracked on with a coursework assignment. Sometimes we see pictures of vegetables on chopping boards – clearly some students were more into healthier eating than others. Sometimes we'd see pictures of people laughing together as one ate the meal they'd just prepared for themselves, whilst another was busily making theirs on the stove in a generic-looking shared student kitchen.

So what? Well, what we were starting to notice, and get an idea for a project about, was how students at our university organise their evening eating. Many societies are characterised by eating together at particular times. Shared meals often serve as a sort of social glue. But how easy is it to organise shared meals when, in universities such as ours, there's lots to do and scheduling time to eat together requires effort? Perhaps we also need to think about whether everyone will be happy to eat the same things – Would everyone like the same food? What about different dietary requirements? Perhaps some need protein for their sports training? There was something interesting in these photos, we figured, to do with how, and whether, social relationships were maintained through eating together in the evenings amongst university students. Policymakers, university administrators, and of course parents all worry about students finding university life isolating. And that could partly be because of the loss of these communal practices.

The point, as we discuss with our 6.30 p.m. photographers, when looking through some of their images together in class, is that these photographs gave us a sense of a social context that was alien to us beforehand. They brought us directly into their social worlds, and that allowed us to start asking questions about how lives were being lived there. We eventually concluded that the images were not enough. They'd tipped us off to an interesting topic. But were we to develop this research further we'd want to speak to some students about their evening meals. And we decided that we'd be keen on using some of these photos to anchor those discussions in the reality of how there seemed to be very many ways of making these meals social or not. The photo analysis was a start, but the next step, we thought, should be to talk about them.

And that takes us to our second way of using photography – what is traditionally called 'photo-elicitation', using images to add depth and focus to the conversations that we have with people. Let's look at two more examples of using photographs to do this. With the 6.30 p.m. images, we decided that this would be a good next step. Here, that step was actually taken.

When Do Young People Think About Climate Change in Everyday Life?

In many parts of the world, worrying developments linked to global climate change are often in the news. At the same time, climate change – or global heating, or global warming, or any of the labels attached to it – involves a complicated body of technical knowledge. This presents the curious social researcher with a dilemma. On the one hand, it's safe to assume that most people in most countries have heard about it. On the other hand, it's not reasonable to assume people – especially non-experts – will find it easy to talk about. Climate change is an extraordinarily complex technical phenomenon and there are many competing and contradictory narratives about how it should be addressed. This was the problem that Sophie Thorpe (2023), who did her master's dissertation with

Figure 9.6 Photos to explore feelings about climate change
Source: Thorpe, 2023

us, faced when thinking about how she might study when and how high school students talked about climate change in their everyday lives. There's a lot of discussion about how young people might be suffering from 'eco-anxiety' but how much, and how easily would they talk about this issue? It's possible that they'd determinedly ignore it in conversation because addressing it seemed overwhelming or they didn't want to seem ignorant.

Rather than ambush them with questions on climate change, she asked some of the young people she was teaching at the time to take smartphone photographs over a five-day period to capture the moments when they thought about climate change. She then used these as prompts for group discussions – taking some of them into class before asking the students involved to talk to their peers about their picture. The photographs her students took were remarkably diverse. They took photographs of disposable paper straws, service stations, car parks, hay fever tablets, outdoor festivals, concrete games courts, garden hose pipes, hall lights, Instagram posts, trees, bees, KFC burgers, and more. And these images certainly didn't align with the obvious ways in which climate change was presented in the media. They also opened up lively and – for Sophie and us – surprising conversations about their ambivalence about discussing climate change; how they felt the need to acknowledge its reality, but at the same, were uneasy about how little they and others were doing to address it. Now, of course, it may well have been possible that Sophie could have staged similar conversations without the photos. But they did help her to focus so that the conversation immediately got to the point. They also gave her students some time to think beforehand about the issue, since they had to do that before they could take their photos. That meant they were more prepared and felt less 'on-the-spot' during the discussion itself. Whilst, as we've said, we can't be sure, we think that, had Sophie not made these photos part of her study, she might have been met with many more 'dunnos' and shoulder shrugs if she'd just asked them to speak about climate change in their everyday lives.

What Do Older People Do in Response to Winter Cold?

Here's another example. With his colleague Rosie Day, Russell carried out a study on how a range of older Britons dealt with the challenges associated with winter cold at home (Day and Hitchings, 2011). In the UK, there's good reason to explore how older people keep warm at this time. Firstly, they are often in large family homes that need a lot of energy to heat. Given that many older people are sensitive to cold, they might therefore be contributing to the climate change that Sophie was also worried about. Secondly, we also know that, with high heating costs, many of them can find winter challenging in ways that can result in various health problems.

You'll have got a sense by now that, if you want to get close to the detail of people's lives, then photos can represent a good route. In this second project,

Russell and Rosie visited some of them at home. After their first interview, each household was given a disposable camera. Then, when a cold spell was forecast, they got back in touch to ask the older people they'd recruited to take photos of things they were doing in response to the winter cold. The idea, rather like our 6.30 p.m. exercise, was that they didn't want to presume that they knew what these older people would do. They also wanted to prompt them to think about the minor details that might turn out to be quite important in understanding how they handled cold weather and whether they were open to changing some of their ways. Afterwards, when these cameras had been returned to Russell and Rosie, they examined their collection of photos before meeting each household once more to talk further about how the winter had gone for them as spring approached.

Figure 9.7 Photos to explore ways of handling winter
Source: Day and Hitchings, 2011

In the spirit of being open about when methods really work, and how they can be challenging too, this is less of a success story. The images were, as you can see, of all sorts of things and the idea was to look at how the whole group felt about certain ways of dealing with winter. The question that Russell and Rosie faced was how they should use these photos in their interviews. When they went back to these households and sat down at the kitchen table with their cups of tea together, should they ask everyone about all the photos? The trouble then would be that some of them wouldn't know too much about the context involved. And explaining all that would eat into the time they had scheduled to talk together. Equally, when they asked people about their own photos, they often got drawn into the detail of that particular situation, leaving them, once again, with less time to explore common issues and themes across the group.

This is not to advise against this approach. It's more to acknowledge how it can take time, and if you want to represent a social group, as well as illustrate what particular individuals do, that will eat up time too. Eventually, some of our photo discussions led to some interesting insights about what people would wear or not when they left the house and faced the cold outdoors; how this was sometimes as much about looking capable as staying warm. They hadn't imagined that would be a part of their project and so asking people to discuss a choice selection of photos definitely helped them to get closer to the lived reality of their lives. But getting there did take some time. We'd also say that a clear brief for participants can be crucial. Some of these older people didn't take any photos because they didn't quite know what we wanted. We'd bought into the idea that this method cedes 'power' to participants who can then more easily 'show us their worlds'. But understandably people often want to know what bits of their worlds we want to see and why – Does a cup of tea really count? Is that really what we wanted? It's a bit like how 'depth means digging' as we discussed in Chapter 5. Being drawn into their social worlds by looking at photographs together takes time. And there may be plenty of dead ends too.

Some More Tricks for Making the Most of It

When we present photo-elicitation to our students, they're often enthused. They find the idea of asking others to take and share photos of their lives seductive. It's one of the most popular ways of working with photographs in social research (see Holm, 2020; Harper, 2002) because it promises an appealing mix of immediacy and authenticity that seems to trump other methods. Even with the spread of smartphones, however, getting people to produce useful photos in social research can be challenging. It can be hard to know how they'll respond to instructions. When they try out photo-elicitation, our students often give their respondents – in most cases their friends and family – little guidance on what to photograph, or they don't give them very much detail on why they are being asked to take photographs in the first place. As with others who use this method, their thinking is often to give people an 'open brief' so that they can really see and learn about 'where they're coming from'. That's admirable. But the result is sometimes that they either don't get any photographs, or the photographs they get are difficult to use.

Working with our students on this topic, and drawing on our own experiences, here are some tips for eliciting useful respondent photographs:

- Provide a short description of what your research project is about
- Explain how the photographs will be used
- Think about what might motivate them to do it (see Chapter 6)
- Give clear instructions of how and when you want the photographs to be taken
- Be clear about how staged and posed you want the photographs to be
- Talk through what you want them to do as well as providing written instructions (lots of us ignore or simply don't read written instructions)

TELLING STORIES AND MAKING ARGUMENTS WITH PHOTOGRAPHS

The ultimate aim of any social research project is to produce some kind of final output for an audience (see Chapter 2). If we're using photography in our research, should we also be putting it in our final research reports – whether that is a term report, a dissertation, a PhD thesis, a journal article, a book? It depends. Thinking back to our discussion about photography as fieldnotes and documentation at the start of the chapter, much of the photographic material produced in this way is really intended only for our own use. We're collecting photographs as 'aide-mémoires' – snapshots that remind us about the site we're studying. We're also using them to help us identify and develop our research questions (Chapter 7). These photographs don't necessarily meet the standards of composition or lighting that make for an informative image for more public consumption; nor do they have to: the photographs taken just need to be useful for us. But, if we're planning to use them in our final research outputs somewhere, then we'll also need to be attentive to how we take photographs that effectively address these readers. So, let's turn finally to how photographs can draw our audiences into the social worlds of those we've studied.

Photographs have a long history of being used as evidence in social research (Becker, 1974; Harper, 2023). Often, they're simply there to provide contextual information; a few photographs are included to show the reader what the places being studied look like. This gives the reader an immediate sense of the case. But more can be done with photos:

- They can be used to animate and explicate the accompanying narrative
- They can be used as evidence to substantiate and ground an overall argument
- They can be used as an affective demonstration of how things are
- They can be used as an opportunity to bear witness and encourage audiences to care

Let's look at each of these in turn.

Animate and Explicate the Narrative

In social research reports, photographs are most often used to provide documentary context. Used in this way, researchers can often just draw on their rough photographic fieldnotes to find 'good enough' images. But we can also do more than this. For example, writing up his study on the emerging urban public cultures of Auckland for a journal article, Alan wanted to give readers a detailed sense of the aesthetics that he saw around him there. This was important to the analytic narrative he was developing. Alan wanted to give his readers a feel for the hospitality spaces along the main commercial strip. His pictures hopefully gave the reader a concrete sense of things, whilst being economical with space (see Figure 9.8).

Figure 9.8 Picturing some restaurants and cafés in Auckland
Source: Latham, 2003a: 1,710

Evidencing an Argument

Photos can also be used to help substantiate an argument. A nice example of using them to do this is provided by Jack Layton's research into city parks and how they are sometimes used for summer music festivals (Layton, 2022). To do this, these parks need to be fenced, so the entrance and exit of festival goers can be controlled. This usually involves the construction of temporary fencing around the section where the festival will take place. His argument, and concern as a researcher, was to tell a more subtle story than one about local populations being disrupted. His study, focused on a particular park in North London, demonstrated that there were good and bad things happening in terms of how park life changed during festivals. He used photos to document the use of the park space over the course of a year. But some of his photos depicting the detail of how the park came alive, in interesting ways, during some of these festivals helped him to make that argument (see Figure 9.9).

Affective Demonstration

The previous two examples are built on straightforward documentation. Some social researchers, however, also draw inspiration from the visual arts in their use of photography. We might think of this as convincing with charisma, as an affective demonstration of a point. For example, one year a group of our undergraduate field class students in Copenhagen decided to focus their project on the theme of waste. They kept all the packaging they accumulated over one day out and about on the field class. Then they assembled, and photographically documented, their shared collection of waste items – smoothie cups, coke cans, cigarette boxes, apple cores, chocolate wrappers, store receipts, and so on – as if it was a museum exhibit. By treating their waste objects so seriously, the students' photo-documentation made a serious point about the amount of waste that is produced each day without us really thinking about it – taking a photo after emptying out their bags was a neat way to do that.

Bearing Witness

Finally, some researchers see their photography as a means of drawing themselves into a closer relationship with, and deeper understanding of, those they are studying. As part of that, some of them work with people to decide how best to present their lives and experiences to the wider world as part of this ongoing conversation. Les Back, for example, sought to bear witness to the rich life of ordinary Londoners in his portraits of East London life (Back, 2004). He and his collaborators worked closely with local people to produce a portrait they

Figure 9.9 Picturing Finsbury Park and its festivals
Source: Jack Layton, 2022

felt properly represented them. Similarly, in his study on the material culture of neighbourhood change in Chicago and Amsterdam, Charles Suchar (1988, 1993) worked with another set of local people to create the photographic portraits and narratives about this change he presents in his articles. Suchar started his research by observing and documenting these neighbourhoods with his camera. This then led him, after building relationships with some of them, to take carefully

Figure 9.10 Documenting a day of waste
Source: Waste group Malmo / Copenhagen students

composed portraits of families and couples in their renovated homes, with these portraits giving a wonderfully detailed and sympathetic view into their worlds. Caroline Knowles and Douglas Harper (2009) do something similar in the study of Hong Kong migrants we discussed in Chapter 6. They combined photography with taking part. Spending time with various migrants involved not just deepening their conversations with them but also building the trust that led to the most

Figure 9.11 One domestic worker in Hong Kong
Source: Knowles and Harper, 2009: 161

compelling photos (in the sense that we could, for example, see them being relaxed and at home in their usual surroundings). Their photographs encouraged wider audiences to appreciate the lives of these workers in their own terms.

There are many ways of using photographs to address your audiences in social research. More ambitious researchers have produced photo-essays where photographs largely replace written accounts, and others have presented their images in galleries and as public art works (see Harper, 2023; Knowles and Sweetman, 2004). The possibilities here are almost limitless, but of course what you should best do with your photographs depends on your warrants – working backwards from what you hope to achieve will help you to know what kinds of images you want.

WHAT PICTURES SHOULD I TAKE? SOME WORDS ON ETHICS

We haven't said much yet about what you should and shouldn't photograph. This is a gnarly question and there's no simple answer. Many people take photos of who and what they see when they are out and about without worrying very much about permission. And there's a long tradition of street photography that treats public and quasi-public spaces as fair game for a photographic study. However, others would say that social researchers should be held to higher ethical standards than simply following the law (in the UK, at least, this is currently allowed). When we're working with our students, rather than present them with rules, we tell them to use their judgement, be respectful of others, and if in doubt ask those involved. Essentially, we're asking them to work in the way we outlined in Chapter 6 – to start by imaginatively putting themselves in the shoes of those they may be studying and to go from there.

What does this mean in practice? In Berlin, we once took students on a walk around an inner-city neighbourhood where a weekly farmers' market was happening. Students took photographs of the stalls and the produce. In the middle, a woman, accompanied by a mandolin player, was singing. Some students gathered around and started taking photos. We suppose this was partly in response to how we had briefed them to record everything. They did this without asking, and without putting money in the mandolin case at her feet. The woman began to get uncomfortable. She was busking, and the students hadn't realised that taking photographs without giving a contribution was bad street manners. The point is you should always use your discretion and common sense. And if you're taking photographs of people directly, you should ask their permission. That could turn out to be quite productive. Indeed, rather than being shy about photographing others, you might use the taking of a photograph as an opportunity to engage in conversation with them (as our students eventually did with the busking woman in Berlin).

CONCLUSION

In this chapter we've examined some of the ways in which photography can be used in social research. We've looked at how taking photographs can be a form of initial notetaking. These photographs can provide an enormous amount of detail about the material texture of a research setting, and they do so with remarkable economy, helping us to think harder, and in sometimes novel ways, about all that detail. Photographs can also be used to organise and focus our interactions with those we're researching. Photo-elicitation presents all sorts of interesting opportunities for shaping our conversations with those we're studying. When we ask people to take photos of their worlds, we gain a new appreciation of their lives, and the spread of smartphones has made this method much more straightforward for many. Finally, photographs from our projects can enliven our research reports in ways that go beyond words. Photographs can animate these accounts by showing the physicality of places and the lives of people in a range of interesting ways that are all worth considering. As with all social research, working with photography is a craft to be honed though, and it's important not to fall into the trap of believing that photos are somehow more real or authentic than other forms of evidence. Still, given that images are everywhere these days, it's surprising how little use most social researchers make of photography. There's much to be gained by being open to its potential.

10
CHOOSING: HOW THINKING ABOUT CASES AND SAMPLES CAN MAKE FOR INNOVATIVE PROJECTS

ON THE POTENTIAL POLITICS OF HAIR

1. 95 percent of women think climate change is a problem, compared to 80 percent of men.
2. Migration to the UK is viewed most negatively by those in the North of England.
3. Gentrification is particularly valued by those who work in the service sector.
4. People with brown hair are the least likely to vote for right-wing political parties.

We sometimes present the above series of statements to the long-suffering students on our master's course about research methods. Enjoying the drama of the moment, and in a similar way to the student poll discussed in Chapter 7, we reveal them slowly, one-by-one. The first three don't appear to trigger any especially strong reactions. Perhaps we hear an intrigued 'huh, really?' if a student feels they have learnt something new. Occasionally there's a sigh of recognition if the statement seems to square with their experience. Most often there's not much reaction at all. These students are pretty smart, and our feeling is they've immediately started to work silently through why these statements might be true, and how societies might respond.

They needn't have bothered. We'd made these statements up. The point, for us, is more that they feel like plausible claims – we are used to seeing statements like the first three in newspapers, in a documentary, online. When our fourth statement goes up, the mood changes. There's sometimes a titter of laughter – 'That surely isn't true, is it!?' More to the point, why would someone bother to examine this connection? We eventually put them out of their misery and tell them they're all inventions. We say we've presented them to highlight how social researchers often work with taken-for-granted ideas about what is an 'acceptable' way of dividing up society or, turning to the aims of this chapter, an acceptable way of 'sampling'. Researchers seldom collect evidence from those with different hair colours when investigating political beliefs – although some shampoo researchers might be quite keen to compare their experiences. In pretty much the same way, there are certain ideas that we, often unthinkingly, draw upon when deciding who or what to study.

This chapter brings them to the fore. How should we go about choosing the right selection of people, or places, or institutions, or practices when we are studying social life? There's a tendency in some social research to 'black box' the process by which researchers go about deciding how and where they'll focus their studies; we are presented with the results of this decision rather than the thinking that informed it. For some researchers, as we'll discuss, choosing happens 'on the hoof' as they think on their feet in response to the opportunities and challenges associated with spending time in particular research sites. For others, there are some quite fixed ways of thinking about how these selections should be made. Either way, considering the ways in which we might approach this task puts us in a better position to do original and effective work.

We'll start with some useful 'rules of thumb' so you can do studies that are acceptable to those you hope to address. Then we'll work through some of the sampling arguments linked to particular methods. This can help if other researchers who do things differently criticise your decisions. After that, we'll consider how we might usefully play around with some commonplace ways of choosing. We'll begin with a trick for coming up with unusual samples and exciting projects before going through some other useful ways of thinking creatively about the challenge of who or what to look at in your studies. We won't be saying more about the potential politics of hair. But we will be questioning conventions in a similar way to that classroom exercise.

THIS IS A CASE OF WHAT?

Almost all social research projects are trying to extract wider lessons of some sort from the researchers' experiences with the people or places they're investigating. Let's start with that. We don't always think explicitly about this or about the trade-offs that we inevitably make between different ways of doing this. But we do have audiences in mind and ambitions about how the results of our studies will travel after they're done. Who, then, will we tell about our projects and what might we want them to do as a result? You might think that you're not bothered about this kind of self-reflection. You might well be saying to yourself right now that you want to just do a study, pass your degree, and move on with your life. But part of the discipline of doing social research is to think about how to convince your intended audience. Thinking about that is also a good starting point when thinking about how to choose who or what to sample.

When you read articles by social researchers, we can often guess at where they want their results to go right from the start. Say they begin by saying political engagement seems to be waning amongst young people and that's a problem. This set-up is already telling us that the study with 18-year-olds in London they're about to introduce should be understood as representing both young people and those who might be politically disengaged. Another way would be to start with place. Perhaps we know that particular regions are characterised by political disengagement too. If we read something along those lines in the beginning of an academic paper – why is it that those in the North of England are less inclined to vote? – chances are that the researcher will soon be telling us about how they went somewhere within that region that, we're encouraged to assume, will likely tell us something about how that local disengagement came about. A third way is to start with an idea being debated by academics and policymakers at the time. Where would be a good place to go to examine the processes highlighted by that idea? If we're interested in a particular kind of social interaction say, who would know about that – where would be a good place to see it in action? A fourth might be to start with a social problem. It's nice to note how many social researchers want to use their studies to give us all ideas about how to tackle societal challenges. OK, great, if that's the case, where might those challenges be especially evident? What are the activities that are adding to climate change? Where is poverty most acutely felt? How exactly are particular groups excluded from certain careers or occupations?

To summarise, then, social research studies are often a case of studying:

- A group
- A place
- A theory
- A problem

And there are more options. Indeed, part of the point of this chapter is to notice and understand how social researchers select the cases they study. But another aim is to spot some of the habits of defining them with which we could productively tinker. Either way, starting by deciding on what you essentially want to talk about in your project can give you a good starting idea about where to go or what to collect. What might your study be 'representing', and what do you want it to represent? Once you've got some ideas about that, you can start to think about how you'd pick individuals, interactions, or places that might be deemed in some way 'representative'. As Becker (1998: 67–8) notes, as social researchers we're always selecting a part which will in some way stand in for a whole. The challenge is to pick a part that does so convincingly.

In social research there's generally a wider point (which takes us back to the warrants discussed in Chapter 2). So, is this an opportunity to test out a theory? Are we studying a group we need to know about in some respect or another? Do they live in a place that we might be worried about for some reason? Being clear and explicit about this process with ourselves can help us to move to the next step. It can also help us to think about audiences, which as we've said from the start is a crucial thing in doing projects that deliver. Who are the people, organisations, or groups who are going to be interested in a particular place, a particular theory, a particular group?

HOW MUCH IS ENOUGH? START BY SEEING WHAT OTHERS ARE UP TO

On that matter of audiences and how we'd speak most productively to them, here's another example to get you thinking. It comes from a paper we wrote about how those working in our home discipline of human geography tend to study social life. We found that, perhaps unsurprisingly, a great many of them were quite keen interviewers. Interviews, as discussed in Chapter 5, occupy a 'sweet spot' in social research – not too fixed and not too open ended – you can control the encounter whilst still having the chance to learn about how they see things. In order to get a sense of how our colleagues did that, we took our own sample – 100 papers from the most recent editions of some of the top human geography journals. For the interviewers, we noted how many interviews were done and what the authors said about how they did them.

Figure 10.1 is a graph of what we found. We present this graph to those taking our master's methods course. In doing so, we've found that their reactions can sometimes depend on the subjects they'd studied before:

For those from a more scientific background – say those who'd done some psychology or environmental science – the idea that some papers don't bother to tell the reader how many interviews had been done was often a problem. Some of them were almost outraged – how is the reader supposed to judge the robustness of the evidence base unless they know this very basic information about the work that has gone into reaching the paper's conclusions!? Others, however, most often those with a background in humanities, are more unfazed by this. For them, we don't always really need to know all these boring details – they tell us they'll

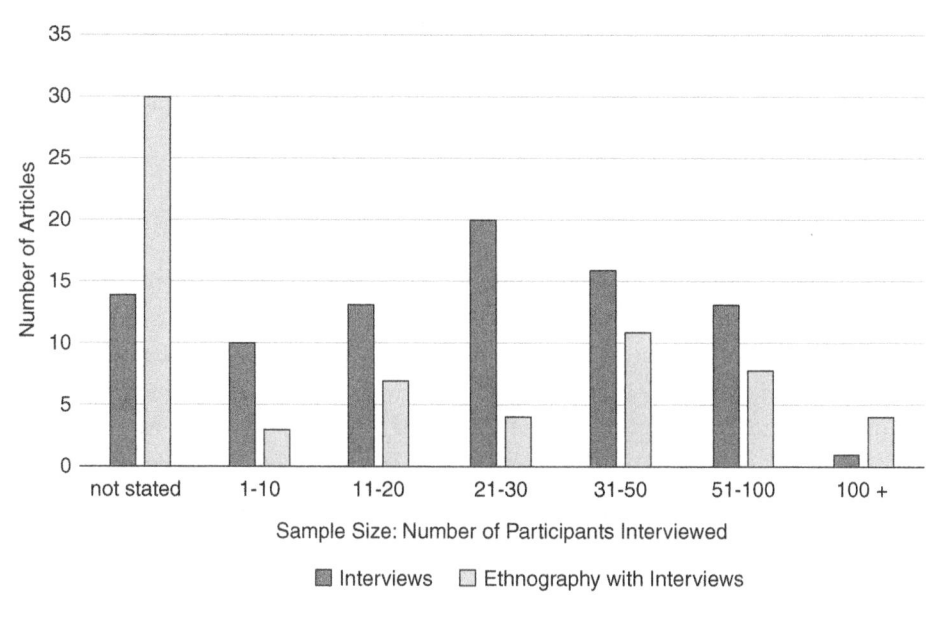

Figure 10.1 Interview samples in human geography
Source: Hitchings and Latham, 2020a: 391

judge the quality of the work by how convincing the argument is instead, and that is just fine! They'll read the paper and see if the author is presenting quotes that really get to the heart of the issue and that persuade them that they are sensitive researchers who have got people to open up.

We tell them we're also interested in 'the spread' of sample sizes – how there's quite a bit of variation in how many people are interviewed. The graph seems to be saying that we don't have a strong convention or expectation for how many people you'd need to talk with before those in geography are happy to publish what you think about what they said to you. For projects that only involved interviews (you'll see that we also included those who did some 'ethnographic' work too – observation and taking part in various ways), they tended to cluster around something like 20 interviews. Having said that, some did over 100 whilst, for others, we've no idea how many people they spoke with. This is also perhaps unsurprising when, as the diversity in our class demonstrates, human geography can be a bit of a melting pot of ideas and approaches – including about how many interviewees is 'enough'.

The implication of both these observations in terms of how you'd do your own projects is perhaps frustrating if you want more concrete advice (sorry – but we'll give you some ideas about that, don't worry!). If you want to know how much time you should spend in a place, how many people you should speak with, or even how many documents or websites to look at in a study, the first thing to do is to see what those you hope to influence seem to find acceptable. So, would they, like the science students, be concerned about the numbers or, like the humanities researchers, look to other ways of becoming convinced? And, if you're hoping to publish in human geography, you've different options for how you justify your sample.

Of course, there's more to it than this. But as a starting point, if you wanted to think in terms of 'the numbers' (as our students understandably often do), see what your audiences would find acceptable. All other things being equal, you'd feel fairly confident that, at least when we wrote the above paper, the reviewers of human geography papers (those who decide whether articles are based on solid evidence and deserve to be published) won't wrinkle their noses if we asked them to consider a paper based on 30 interviews. Things could easily change in the future of course. We might start to demand bigger samples because we want to be sure that the authors have done plenty of work before bothering us with their results. Equally, work pressures might mean reviewers increasingly roll over, recognising that there's not the same time to do so many interviews anymore. And it might very be different for those working in other disciplines. It's also quite possibly the case that those in government might want to know we've spoken to more people before they are happy to listen to – and potentially act on – what we've learnt.

Beyond that, it's nice to think that your audiences are made up of fairly reasonable people who understand the challenges of doing a project. So, if it will likely take six months to get hold of, speak with, and then think hard about what, say, 20 people say about a topic, and you've only got six months to do your project, then 20 it is! In our university, we tell our students something like that when they are getting ready to do their dissertations. Equally, if you wanted to do a really focused study and there are only 10 people who have the characteristics you want to examine – say you'd decided that you wanted to look at those who had set up a particular kind of business (and one of them is in no mood to help you) – then it looks like you are doing a project with nine people and the readers of your report should, you'd like to think, be alright about that.

Here are some other common arguments about how to decide when we've done enough:

1   When we've enough 'data' to feel confident about speaking on behalf of the group or place or set of documents that we want to represent. And, as we've discussed, one way of getting that confidence comes from seeing what those in our respective fields think is enough. Also, what do we imagine those we might hope to influence would need to accept us as spokespeople? Some thought about what exactly we're focused on can help here too.
2   When we've reached 'saturation' – people in your sample seem to be saying the same things over and over or we're seeing the same thing again and again and not learning anymore.

(to be honest, we don't entirely believe in this idea – there could always be someone just around the corner with something new to say, or the next document could always be the one that presents things a bit differently – but the idea that we should stop when we've reached 'exhaustion' or when the time we've got to do the data collection for our project has run out sounds about right. Having said that, if you've done all that's possible, as with the business leader example, then hopefully you're fairly full of thoughts by the end as there's no one left!)

The truth of the matter is that most people stop when they feel they've done a reasonable amount of work (Mason, 2010). But it's good to think through these issues. When we speak to our students when they're getting ready for doing a project, it's common for them to ask the dreaded question: how much must I do? Staller (2021) also found that (see also Baker and Edwards, 2012, on interviews). We like to think this comes from a place of eagerness – they want to do a really good job. But they could also be keen to know what will get them the grade they want. We're aware they have other things going on in their lives; though we can't see how any of that could be more fun than social research! Either way, the advice we give to them is to look at what others who've done well in the task they've given themselves have done – writing a paper for a particular journal, getting a good grade in the student project they are doing. You might face particular challenges that mean things will turn out a bit different for you; all projects throw up their own individual obstacles and challenges, but that's a decent starting point. For Becker, there's 'no magical number' to get you 'out of danger' (2012: 15). Still, giving some thought to what certain audiences would find acceptable is a good way to begin.

DIFFERENT METHODS, DIFFERENT ARGUMENTS

In a similar way to the above discussion about the benefits of working backwards from where you want your results to travel, there are also ways of thinking about choosing that fit with different methods. In other words, there are different visions of how 'choosing' should work for you that naturally follow on from what different methods are trying to do. Knowing which arguments go with which methods can at least help you to defend yourself when challenged by someone used to a very different way of thinking about how we should do our choosing. There's no superior school of thought here. It's more that different ones emphasise different aspects. We've talked about a number of methods already: observing what goes on; asking people questions in a survey; identifying, and then reading through, collections of words; speaking to people about their lives and views. Here are some of the ways in which they tend to do that:

Argument 1. I've Got to Wait and See

Yes, well, I may have only been to one place, but it takes time to do what I do. Anyway, back off, I can't entirely know what exactly I'm studying in advance – I will wait and see what is most interesting and collect lots of evidence about that, all being well.

Our first character is what people often call an 'ethnographer' – someone who sets out to learn from their chosen social context by spending time within it with an open mind. Like the observers of Chapter 3 or those who took part in Chapter 4, these guys allow their 'samples' to develop. They'd say we'd be mad to specify in advance how exactly the topic we hope to explore will feature in local social life. And so, to some extent, they'd say that we've got to wait and see. If they had to make a call, instead of thinking about numbers of people as we did above, this group would rather think about amounts of time. So, if you like the idea of doing a study of this type, you'd be as likely to talk about how many times you took part in an activity or how long you've been living somewhere. If you were after some numbers, this would be about how many months you've lived there or the number of times you did a particular activity with people. This is all based on the idea that you're seeing plenty of things that help you understand that context when you are there (not wasting your time by not thinking much at all about your study). We'll talk more about the value of being more specific about what you're looking at shortly, but, for now, that's how they might present things at the start. They'll go and then follow their nose.

Argument 2. I'll Tell You the Story and See What You Think

OK, so I can't speak to everyone. I get that. So, I'll often justify a focus on a specific group/issue, and I'll talk about how I got some of them to speak with me and how that went. Then you'll believe me when I try to represent that group or issue, I hope.

This is what we think a social researcher who uses in-depth interviews would often say. They'd tell you the story of how they did their study, how they ended up with a particular set of people, and how they interacted with those they spoke with. This is partly because whether we believe them, when they make claims about how that group sees things, rests on them convincing us that they've done a good job of getting to know that group and of thinking really hard about how they are responding to being asked to speak about certain topics. They'll also show us through their quotes and accounts of what people said that they've really understood the group (those numbers are not worth much if you didn't get the depth that we talked about in Chapter 5). They'll also often tell us about whether those they spoke with are 'typical' of the wider group, though they'll expect us to embrace the fact that their work takes time so they can't talk to everyone. The chances are, they'll suggest, no one will have spoken with this specific selection of people about this topic before, so, whilst their conclusions are probably provisional, this is a decent start.

Argument 3. I'll Make a Call Based on What's Available

I'm interested in the ways particular organisations or groups represent certain things. [Or *I'm interested in the different ways different groups or institutions represent the same thing.*] *So, I'm pragmatic (partly since I must go with what I can access).*

How might you handle the choosing issue when looking at the representations that are out there in the world already? We've already seen in Chapter 8 that you can do this in lots of ways. But what unites them is a sense of pragmatism. You do what's sensible in response to the material you're examining in your study. We must deal with what's already out there, after all – from social media posts to newspaper articles. What you'll need to be sure about though is that you've got relevant stuff to get your teeth into – that you've devised a way of usefully using the time allocated to doing your study to good effect. If you've 12 policy documents that you hope to scrutinise to know how particular governments are thinking about immigration, say, you'll need to be sure that there are lots of interesting phrases and ways of talking about immigrants within them. If you realise they don't actually say all that much about it, you might then have to think on your feet by extending your sample or looking at how they talk about more than one topic.

Argument 4. Oh My God – This Is So Important!

This is really important for me. People are so damn different! I've got to get this right! Thankfully there are accepted procedures ... and the more people (and the tighter the focus), the more reassured I'll be.

Those who do surveys have well defined rules for deciding how many, and who, they want to participate in their surveys. They have statistically robust formulas that tell them the number of completed questionnaires you'll need if you want to be confident that the patterns found in your sample of people in your city, say, would also be found if you asked everyone there. These guys are also keenly aware of the differences between people; partly because their results allow them to see and explore them. They will also have strict rules about how to select who will be asked to complete a questionnaire, which is important to maintain the statistical representativeness of the sample. They'll be thinking very hard about the different types of people who should answer their surveys: how they might distribute them so they can try to speak on behalf of, say, all students, rather than just those who were happy to fill in a form at the end of lectures. If they distribute their survey to students in the morning, for example, might that mean that only the students who are awake and keen on their studies fill it in – so is this a study of keen students and not students more generally? And, partly because they don't engage with the people themselves, they need to think upfront about the circumstances that may encourage them to give certain answers.

Shorter Interactions, Bigger Numbers

If we had to summarise the above positions, we think this is essentially about a trade-off based on the amount of time you spend with people. Almost all social researchers take pride in the amount they engage with the people, places, and practices they're studying. They just do that in different ways. The survey researcher is in a position to demonstrate their commitment through bigger numbers partly because, if all goes well, they can generate their material relatively quickly. After spending a long time getting their survey design right, once they've sent it out, they could soon receive a lot of responses to help them explore their patterns. Meanwhile, the interviewer knows that it takes a long time to do and analyse their interviews, and they want to do them well, so they work hard to pick the right people. The ethnographer knows that a social context doesn't immediately reveal its secrets so better to stay in one place and then let the magic happen.

We know of a PhD who did her social research project with only seven people. Seven people for three-to-four years of work!? What on earth was she doing for all that time? Well actually quite a lot. She really wanted to get to know the people she was studying because she wanted to know how aspects of their ethnicity had featured in different stages of their lives. And so, to get that rapport and to build those relationships, she spent quite a bit of time with each of these seven. So, more isn't necessarily always better – better (in terms of getting the right material and working in line with the sampling argument that fits with your method) is better!

TURNING ANSWERS INTO SAMPLES

So far, we've given you a broad sense of how to think about choosing who or what to study – from all the people out there in the world, all the places you might go to, or things you might read. What to pick? We've tried to step away from some of the usual ways in which 'sampling' is discussed to give you a candid account of how these things actually work in practice – the insider scoop on how it happens (if you like), rather than a set of abstract rules against which you should judge yourself. That said, let's turn to some of the tricks that can help us to choose inventively.

You'll remember how we began the chapter with how we get drawn towards certain ideas about who to compare in a social research project – in a study of political persuasions, thinking about people with particular hair colours felt weird, whilst examining the effect of where they lived seemed all right. As discussed in Chapter 6, we usually ask our master's students to interview someone they know (often it ends up being a friend or relative) about the issues they've come to consider with us. It's a fun exercise – a nice chance to start putting some of the ideas into practice. A few weeks later, when we turn to sampling, we ask them who the 'population' the person they spoke with might be representative of. In this way, we're asking them to think about how their interviewee could become a 'case of something' in the way we talked about earlier on.

Though we ask them to be as inventive as possible, the truth of the matter is that some of the above conventions about what constitutes a 'proper' sample for a social research project are hard to shake off. Sometimes we even get confused expressions from them before they say things like: 'well she was a woman'; 'I guess they were part of a young professional group'; 'um, someone in their sixties maybe?'; or perhaps 'someone with a high level of education'. We call these the 'usual sampling suspects' in our class – age, gender, and education are often things that get explored in research, which is fair enough since they generally do make a difference.

But, so we tell them, there are other options too. And they could perhaps be even more interesting to explore precisely because we don't immediately think of them. Next, we ask our students to think back to their interviews and to consider the most interesting things that happened within them. Our idea is that, if we allow ourselves to linger over these instances, we might start to spot other sampling strategies that could be all the more inventive because we're not falling into the 'usual suspects' trap.

Here are three samples we've come up with:

People Who 'Don't Know Much' About Climate Change

As discussed in Chapter 6, plenty of our students speak to their parents: it's easier to recruit 'respondents' if you see them every day at home! One of the challenges they often talk about is how (since they'd decided to do a whole degree because they feel passionate about, say, environmental topics) it was often quite tempting for family members to defer to them. Mums and dads moan,

'Oh that's your sort of thing much more than mine, though I do see it on the news sometimes.' Initially, we might imagine this to be the kind of person we wouldn't want to study; surely, they'll not have all that much to say about climate change if they don't know much about it? But perhaps it might be exactly this sort of political 'dodge' that could be worth examining (see also Chapter 5). If we want to trigger a groundswell of interest in, and commitment to, tackling global warming, say, these could be exactly the people we'd want to understand. Could we therefore do a study of how those who say they 'don't know much about climate change' speak about that disengagement? Well, we think we definitely could and, partly because of this unusual sampling approach, it would be very original and valuable.

People Who 'Really Care' About the Mistreatment of Migrants

Another common choice is to interview someone from the same course (again – easy access!). One of their courses, as you know, is about migration. These pairs often end up embroiled in some passionate exchanges, and they can often enjoy getting to know each other in this way – bonding over how they came to care and supporting one another as they let rip about how badly some groups can be treated. When we talk about that in terms of their sampling, this, for some of them, seems like a problem at the start. How can we say we're learning about how those of a particular generation feel about a topic if we've only spoken to those who really care about it? Should we perhaps be recruiting some who don't care so much to deal with this 'bias'? We say that's not a problem if we just make that our focus. So, perhaps we should do a study that is explicitly about those who care about migration. How do they manage that commitment in practice? Is it gingerly revealed because they know that others might not share their politics and things could get nasty? Again, we can imagine some very productive interviews here. There's a neat study here on how political and ethical commitments are shared and potentially spread.

People Who 'Love Soap Operas' About City Life

Another of the topics that our students interview about is urban change. Some of these students can get quite agitated about issues like 'gentrification' – how particular neighbourhoods become fashionable in ways that mean the locals get pushed out when things then get too expensive for them. The trouble is that some of their friends and family haven't thought too much about that. More promisingly, however, some of those they spoke with had seen that the types of people featured in their favourite soap operas about an urban community had changed. More than that, they could reflect in some quite thoughtful ways about how different kinds of people were getting along in these TV show. Could that be a sample? Well, yes, we could do a very nice study of how people see social change in cities through the world of the soap opera. Focusing on those who watch a particular soap opera could make it, unlike those who dodged the idea of speaking about climate change, less threatening to discuss since sometimes the whole point of soap operas is to enjoy talking with other fans about the happenings within them.

Now we are not saying that we should all do these studies. It's more that we've sometimes witnessed a disconnect between what our students find most interesting and what makes for a 'proper' sample in their mind's eyes. As our three examples show, allowing yourself to build a sample around what is most interesting, instead of what instinctively feels appropriate, can be a good trick for coming up with original ideas for a social research study. And there are plenty of potential 'homogeneities' to pick from here (Robinson, 2014). Though there might be some 'recruitment' challenges ahead of us (how do we get hold of these sorts of people?) these are not insurmountable. And we can imagine people being intrigued by the unusual focus. Certainly, we can see ourselves being more interested by a researcher saying that they want to speak to us about our favourite TV show than our supposed 'opinions' (see Chapter 7) on urban politics.

BUT DO I WANT TO DO WHAT THEY'RE DOING? SPOTTING OPPORTUNITIES FOR UNUSUAL SAMPLES

Here's another way of starting to think differently about how to choose who to study. It starts off with a contradiction. Bear with us. We said earlier on that one of the best ways of deciding on how many people you should involve in your study partly depends on conventions and audiences – what others in your research community think is reasonable and the numbers that those we may hope to influence might feel that they need in order to listen to us. That's all true. But sometimes toeing the line can mean missed opportunities. We're thinking now not so much about the numbers but more about how particular sampling strategies have come to predominate when we turn to particular topics. This is rather like the discussion of 'images' that we presented in Chapter 7, but it can also have implications for our sampling.

Noticing how others have done their sampling, and then mulling over what those approaches miss, can represent another route towards exciting social research. Here are a couple of examples to demonstrate this point. Both of them relate to recreational running, a topic that, as you know, we've both been interested in for a while now. Both of them, to use a modern phrase, also sought to 'flip the script' in terms of how they chose who to study.

Example 1. Who Cares About Urban Air Pollution?

A master's student working with Russell, Antonia Hodgson, became, as part of her studies, keen on doing a project on air pollution in everyday urban life. Fair enough – that's a big issue in lots of places. As is often the way, the first thing she did was to do lots of reading about this topic. That told her plenty of interesting things about how some of the 'usual sampling suspects' felt about the issue. She noticed a lot of interest in those who lived in particular neighbourhoods. That makes sense when we know that pollution can be highly localised. In that context, it feels obvious that we might want to learn from those who live with quite a lot of it.

But then she took a step back. Do we all live like that these days? Though picking residents from particular areas gives you a focus, are city dwellers really spending most of their time in and around their homes? Is that the place where they most often encounter air pollution? A lot of us are a bit more controlling when it comes to how and when we are outdoors. We go outdoors for particular activities and the amount of time we are outside because we've just nipped to the local shops near where we live might not be all that much overall.

Who then, if we started to think about lifestyles instead of location, might be worth targeting? Well, so Antonia eventually figured, perhaps recreational runners could be a good choice. After all, they often spend significant amounts of time running outdoors and they're presumably more interested than most in their personal health too. She also found out, as she got into this idea, that breathing heavily, as you would when you're running, can further add to the health risk. No one had particularly looked at recreational runners in this way before but, given that this practice is becoming increasingly common in many cities, perhaps we should?

The next question was about whether we could refine the sample even further, so as to feel confident about representing the group and sure about speaking with those with plenty to say. By following the flowchart in Figure 10.2, Antonia came up with quite a neat study. Its originality was largely based on noticing how sampling was often done when others did social research on this topic and then flipping the sampling script (Hodgson and Hitchings, 2018).

So, what groups could be good to sample?
Studies of cultural groups have often focused on where people live

↓

What other groups might have things to say about urban pollution?
Runners should have an interesting perspective on exposure

↓

Who might have the most to say about that within the sample?
Runners of longstanding because they will have learnt to live with it

↓

Who might we focus on within that?
Runners who run in both the city and parks ast hey'll have thoughts about the differences

Figure 10.2 Choosing runners for a study about air pollution

Example 2. Who Cares About Shared Experience?

As we've said, in many places running is an increasingly popular practice these days – partly because it fits around our busy schedules when we can't expect the team-mates commonly required for sports to be free and also because we can get going as soon as we leave the house. The trouble here was that many previous studies with runners had, understandably enough, tended to recruit from running clubs. This is understandable when, as we'll discuss, it can sometimes make sense to work backwards from those you can get. And running clubs also offer rich pickings for social researchers who can just go along to one of their events and ask nicely if anyone is willing to talk with them. If you did it that way, you'd probably get even more volunteers because they wouldn't want to look comparatively unhelpful in front of their friends, we'd imagine.

But how does that all fit with the idea that running is becoming popular precisely because we don't need to wait for others to be available or go to meet them somewhere before we start? This didn't sit well with us. Indeed, we thought it was quite possible that the conclusions that others were drawing about how nice it is to become part of a collective 'running culture' didn't really apply so much anymore. We needed to try a different sampling approach.

The problem though with recruiting the kinds of recreational runner who were starting to predominate was that they might not necessarily see themselves as suitable for a study; they were just finding an efficient way to get some exercise. How then to recruit those who didn't sign up to the idea of 'being a runner' – those who we eventually called the 'non-runner runners of London'? They'd immediately shut us down: 'Oh you don't want to study me – I just go for runs sometimes.' That required a bit of work – as being inventive with your samples sometimes does! It involved some cajoling as we worked through our social networks to recruit some of this growing group. We also wanted to speak with those who'd been doing it for a while – based on the assumption that they might have more to say – and compare those who ran alone either on treadmills indoors or outside. This was because our bigger project wanted to compare, like Antonia, how different environments were experienced (Hitchings and Latham, 2017).

Both projects came up with interesting conclusions partly as a result of sampling differently. Because the first study focused on practices, rather than places, we learnt how, when you are involved in an activity, and you think that activity is doing you good, the idea of being at risk from air pollution can easily be pushed out of the picture. Because the second study focused on those who were not part of running groups, rather than those who were, we learnt about the joys of solitary running as much as the camaraderie that could come when you ran with others.

Either way, the point is that sometimes the whole originality of your study can come from going against the grain of how sampling has previously been done on your topic. So, another trick is to notice what groups others have focused on and to ask: what if I did things differently?

So, what groups could be good to sample?

Studies of cultural groups have often recruited from running clubs

↓

What other groups might have things to say about the experience?

Runners who usually run alone since this is where the growth is

↓

Who might have the most to say about that within the sample?

Runners of longstanding because they will have learnt to live with it

↓

Who might we focus on within that?

Runners who run either indoors or outside as they'll have thoughts on the differences

Figure 10.3 Choosing runners for a study about social trends

WE ONLY EVER STUDY FRIENDLY PEOPLE! ON MAKING THE MOST OF WHAT YOU CAN GET

Apart from things like censuses in which governments require that citizens provide information about their lives so they can make better policies, a great deal of the material collected by social researchers depends on goodwill as discussed in Chapter 6. In other words, an unspoken truth about social research is that many of our studies are effectively studies of friendly people. Say we were doing a study about anger – we'd have to think quite hard about catching people at the points when they've calmed down enough to consider it. Either way, thinking through who you can most easily get hold of and then working backwards from that is an option.

But What Kind of Student?

Here's an example. Every year we supervise dissertation students interested in everyday life in the UK. Many of them want to explore topics such as whether people are trying to live sustainably, how they deal with others in cities, what they do with their technology. So far, so interesting. The next question is who to approach. Despite some lofty ambitions, when we start working through who they might be able to access, it's not unusual for some student to lose their nerve or for other life pressures to get in the way. They eventually settle on the idea of studying other 'students' as a way of giving themselves a focus. They know plenty of them, after all, and chances are they'll be supportive and willing if approached by someone with a similar background.

Take one of our undergraduates who decided that she wanted to examine the relationship between social class and the likelihood of people making more sustainable food choices – effectively whether working-class people felt these concerns were the preserve of the middle classes or whether they thought about them in the supermarket too. Eventually, in the above way, she settled on studying working-class university students. Her next task was to work backwards from that. Why might students be particularly interesting here? Well, perhaps we might imagine university to be a turning point for people. It's at this life stage that many young people suddenly take charge of what they eat when previously their parents often sorted out their meals. Great! So, we're starting to develop a neat argument for a relatively focused study.

But could we go even further? We asked her which students she'd be most likely to recruit. She said that many of those working-class students she knew had managed to get into some of the top UK universities. Actually, she'd got to know some of them because of their similar backgrounds. Could that make her study even more focused and interesting? Well, yes! We know that, in the UK, the top universities are still comparatively full of those from more privileged backgrounds. That helps with the focus! So, now we've a study about how concerns about sustainability feature in the food practices of working-class students as they start to take charge of these matters. We've also now decided to further focus on those studying at universities where they're exposed to the potentially surprising food habits of some of their middle-class peers.

Sometimes this process happens as you go (see the above account of how the ethnographer sees sampling), but another trick in developing a nicely focused project can be to follow this sequence:

1 Who can you get?
2 Can you make it more focused?
3 What could that make them a case of?

Working backwards from who or what you feel you can get is something we suspect happens more often than many researchers let on. Still, turning what can be dismissively called a 'convenience' sample into something more strategic is a neat trick. Often, it's a sensible response to the situation at hand; you just need to think hard about what they're a case of!

WHAT'S WITH ALL THE PEOPLE?

Here's a last strategy for thinking in inventive ways about what your study's focus could potentially be. This one is a bit of a challenge for a book on social life, but that's exactly why it's a neat final trick to consider. You may have noticed that the 'usual sampling suspects' we've discussed above are focused on different categories of people. We've even reproduced that idea in our attempts at starting to be a bit more creative too – these have been people with interesting experiences or views ... but they're still people! That makes sense in a book about studying 'social life' because our focus here, by definition, should be about people, right?

Our last trick is about fighting the urge to see social life as essentially made up of people with a range of pre-existing attributes. Could the 'usual sampling suspects' actually be sidebars in the real drama of social life as individuals – regardless of their age, gender, or class – get swept up in particular processes? OK, so what could social life be essentially composed of, if not different groups of people? There are actually lots of options here when we stop ourselves from getting fixated on all these human 'populations' (see Mason, 2018), but here are a final three examples:

1. Interactions

It's weird how often social researchers end up separating people off from the wider worlds they inhabit. In Chapter 9 we saw how photography can sometimes help with that. This is especially when there are clearly rules that we, often unthinkingly, find ourselves reproducing in different contexts. Could they furnish us with some other samples? For those doing observation, we might, for example, go somewhere to see what kinds of rules are in evidence. Eric Laurier and Chris Philo (Laurier and Philo, 2006), for example, wanted to understand whether cafés were places of sociability these days – do people sit alone on their laptops there or do they go because they want to connect to others in some way? Well, that's something to examine and, for them, that meant video recording life in some Scottish cafés to examine interactions between erstwhile strangers. They were sampling for interactions. If you were doing some kind of observational work, this is a good thing to think about. Identify some interactions and then collect as many examples as possible – either in your notebooks or perhaps through video – to then compare. In this case, observing allowed Laurier and Philo to learn about the conditions in which people did or did not interact. If you have a baby with you, so the study revealed, they'll often draw you into a fuller encounter with others if you are sitting in a Scottish coffee shop. So can pets. By sampling for interactions, rather than people, we learn new things about how particular places or situations work.

Figure 10.4 Interacting with babies in buggies in cafés
Source: Laurier and Philo, 2006: 199

Figure 10.5 Queuing for showers at summer music festivals
Source: Russell Hitchings

2. Practices

Another way is to start with activities. This is an idea that Russell ran with in the festivals study we talked about in Chapter 7. This study was partly about how, regardless of how we'd ideally like to live in line with our values, we often get drawn into particular ways of dealing with the demands of everyday life. One of these is showering which in countries like the UK, as we discussed, is a growing drain on increasingly scarce water resources. So how to study that? In his project with young people at summer festivals the idea was to catch them at the point at which they were suddenly aware of how 'addicted' they had become to everyday (sometimes even more often) showering since their much-loved showers were suddenly absent. By focusing on those who did lots of showering, they explored how the practice of frequent showering had 'captured' people. In this study, social life was made up of practices that take hold of us.

3. Experiences

Our third example centres on moments in people's lives when new ways of living and thinking came about. In some respects, this is rather like the narrative interviewing of Chapter 5. People often remember moments and turning points in their lives and so that means they might have plenty to say about how it was to live through them. A good example comes from a PhD student Russell has been working with. Hao Wu is interested in queer life online in China. Rather like Antonia's

Figure 10.6 Turning to queer social media at particular points
Source: Russell Hitchings

project in which she benefitted from questioning how others had defined their focus in studies on a similar topic, he found there were lots of accounts of what social networking apps meant for gay life. But he was also interested in how things have changed, as much as how people currently deal with these apps. So, how to handle that? His focus turned to the moments when different aspects of queer life there moved on and offline. He is sampling for experiences (associated with the times when lives move on- or offline) rather than staging a general discussion of how relevant apps could be both annoying and exciting. And that, we think, promises some far more personal and relevant accounts.

So, it's worth thinking about what your focus is. This might seem obvious. But it can easily be overlooked and there are plenty of options to choose from. If we allow ourselves to think creatively about what we're sampling for in this way, we can reap rewards. Sometimes the focus will emerge over the course of your study but check-in with yourself as you go about what it is. Once you're clear, you can think about how to ensure you're seeing or hearing about or taking part in as much of it as possible – be it an interaction, a practice, an experience, or something else. Either way, a good idea, once you've decided on the topic you want to research, can be to (instead of turning to the 'usual sampling suspects') ask something like:

- What could be an interesting interaction related to that?
- What could be an interesting practice related to that?
- What could be an interesting experience related to that?

You might find yourself with an unusual and potentially very promising focus.

'IT'S NOT BEEN DONE BEFORE!' / 'SOMEONE'S ALREADY DONE IT!'

We're just about finished with choosing and sampling. But we couldn't end without saying something about the above two statements. The first we often find ourselves encouraging our students to remember. The second we often find ourselves having to tackle if they've started to panic. Both say something about how it's useful to see your study as part of a broader conversation between researchers, and indeed within society, about social life.

'It's Not Been Done Before' – A Statement to Remember When Sampling Worries Arrive

Sometimes our students get increasingly worried that they can't reasonably make statements that fit with some of the ambitions we started this chapter with. Say they've done only a small number of interviews with people they know – that's surely not enough to speak on behalf of how young people think about their topic?! Say they've worked in a bar because they want to get a feel for how different groups interact there. The project worked out fine, but they are increasingly anxious about how their bar might have a unique culture. Even the one next door seemed to have very different interactions going on within it – 'Oh my goodness, I'm going to fail!'

We say that is all true and something to be acknowledged. But it's not something to worry too greatly about. Why? Partly because, if you see your study as part of a gradual journey towards understanding how young people feel about a topic, or how people interact in bars, then you're still helping with that! You're part of the conversation. Avoid claiming that all young people think in a similar way or that all bars work in a particular way, and instead say that your study suggests that some of them do, but that broader claims require further testing. Others might want to see whether your findings hold true for the bars where they live or for a different set of young people. Your study is neither the last word on the topic nor a total failure. Yours is one sample or one case amongst many – a single step on a collective journey towards greater understanding.

'Someone's Already Done It' – An Opportunity more than a Catastrophe

The other statement is one that we need to manage, more than one we'd encourage you to turn to when you need to calm down. It's not uncommon in a project to discover mid-way that someone has done something similar to you. Sometimes you've missed it when you were doing your reading before. Sometimes someone else had had a similarly good idea just before you and their results had just been published. This can understandably freak a person out.

We say that is all true and something to be acknowledged. But it's not something to worry about too greatly. Why? Well, their study will always be slightly different to yours; they might have done it somewhere else, with a slightly different group of people; perhaps things have changed a bit since theirs was done. Indeed, the fact that they've done a similar study means you've clearly hit upon a valuable topic. Now you've got someone to compare findings with; you can see whether your results are similar to theirs and then reflect on that comparison. Together you are providing a fuller picture of the topic you've both been examining and that's no bad thing. Thinking in terms of a conversation helps again. Yours is one sample amongst many, a single step on a collective journey towards greater understanding.

Maybe repeat that last statement aloud whenever you need!

CONCLUSION

So, there you go. In this chapter we've tried to give you an honest account of how to go about choosing your case study or sample and a sense of how you can be inventive in doing that too. The decisions we make about what exactly we're going to study – who we are going to talk to, what kind of things we are going to ask them, what we are going to observe and so on – are crucial to social research, and we've tried to demystify the process a little. The act of choosing what to study isn't something that good social researchers intuitively know how to do. Again, it's a skill that's learnt and developed. We called the chapter 'choosing' partly because we know that the idea of formal 'sampling' can be off-putting. But essentially 'choosing' and 'sampling' are different ways of saying the same thing – we need a focus for our studies so what should it be? In our experience, thinking through the possibilities of what to choose is one of the most intellectually exciting aspects of social research, partly because it's often glossed over. Rather than a source of worry, thinking carefully about these issues will ensure you're doing good work that also appeals to your audiences. But, more than that, as we spent the latter half of this chapter discussing, if you allow yourself to linger over, and play around with, different ways of defining who or what you're studying, you can come up with some excitingly novel studies.

11
WRITING: HOW TO PRESENT THE MATERIAL WE'VE COLLECTED

WHAT'S OUR AUDIENCE?

We've been working with a former research student, Michael Nattrass, on how people currently share roads in the UK, and whether they might share them more amicably. As part of his work, Michael videoed people cycling in a smallish city in northwest England, before asking other local road users to evaluate clips depicting some of these cycling practices. Here's an extract from the introduction to a paper we wrote about what he found out (Latham et al., 2024):

> Studying infrastructures may seem like a daunting prospect for those interested in the lives of those who interact with them. The idea, after all, is often that infrastructures should fade into the background of everyday life as facilitative conditions that help societies to function. Meanwhile, whilst a recent focus on infrastructures in human geography has produced much innovative work, beyond general calls to approach infrastructures ethnographically there has been relatively little systematic reflection on how researchers should respond to such calls in practice. With that in mind, this paper aims to substantiate the claim that, whilst infrastructures may indeed be challenging to foreground in our studies, a carefully calibrated research design can provide original and insightful understandings of how they are collectively negotiated by those who live with them.

This is not the most exciting of paragraphs (sorry!). There are no grand reveals, and the style is kind of dry. If we were trying to engage non-academic readers, we might have lost them by the second sentence. Most people have some idea what an infrastructure is – it's a common enough word, after all. But, by that point, we're already starting to make assumptions about the reader's knowledge – that they know something about how social researchers think about infrastructure (as 'facilitative conditions that help societies to function'). Then, by the time we arrive at the third sentence, we're clearly addressing a specific set of researchers ('human geographers') in terms of how they tend to study infrastructures ('ethnographically'). Unless the reader (a) has an existing understanding of how these human geographers have been studying infrastructure and (b) is interested in thinking about how they might do so better, they are unlikely to get past the first three sentences. So, is this a bad piece of writing?

Social researchers are often mocked for writing badly. Some even argue that's a conscious strategy for getting ahead in the academic world! As a student or early career academic, some social researchers learn to write in ways that are purposely obtuse, partly because doing so signals that they've become legitimate members of their chosen scholarly 'in-group' (Billig, 2013) by showing they've 'learnt the language'. This was not what we were doing in our excerpt (at least it wasn't our aim!). But perhaps we could have started with something more compelling:

> On a chilly September morning, Arthur, a retired university professor, steers his bicycle up onto a sidewalk. Slowing up, he weaves between two pedestrians, then drops neatly down a curb into a three-way intersection making use of the traffic light walk phase to avoid the cars. Nothing in this cycling sequence is legal. But on being challenged to explain his route by an interviewer, Arthur has a justification for his choices immediately at hand. Using streets is both an everyday activity and source of, sometimes violent, dispute and disagreement between different travellers. And that is all about their interpretations of the right ways of sharing them. Shown a video of Arthur's cycling, Anna, a non-cycling school administrator in her early 40s, is horrified by his apparent disregard of the 'rules'– 'There's no [justification] for that kind of behaviour', she exclaims, 'he's just being selfish!' In this paper, we examine these different interpretations and consider the implications.

That's a more engaging start. There's more action – a guy riding his bicycle (maybe recklessly, maybe not), someone else judging what he's doing. It has more recognisable actors – the cyclist Arthur and the non-cycling Anna. And we're immediately drawn into the drama over the right and wrong ways of cyclists using street infrastructure (how are they going to resolve this?!). If you're a non-academic, you might be more likely to keep reading. On the other hand, if you're an expert on infrastructures, you might well be asking, 'Well what *exactly* is this paper about, and why should I, a busy researcher, be spending my time reading it?' For this kind of reader, the first introduction is actually (for all its flat matter-of-fact-ness) more compelling, a better hook to get them to read the rest. So, here we have two paragraphs both of which do the same thing – introduce a study on street sharing in Carlisle – but which do so in strikingly different ways. Rather than thinking about these paragraphs in terms of 'good' or 'bad' writing, it's more helpful to think about them in terms of how well they are tailored for specific audiences.

In this final chapter we'll explore how to present the results of our social research. Though there's a growing menu of options in terms of engaging the world about what we've found, we'll concentrate here on writing, and on some of the most common features of social research reports. Our essential point is that when we write about our research we're always doing so for an audience. For some of us, that audience might be frighteningly small – a couple of dissertation or thesis examiners. But it can be much larger too. For an academic article it might be a small group of people already very knowledgeable about the topic. A report might be read by both experts and engaged members of the public. If we wanted to produce a story for a newspaper, popular website, or magazine, the readership could be anyone who happens to stumble across it. In each of these cases, there are conventions and expectations about how your research findings should be presented. An academic audience often demands that you cut straight to the intellectual point. By contrast, a more popular piece might expect a 'folksy anecdote' to draw them in – what is known in publishing circles as 'a Malcolm' after the popular science writer Malcolm Gladwell, who's a master of crafting beguiling introductory hooks (Johnson, 2024). It's worth thinking about what different devices do (Becker, 2007).

This brings us directly back to the warrants that guide our research (Chapter 2). Remember that a warrant is the overall purpose that motivates our work – so that's about, firstly, what we hope to achieve and, secondly, what that means for what we'll practically do. Reflecting on our warrants helps us to focus on how to write too. With that in mind, this chapter is about taking all that material that we've collected in our research projects – our interview transcripts, observational notes, counts of how people responded in our surveys, and more – and turning them into an effective final report. We think that it makes sense to start with some of the devices we most commonly see in social research writing, since our students most often wonder about those. Firstly, we'll look at ways of using quotes. Secondly, we'll turn to sharing short depictions of moments from our research experiences and contexts, what are often called vignettes. Thirdly, we'll say something about the use of numbers in our final accounts and, fourthly, briefly think about what diagrams do for us. After that, we'll consider how the words that we use should fit with how we see ourselves, ways of working with references and theories because our students often worry about those, and end with some writing tips. This chapter isn't a step-by-step guide to producing a good dissertation or research article (there are plenty of those already). Neither does it offer very many fixed rules about how we should do our social research writing (sorry again!). This is because, as you'll have hopefully gathered by now, we think that the best start when deciding 'how to study social life' is to reflect on what different strategies are doing for us, which is surely a much more enticing prospect than just doing what you're told.

QUOTES

Many of the methods discussed in this book leave us with the words, either spoken or written, of those we've studied. There are our interview transcripts. There is the talk we've overheard or taken part in when doing activities with people or listening to how they were interacting already. There are the responses to our open-ended survey questions, which, let's face it, are very much like talk. There are the written views and accounts we may have found in documents and on websites and then closely examined. In Chapter 8, we gave you some ideas for exploring and analysing this material in a systematic way. But once we've done that, how should we present it to our readers? We cannot present it all. Many projects end up generating thousands upon thousands of words. Even the most patient of readers won't want to wade through all that. Our task is to shape this material into a document that conveys something essential and important about what the study has discovered. How should we use quotes to do that? Should we?

Quoting at Length

Many social researchers quote people at length. Going back to the interview with Janine, the Hong-Kong-based, Filipina domestic worker quoted in Chapter 6, Knowles and Harper (2009) give us extended quotes so that Janine can 'tell her own story' in her own words and without interpretative interruption. Let's re-join her account:

> 'People have different ways of housekeeping, and so on.... It's like when you are preparing food for Chinese you just have to, OK, bring all the plates, cutleries and the chopsticks and that's all.... And soup, you know first, but in Western family, no. You have to serve wine glasses first or cocktails and bring everything; after that the main course, the soup and there's a mat. So there is really a big difference. Yes. When it comes to household, really, Chinese is simpler, but you learn. They are going to teach you the way they want.' (p. 163)

This is compelling stuff. And it's tempting to think of engaging blocks of quotation like this as a kind of gold standard. These extended quotes have something of a 'sacred quality' (Bissell, 2023: 191). We feel like we're right there with the interviewee as they start to 'open up'. There's also a 'palpability' to it – we're getting an account that is rooted in the detail of Janine's life – she's certainly not brushing Knowles off with talk of generalities (Small and Calarco, 2022). Rapport certainly seems to have been established since they are talking together so candidly. These quotes also imply an authenticity (and with that a degree of unchallengeable-ness) about what is being said. These are real people speaking directly to the reader. This, of course, is the effect these researchers are after. And it explains why this quotation style is so popular. But, if we're trying to be careful, self-aware, social researchers, we should recognise that the 'authenticity' of the extended quote is carefully curated and crafted.

When researchers select and present an extended quote they have, out of necessity, left out (excluded, if you're feeling dramatic) many others. So, the selected quote is to some extent being used to stand in for the whole of the interview. The quote is also often standing in for the experience of the other interviewees who there isn't space to quote too. In doing so, we've hopefully avoided the 'cherry picking' we talked about in Chapter 8. Further the quote will itself have likely been cleaned up somewhat and spliced together. Unless we are just as interested in their reactions as what they've told us (see Chapter 5), it's rare to see a block of raw interview text from a transcript including all the fillers – words and phrases like 'uhmm', 'you know what I mean', or 'like' – or to see evidence of the interviewee losing their thread as they circle a theme trying to find the right words, or are just being plain repetitive (we all often are when we're talking to people). There's nothing untoward about this – we're used to this from interviews in magazines, newspapers, television, and podcasts, all of which usually edit their quotes in some way. And presenting the quote just as it appears in the transcript risks making those we're researching appear inarticulate or – worse – stupid, as well as marking it harder for the reader to follow.

Avoiding Quotation

Despite the appeal and allure of authenticity provided by the extended quote, a second approach to using interview and other word-based material is to avoid direct quotation. Instead, the researcher paraphrases what was said in surveys or interviews. Take, for example, Elizabeth Shove's (2003) use of interview material in her book on how increasingly resource hungry patterns of living have developed in many countries:

> When Jane was a baby, her mother bathed her in the kitchen sink. There are pictures to prove it. However, her first real memory is of sharing the tub with her older sister, Sally. This was recalled as a daily ordeal, one that continued until Sally graduated to the shower at the age of about eight or nine. Jane soon followed suit. The right to shower alone

signified freedom and independence: it was a rite of passage on route to adulthood. As a teenager, Jane had lots of long, thick hair and a set of expectations that obliged her to shower for thirty minutes during an hour-and-a-half ritual of 'getting ready'. Appearance was a central concern, and the nature of her unruly hair was such that it 'needed' shampoo, conditioner, detangler and more. (p. 109)

Here we learn a lot about Jane – and her relationship to showering, the topic that Shove is concerned with. But we learn about her through Shove's interpretation. This technique aims to convince readers not through claiming some kind of unmediated truth or showcasing authenticity (as with the extended quote). Rather the reader is convinced through a combination of the thoroughness and detail of the summary, and the description of multiple examples to build an overall argument or narrative. We also have the sense that Shove is cutting to the chase for us – she's winnowed down Jane's account so that the 'take-home' message is apparent, which is probably more appealing for those with less time to get to know individuals.

General, Not Individual

A third approach is to avoid referring to individual interviewees or respondents at all. If the focus is on a topic that explicitly extends beyond the person – like, in the next case, a social practice – then avoiding talking about individuals is helpful; it keeps the readers' attention on what is important for developing the point the researcher is making rather than putting the spotlight on how things are for specific individuals. Take this quote from Russell's (Hitchings, 2011) study of London office workers and their relationship to the outdoors (discussed in Chapter 8):

Still anecdotes abounded about opportunities occasionally taken to venture outside at lunchtime and pick something other than the on-site canteen. Interestingly this was often combined with errands as a way of going outside without losing senses of purposefulness that could be important to sustain if you wanted to keep going afterwards. On these occasions, there would be times when, because the weather outside had already faded into the cognitive background, it could be a shock when respondents were confronted by the potential social and physical discomfort of, for example, getting wet on leaving the foyer. (p. 848)

In this extract – and in the paper as a whole – he rarely names people. Instead, the reader learns about how his chosen social group – lawyers working inside central London office blocks – live with the outdoors as a collective. This way of presenting interview material might seem coldly analytical (it certainly doesn't draw you into the lives of the people involved in the way that Knowles and Harper do).

However, some audiences will be less interested in the experiential detail of personal life stories. They'd rather know specific things about specific phenomena. Russell wanted to convince other environmental researchers and policymakers of the validity of his paper's account of how air-conditioned offices combined with the demands of professional life to effectively trap people indoors. To do this, he figured he should stay focused on the collective experience, downplaying individual narratives because he felt he needed to draw broader conclusions about the social group for these audiences to be interested.

We've three different ways of presenting what people have said to us in social research here. And many research reports use a mixture of the above techniques. There are others too. Some of those interested in how people deal with the interview itself would also include the questions that we posed and also all of those 'ums' and 'ahs' pauses (because that tells us about how the individuals are handling each other). Whatever your approach, the key skill is about identifying when you should lean into different ones rather than becoming fixated on any one style of presenting people's talk. Another way is to note the conventions that characterise the field to which you want to contribute – what are their current 'quotation cultures' (Hitchings and Latham, 2020a) and do you want to tinker with them? In our experience, people often expect to see some quotes to 'bring things to life' and we often dutifully give them those. But how and whether we should always bring things to life in this way is another matter (see Eldh et al., 2020). Students often ask, how many quotes do I need? How long should they be? We tell them to think about their project aims and intended audiences. Having said that, we say it's usually useful to consider how individual accounts relate to the wider sample of people being studied (Small and Calarco, 2022), and to definitely resist the temptation to serve up the best quotes and hopefully position them as representative without having spent plenty of time before on analysis.

VIGNETTES

A second common presentational approach is to use 'vignettes', short accounts of experiences or observations. They do many of the same things as quotes such as 'bringing things to life' by teleporting the reader into the contexts being studied (Hitchings and Latham, 2020b). Done well, vignettes really capture our imagination. But they can also eat up precious words in our reports so we must, once again, be mindful of how they're working for us. We've talked about Alan's study on public life in Auckland (Chapter 9). Here's a vignette from a paper he wrote afterwards:

> Armadillo. Karangahape Road. A Thursday evening. Paul Rennie Brown is drunk again. Okay not really drunk. Happy. Voluble. Okay, a little more than happy and voluble. He's LOUD. Well actually – to be fair – everyone's

loud. Loud in a pleasant, raucous, Chardonnay-ed, Sauvignon Blanc-ed, kind of way. All eleven of them. A group of 40 plus somethings. All single, a string of sticky, confusing, messy, divorces behind them. Solo parents with no kids, as Paul likes to call them. They are having a dinner party for no other reason than that Paul thought that they might like each other. It might be fun. Come along. Enjoy yourself. Make connections. Paul likes these New Age-y management book phrases. It is part of his charisma, his attractiveness. It keeps things interesting. Conversation flows, although it isn't really about anything much. Nothing immediately Earth shattering. Linda, an uptight looking woman wearing a little too much make-up, looking just a little too pale, is telling anyone who will listen how she hates smoking.

> 'I used to go out with a guy who smoked in his car. After a while I refused to go in his car.'
> 'Well, I always take the cigar out of my mouth before I kiss a woman,' replies Karl in an effort towards reconciliation.
> 'Most of the people I associate with don't smoke. I would be in hospital if I smoked.'

Karl is German. Well, was German. Many years ago. Now he's a New Zealander, although he does occasionally get puzzled about why Kiwis get so worked up about such trivial things. Like smoking. Smoking in bars? That's what you do in bars. Anyway, there's other things to talk about. Like Linda's story about her grown son living in London. Rudd telling how his father was a miner in [the Netherlands]. Talk about business. Other evenings in similar restaurants. Lots of things. Tonight was a great night. (Latham, 2006: 101)

What is this vignette doing? Firstly, it's evoking a moment, an evening out in a restaurant. Secondly, it's introducing a category of people; the gregarious, apparently economically prosperous, middle-aged professionals who populated many inner-city Auckland restaurants back when Alan was researching them. This is the cast of individuals – Paul, Linda, Karl – involved in the study, and that piques our interest. Thirdly, it's describing a place, or rather a nested series of places, Armadillo (a restaurant), Karangahape Road (where the restaurant was found), inner-Auckland (the broader area that Alan hoped to speak about). Fourthly, it is starting to set up a research problem – the puzzle of why we should be interested in these people and places (understanding the variety of reasons why people come together in urban Auckland). But it's also a piece of writing that's having a bit of fun. The purpose of the paragraph is as much as anything to convey a sense of what it is to be out, with friends, a bit 'half-cut'.

Compare that to the following excerpt from a paper by our colleague, Tatiana Thieme (2021), on the 'hustle economy' (how people respond to immediate everyday challenges in order to get by) of young garbage collectors living in informal settlements in Nairobi, Kenya:

> [A]round 5 a.m., a ribbon of light appeared under the doors of ground-floor dwellings as some of the *mamas* started their morning chores, cleaning, going through the multiple steps involved in making morning tea (fire, boiling water, boiling milk, tea leaves, stirring constantly). It was still dark, but the night was over, giving way to the crescendo of the morning bustle. Tilted young bodies left flip-flop footprints in the dirt paths as their slight frames carried heavy jerry cans of water fetched from the local water points; uneven wooden tables were set up as working surfaces for the first hour of preparation involved in making *mandazis* (fried dough) and *chapatis* (flat bread) – mixing the flour, oil and water, working the dough, and separating out the small balls of dough before frying. Near the Kibichoi primary school, the water point and the corner where collected garbage was stacked until the truck arrived to take it away, Geoffrey's *mandazis* was well frequented. He had been making and selling *mandazis* for the past twenty-eight years, and his attention to his craft was coupled with efficiency and dexterity. Without precise measurement he managed to make each small ball of dough equal in size to all the others, forming uniform hand-cut triangular shapes that became differentiated only once they flared up in the hot oil before being carefully displayed in the wooden crate next to the working table. (pp. 35–6)

Tatiana is deliberately using the vocabulary ('the mamas') of those she is working with in our second vignette. This establishes her credibility in terms of being able to speak for the context at hand (she's using their language). In a similar way, that she can talk in terms of generalities further reinforces this idea (she's been there long enough to have a strong grasp of how exactly local life goes on). The detail helps with that too (wow – she's watched that guy make mandazis many times!). Beyond that, she's also drawing us into her experience there (she'd accompanied some of these garbage collectors and their shift was coming to an end) and she's also hinting at her analytical focus (how this kind of work was carefully choreographed as they all played their part to make the community work through their interlocking 'hustles').

Just like quotes, vignettes do different things for us (drawing us in, setting up research problems, establishing our authority). And you'll need to know what your aims are in order to use them most effectively. In terms of how social researchers have discussed vignettes, they say more about how we can use them to encourage those we may be studying to talk with us. But some of their observations there apply just as well to how we should think about the imagined audiences for our research reports. When using them to engage participants, people worry about how vignettes might mean that we 'lose' people (Hughes and Huby, 2004) – in other words, whilst contextual detail can capture the imagination, there comes a point when people will disengage, saying 'OK – good for them … but that's nothing really to do with me.' Alan is skirting this kind of disengagement in telling us about Karl's attempted jokes; Tatiana is too with her interest in hot oil. On the other hand, those details give us the 'palpability' that convinces us that the researcher has properly made the effort to put themselves 'in the shoes' of those being studied that some see as the hallmark of good work using these methods (Small and Calarco, 2022).

Whilst it can feel churlish to dispute the veracity of an engaging vignette when the writer has gone to all the trouble of producing one, some audiences will still question whether they need to know so much about one particular instance, place, or situation. And we should think about what your vignette is doing – explicating a process, establishing authority, whetting the appetite. That has implications for what we leave in or out. Vignettes eat up precious words so use those words wisely. We should also remember that our job is probably to do more than just appeal to our audiences on an emotional level when we're hopefully presenting the results of deep reflection of some sort. Our colleague Jennie Middleton (2024) has discussed how we can be tempted by 'analytical leapfrogging' – presenting the engaging vignette as though it represents the findings even though the analysis is yet to happen. Vignettes are certainly an effective trick to draw audiences in by encouraging them to empathise. But we're not journalists, so our prime aim should be to use that as a hook into the presentation of our 'proper' results from a study that took some time (Silverman, 2015). There's good reason to pepper our social research reports with vignettes but that main event – the 'meat' of our paper to which we're adding the pepper, if you like – should still be the results of our analysis.

NUMBERS

Many social research publications bulge with numbers, tables, and graphs. Often these are the result of surveys that have put the same question to lots of people. We're not going to talk about all the statistical tests that you might do here – partly because we're not good at them – but we do think it's worth thinking briefly about what's happening when we trade in numbers when we present our results. Here's a table on what Mohamad-Hani Temsah and their colleagues found out about what healthcare workers in Saudi Arabia felt about whether AI might become part of their everyday professional lives (Temsah et al., 2023).

Seems straightforward enough. They've asked a bunch of people, and according to that bunch, these are the main challenges in making AI more popular in local healthcare (for those who'd like them to think about using it more). But we

Table 11.1 A table from a research article

Factor	Frequency	Percentage
Lack of credibility/Unknown source of information of data in the AI model	496	46.9
Worry of harmful or wrong medical decisions/recommendations	425	40.2
Not available in my setting	403	38.1
AI chatbots are not yet well-developed	397	37.6
Medicolegal implications of using AI for patients' care	326	30.8
I do not know which AI model can be used in healthcare	311	29.4
Unfamiliarity with using AI chatbots	296	28.0
Worry about patients' confidentiality	273	25.8
Resistance to adopt AI chatbot in medical decisions	249	23.6
Worry of AI taking over human role in healthcare practice	218	20.6
Others (e.g. lack of personalized care and inability to adapt to prognostic factors)	43	4.1

Source: Temsah et al., 2023: 5

need to be careful with these numbers too. We can see how it might have made the process easier for those they spoke with to give them this selection of options to pick from. But there could have been other options. And we are positioning this as something they're in charge of too. The fact that a good number saw this as something that is out of their control rather undermines that idea. So, it could be easy to look at this table and claim that, if we want to get more healthcare workers to adopt AI in Saudia Arabia, we need to tackle the top row (so credibility is key), but that's assuming the people who answered the survey are decision makers (and that the survey covers all the options).

None of this is to criticise their study, which we've picked more or less at random – it's more that we need to recognise the work that's gone into such a table, along with the work that such a table does. A table is a kind of 'scientific transformation', conjuring up 'apparent truths' that feel like the outcome of rigorous work. But for Howard Becker (2007: 42), for all their pretence of telling us the bald 'facts of the matter' these devices bear the imprint of the researcher more than most because, in order to get the numbers, they've already defined how we should look at the issue. We can spot the selections that people make when they edit their vignettes – when we're making numbers the editing just comes earlier here. With all that said, for those who are adept at dealing with tables the results are quick to process. So, as long as you are sure that your conclusions don't reach beyond what the numbers are actually saying and you don't assume that 'number talk' of this kind necessarily equals authority (Lareau, 2021), they're a good option.

Sometimes that's easier said than done. Not infrequently we see students present the results of interview studies as percentages. They say, for example, that

15 percent of those they studied felt that, say, climate change is terribly worrying. We invariably ask something like, 'So you mean three of the 20 people you spoke with?' The percentage doesn't fit when they can't be absolutely sure that their interviewees shared an opinion based on discussions that were allowed to wander, rather than pin people down. And there's nothing wrong with 'owning' the small sample in such a study when talk takes time. So, don't be shy to speak in terms of small numbers. A colleague of ours calls the tendency we're talking about 'the worst of both worlds', because students aren't showing they appreciate the strengths of interviews and they're wrongly assuming that talking in terms of percentages makes them seem scientific. Use numbers when it helps you to convey your findings but don't force them into the discussion because you think that sounds better.

DIAGRAMS

Next up: diagrams, namely visual devices that stand in for, and describe, something within the world. Diagrams are used extensively in everyday life – think about the instruction manual you might get with a new electronic device, or the assembly instructions that come with a piece of furniture. But they aren't perhaps used as much by social researchers as they might be (Becker, 2007). This is surprising as diagrams offer some real advantages for researchers.

Take, for example, Tim Schwanen's (2007) use of a diagram (see Figure 11.1). He's describing the material configurations of family life by showing us the cycling practices of working families in the Netherlands. Drawing on interviews and a survey with parents about their different 'chauffeuring' activities, he uses two simple axes, time (on the Y axis) and place (on the X axis), which is also a proxy for distance. The diagram describes a morning in the life of a working

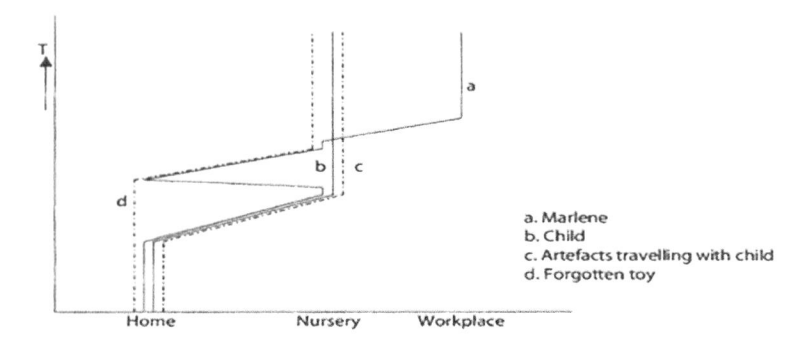

Figure 11.1 A diagram about a working family
Source: Schwanen, 2007: 18

mother (Marlene) with a pre-school child who attends day-care. The diagram takes a little effort to read (in that respect it is no different to the tables we discussed above), as the reader has to work out how the diagram works. But it also provides distinct advantages.

Firstly, and most obviously, the diagram is a technique of abstraction. It distils out from the flux of life a representation of relations between key elements of that life (that Marlene's workplace, home, and childcare are in different places; that the distance between them needs to be negotiated by her and her child; that physical things such as toys and notebooks travel with them). Secondly, and relatedly, diagrams work as valuable techniques of analytical simplification. There's a lot of detail left out of Schwanen's diagram: it doesn't tell us about the effort of getting a pre-schooler out of the house; it doesn't tell us what Marlene is doing whilst at work; it doesn't say what the father is doing; and so on. But this simplification isn't an omission or oversight – Schwanen has learnt about these things from his interviews too. Rather the simplification provides a close-up of the things that matter for Schwanen's analysis: that attention to material objects is important; that it takes effort to co-ordinate over time and space; that relationships between people shape their mobility patterns. Thirdly, diagrams offer many possibilities for comparison, be that across societies, organisations, people, or groups (Becker, 2007). In Schwanen's case, the comparison is between categories of people – parents, men and women, cycle commuters and automobile commuters. In this diagram, we are being alerted to how complicated family co-ordination can be and how, in this case rather charmingly, Marlene will rush back home if a much-loved toy is forgotten when she drops her child off at a Dutch nursery. Moving objects (as well as other people) around matters.

So, diagrams are a useful device for summarising and describing our results in ways that reach beyond text. They can also be useful in situations when we're not asking people to sit down and read all about our findings because they offer compressed simplifications that travel more easily. We can put them up in our presentations and, if we find ourselves lost for words, the diagram is waiting to help us work through what we've found out. We've noted that our student researchers can be nervous about making diagrams. And we know they've fallen a bit out of fashion. Some find them heartless – 'You want me to translate all the challenges and issues people face into a shape?!' Making diagrams can also seem a bit grand, suggesting that we, the experts, can boil all that research material down into a figure with arrows and annotations. Still, we think that diagrams can often be worth a try. They offer the inventive social researcher some really distinctive ways of presenting and arguing with the material they've gathered (Becker, 2007; Latham, 2020). It's worth taking the time to at least consider whether there may be a diagram hidden in all the material you've collected that you could potentially coax out.

HOW TO THINK ABOUT THESE DIFFERENT DEVICES

Though your options for presenting your material are often already prescribed by the methods with which you've engaged people in your project, there's still scope for thinking about the work that different devices do. When should you tap into the particular power of each? The above selection isn't exhaustive – what about charts, what about statistical tests? Our point was more to get you thinking about their comparative strengths – what they do for both you and your reader. Arguably, you might want to work backwards and choose your method based on the results that might be most well received by the audience you've selected. In that respect, sorry for leaving this to the last chapter since perhaps it should have come at the start (though see Chapter 2)! In any case, here's a set of questions to help you decide on your devices:

- What do others in my field do?
- Who are my audiences?
- What will they be interested in?
- How much time do they have?
- What do I want them to think of me?
- What do I want them to feel?
- How will my devices establish my authority?

THE IMAGES WE LIVE AND WRITE BY

On that matter, let's think a bit more about how our presentational strategies align with our purposes. In Chapter 6, we considered how social researchers frame their relationships with those they're studying and what that means for how their encounters with people unfold. These framings also carry through into how social research is written up. The key, once again, is to be self-aware about the images we have of ourselves and of the nature of our work. As one way of exploring this, we sometimes stage a short classroom discussion about the words that our master's students might use to describe their research and, more specifically, the people they've studied (or learnt from, or worked with – these phrases matter!) as part of that. So, what should we be calling them? Here's a list of possible options that we've brainstormed:

Pseudonyms
Real names
'Respondents'
'Interviewees'
'Interlocutors'

Which one to go for? You'll likely have a sense of our answer by now – it depends! OK, but on what? Well, would you say that, in your work, you were acting like a scientist who aimed at being appropriately neutral so that people's perspectives could more easily come forward without any influence from you? Were you joining a particular set of people in bringing their perspectives forward to the wider world – a sort of ally or advocate? People often say to use pseudonyms when writing and we generally do that ourselves. That way we can talk about individuals and remind the reader that these were 'real people' whilst also reassuring those we've spoken with that others won't be able to recognise them afterwards. So, there's quite a lot to consider here. Then, we put our first list alongside another (this time of possible ways of seeing ourselves):

Storyteller
Neutral listener
Scientific researcher
Scholar-activist
Empathetic friend

Then we ask them to match them up (we haven't done that for you here – where would be the fun in that?). Your choice is about how you see yourself again. There are trade-offs between each of these options, of course – you can't be so neutral and scientific if you're prioritising your role as an advocate. If we are talking about groups of people you've got to know over some time, it would feel odd to call them respondents when that would also undermine the alternative authority that comes from all the time you've spent with them. It's like the perennial question that some students nervously ask – should I write in the first person? In doing so, they're getting themselves worked up about losing the air of being appropriately scientific once again (which somehow feels wrong to those who've done 'science' projects before). In social research, that's one amongst many ways of writing about your relationship with the people you've studied. Our response is they should pick the right ones for them and then be consistent.

THEORIES ARE JUST SIMPLIFICATIONS

So far, we've been talking a lot about your audiences and how they'll likely respond to the material you show them. That brings us nicely to our next topic: how you condense things down more generally. All of your audiences will be expecting that. And, as we see it, we've got a responsibility to come up with some sort of abstraction in our work; even if it is to say things are more complicated than we thought. We've gone to all the effort of doing a study, after all, so we'll want to tell people about the most important things we've found. It's part of our job as social researchers to spend a good deal of time lingering over what people are doing in particular places, what they're saying to us, or how they speak about different topics, and then eventually reduce it all down into some sort of 'take-home' message for some audience or another. So, we've got to do some simplification. We've talked about 'analysis' in Chapter 8 when we considered how we might identify 'themes' to make this more manageable. But what to do after that point – do we just give an outline of what we found through those means?

One way of giving yourself some 'analytical bite' is to draw on particular 'theories' to help you think about all the material you've collected. Theories in social research are generally understood as ways of looking at the world that some academics rather like, and others are less sure about. They are simplifications too, but they are also recognised topics for debate. And that's, we'll admit, where we sometimes get a bit jittery. When we tun to 'theory' the academic jargon that comes along with it can end up shutting down the potential for you to speak to others. 'What theory are you using?' is a common question that some of our students – at all levels – worry about having to answer. Theories in some of the scenarios that concern them can be like badges of honour. They show belonging. You'd feel confused and lonely if you didn't have at least one, and that's partly what they're worried about. For some social researchers, developing and elaborating on theory is the most important thing for them to do. And we can see the appeal of starting out with assumptions and ideas about what to look for ('theories' are effectively that). Theories give you a focus, a guiding sense of what you're studying when you design your studies. This focus can be attractive when, as we've discussed in earlier chapters, a lot of (potentially bewildering) material can come out of some of these methods. But, as our favourite author reminds us (Becker, 1998: 4), that can take you towards a particular set of audiences:

> I have a deep suspicion of abstract sociological theorizing; I regard it
> as at best a necessary evil, something we need in order to get our work
> done but, at the same time, a tool that is likely to get out of hand, leading
> to a generalized discourse largely divorced from the day-to-day digging
> into social life that constitutes sociological science.

Becker is effectively saying that too much theory means we'll end up speaking to other academics because they're the ones interested in it. Over and above whether you 'need' a theory (we'd also argue for exploring topics that should just be looked at with an open mind about where that takes you) what we'd say about 'theory' is that how much you write about it in your final research report should depend on your warrant. If your audience is concerned with the practicalities of the topic or case you're researching – maybe policymakers or engaged members of the public – then dwelling on the theoretical framing of the research won't be very productive. If your primary warrant is to contribute to public understanding and debate on a topic then you should stick with what you found out. Dwelling on the theorical nuances and niceties will just get in the way. If, by contrast, you're writing a research report for an academic audience – be that an article, an undergraduate dissertation, or a PhD thesis – then theory is often looked for.

So, be aware of the trade-offs. Russell vividly remembers a time when he went to speak to some local government officials about how they might respond to his findings in that office worker study of his. He began with some relatively excited talk about the theories he'd decided to use in his project. He couldn't help himself. He'd spent a lot of time thinking about them. And doing that was often well-received in university corridors and academic conferences. But now their faces were blank. Of course, they were. Why did they care? Their jobs were about managing city greenspaces not debating social theories. Suddenly all the academic terms he'd been working so hard to master disappeared as crutches to help make his study seem impressive. He was left stranded with the challenge of giving a straightforward account of what people said in his study.

Students often wonder about how best to handle the idea of working with theory in their work. Whilst there are many ways of doing so, here are some pointers about 'theories' for you to consider so that it doesn't – as Becker worries – get 'out of hand':

1 *They're an option.* You don't necessarily need to badge your social research project as about testing out or applying theoretical ideas that you've come across. They can help to give you a focus, but you don't have to put them front and centre in your study.
2 *Don't be scared of them.* When academics sometimes judge each other on how good they are at abstract debate, theories can start to seem quite scary. See them for what they really are: they're just simplifications. If you're worried, think about them in terms of 'working assumptions', 'problem definitions', 'pictures of social life'.
3 *Know when they matter.* That's where Russell came a cropper in the above scenario. Theories can matter a lot for academic audiences who are keen on seeing how well you can evaluate different ways of looking at your topic. Others might not care one bit (or be at most tangentially interested in how we tend to think about, or define, a problem) because they really want to know what we've found out in our studies.
4 *Don't have too many.* You might expect this view in a book focused on learning from the methods but, if you want to be guided by theories, don't have too many. If you do, you'll never be able to do them all justice in terms of testing each of them out whilst also learning from the results of the various interesting techniques we've discussed.

HOW MANY REFERENCES?

Whilst we're talking about how, and when, to engage with other writing in our work, let's briefly say something about references. Research projects don't happen in isolation. They're generally designed to be in conversation with previous research and with a range of academic and public debates. No matter how unique we feel our project is we're always building on work that's gone before (and see Chapter 10 on why thinking in that way is a generally good thing). So, how much should you discuss the work of others in your final report? And how should you do that? We haven't said much on this so far in the book, partly because we're all about getting out and finding things out for ourselves, and partly because there are plenty of books already on writing (called 'literature reviews'). But we know that effective reports should make links to what others have done. Or, put another way, social research writing usually needs references.

Now references can be challenging. You don't see them in newspapers, magazines, novels, or popular non-fiction. That being the case, it's not surprising that new social researchers can be unsure about how to use them. Often, rather than thinking about *how* references should be used, we find our students asking us *how many* references they should use in their dissertations, research reports, and so on. If we need to situate our research in the context of what others have done, referencing other authors allows us to do that precisely and economically. References also help us gain authority with readers – we've done the reading for people to trust us on the topic. But effective social researchers are self-aware about how they use references. More referencing is not (necessarily) better. You'll end up looking stupid if you cite irrelevant publications. Or if you positively cite poorly designed studies. Or if you cite too far back when talking about recent developments. Also, we don't want the references to crowd out our accounts of what we've found.

So, in response to the 'How many references do I need?' question, we say that a better question is 'Where should I put them?' Sometimes it can be tempting to repeatedly cite others throughout. We think this is because our students are used to writing essays in which they're encouraged to cite liberally. It can also be hard not to tell the reader about a link between your findings and the arguments of others when you spot it ('Look, I've found one!'). But you've hopefully proved that you've read lots of relevant studies earlier on so that box has already been ticked. In answer to our reframed question (neat swerve on our part), we say reference plenty at the start and return to these ideas at the end. Don't worry so much in the middle. That's where we're learning from how you've done interesting things with some of the methods discussed in this book. At that point you don't want to take yourself away from your quotes, your numbers, your diagrams, and your pictures by returning all the time to the readings we already know you've done.

HOW TO IMPROVE THE WRITING

Before we finish our writing chapter, we should address the elephant in the room. We've said nothing yet about how you go about actually writing your research report. People often talk about writing as something you're either good at or not. And some people certainly do seem to be better writers than others. The question is, how did they get to be better? The novelist Ernest Hemingway said 'all writing is rewriting' (Germano, 2021). So, even the most talented writers need to work at it. But how should you go about that rewriting? Let's return to our paragraph from the start of the chapter. The version we shared is the final version. But getting there took a while! It had gone through at least eight drafts before we ended up with that. Below is an earlier version. We deleted the struck-out words, and the underlined ones are those we added:

> Studying infrastructures may seem like a daunting prospect for ~~those~~ <u>researchers</u> interested in the lives of those who <u>routinely</u> interact with them. The idea, after all, is often that infrastructures should fade into the background as facilitative conditions that help societies to function. Meanwhile, ~~a great deal of innovative work in human geography~~ whilst <u>a great deal of a recent human geography interest in</u> ~~the infrastructural~~ infrastructures has produced <u>much</u> innovative work, beyond <u>general</u> calls to approach infrastructures ethnographically there has been relatively little ~~systematic reflection on~~ <u>discussion of</u> how <u>exactly</u> researchers should respond to such calls in practice <u>so far</u>.

We've made twelve changes – reorganising sentences, changing some phrasing, cutting superfluous words. We did this by reading each sentence out loud together before thinking about next steps. We'd usually meet in a coffee shop (sorry to the customers sitting nearby). Then one of us would do the reading. He'd stop at the end of each sentence, and we'd discuss whether it made sense and whether it could be clearer and more engaging. We probably looked a bit strange. But it was a nice thing to do as we tried to make our writing as convincing as possible. This might not sound very scientific. And in all honesty it isn't. Good writing is just as much about having the patience to stick to the task of making your manuscript better. Whittling away at your writing in the hope that it's slowly improving can be hard, but it's worth it.

Here are three final writing tips from us:

1. *Write a first draft of a section of writing in one go.* One of the tricks of becoming a good writer – and also ironically enough an efficient one – is not to be too attached to what you've written. If you recognise that anything you write is going to be edited, rewritten, and redrafted, that makes the first draft a low stakes affair. When you're ready, sit down and write a first draft

of a section of writing. Don't go back and edit, just write it. You might want to do that long-hand in a notebook too. Sounds a bit old-fashioned, but this stops you from being tempted to stop and edit, and helps you to keep the flow between points. Then type it up and *voilà* you've your second draft.

2 *Once you've a decent typed draft, print it out* (all the sections that might result from following tip one). Then lay it out page by page on the floor. You might need to find a decent sized room to do this. In any long piece of writing, which the result of a study of social life often is, it's hard to keep track of how the different sections fit together – if they're the right length, if they follow from one section to the next, if something is missing, and so on. Physically laying the pages out allows you to get an overview of where your draft is at.

3 *Some time towards the end of the process, get a 'fresh pair of eyes' on it.* If you're working to a tight deadline this can be a challenge. But often when we're writing we get tangled-up. We know what we want to say. But we can't find the right way to say it. Or we lose sight of our intended audiences and how they'll likely respond. When you're 'too close' to your writing, you can't see things anymore (typos, argumentation problems, terms you need to explain). The fresh 'eyes' can be other people's; it's a good idea to get someone you know well enough to tell you when things don't make sense, or they can't follow things. Or it could be more about refreshing your own eyes, forcing yourself to take a break because you'll spot the issues more quickly when you return. Another trick is to read things in a different way. Read your writing out loud when you feel you've a nearly final draft. Worked for us in the coffee shop!

CONCLUSION

And that's it! Working through all the material you've gathered and turning it into an engaging report is a challenging stage in social research. But it can also be the most rewarding. You sit down and you slowly transform your ingredients – excerpts from field notebooks, interview transcripts, coding reports, photographs, annotated documents – into an effective account of what you've found and how others might respond to that. There's a kind of magic to this. But you can still work at creating the magic. Our starting point is to think about what you want your studies to do and how chosen audiences will likely respond. To give you one final classroom exercise example, we ask our master's students to send us a 'perfect paragraph' of good social research writing. What's often interesting about this is how, when we discuss some of them together, it can be hard to articulate exactly why it's good. They know quality when they see. But, to ensure we've got that quality too, we need to work through the means by which we get there.

CODA: THE PEOPLE WHO INSPIRED US AND IDEAS FOR FURTHER READING

There's a huge literature on social research methods, and frankly it can be a little overwhelming. Because of that we've avoided using too many references in this book. Instead of burying you in readings, we'd rather you'd try some of the exercises we've presented. Social research is a craft honed through practice, after all. Still, some might be keen to know a bit more about the activities we've discussed in each chapter. You might also be curious about the inspirations for the accounts we've presented within them. To help those readers out, this short coda gives you an annotated list of some the books and articles we've either drawn on extensively in particular chapters or see as key starting points for digging into the literature on the topics they cover. As with everything in this book, we're not aiming to be comprehensive. But this is enough to get you started. At the end, we've also provided a short list of some methodologically oriented journals for those who really want to get their teeth into what others are saying about their experiences with particular techniques. As we see it, it's sometimes better to start by trying a method out before looking for others who've experienced comparable challenges (why should the reading always come first?). We think these journals could be especially good for that.

Chapter 1. Introduction: What Is the Point of this Book and How to Use It

The inspiration for this book is Howard Becker. An accomplished sociologist, in the second half of his long career he wrote a series of 'how to' books for social researchers. The biggest inspirations for us were *Tricks of the trade: How to think about your research while you're doing it* (1998, Chicago University Press) and *Telling about society* (2007, Chicago University Press). In those, rather than focus on idealised models of how social research should be carried out, Becker begins with the concrete strategies and techniques that social researchers like him actually use – from coming up with worthwhile research questions, to what questions to ask in interviews, to finding useful case studies. We have tried to emulate Becker's approach by also working through concrete examples to show how social researchers go about their work, by thinking really hard about what particular activities are doing for us, and by questioning conventions. We've also tried to popularise his approach a little through a focus on specific problems we've encountered ourselves, as well as the issues that seem to worry our students. David Silverman's *A very short, fairly interesting and reasonably cheap book about qualitative research* (2013, SAGE) also helped us to feel confident about writing about methods in the way we have in this book.

Chapter 2. Warrants: Starting with What You Want Your Study to Achieve

The inspiration for our use of the term 'warrant' was Jack Katz's 'Ethnography's warrants' (1997, *Sociological Methods & Research*, 25(4), 391–423). Katz only focuses on ethnographic research. He's puzzling out the idea of how ethnographers – social researchers focusing on the texture and meaning of everyday life worlds – justify what they are doing to others. Katz expanded the range of warrants in a following article, 'Ethnography's expanding warrants' (2012, *Annals of the American Academy of Political and Social Science, 642*(1), 258–75). Becker's *Telling about society* was central to our thinking about audiences and methods and how we sought to link warrants and audiences. In each chapter, Becker examines a different way of engaging audiences in social research, and how different audiences might respond. Becker is also very good at encouraging us to look beyond social research conventions for ways of representing how societies work.

Chapter 3. Observing: On Learning to Learn from Different Social Scenes

Observation often gets bundled together with participant observation. The two books that we found most helpful for thinking about observation were James Spradley's *Participant Observation* (1980, Holt, Rinehart and Winston) and Robert Emmerson, Rachel Fretz, and Linda Shaw's *Writing ethnographic fieldnotes*, 2nd edition (2011, Chicago University Press). *Participant observation* provides excellent tips on how to orient and organise field observations. As a budding social researcher, Russell used some of the tables to organise his initial observational work during his PhD. When many social researchers can be weirdly secretive about their notetaking, *Writing ethnographic fieldnotes* does a fantastic job of demystifying the process, describing in straightforward language how you might develop and improve your notetaking skills; it also includes advice on working up notes into more polished accounts. Christina Nippert-Eng's *Watching closely: A guide to ethnographic observation* (2015, Oxford University Press) provides an excellent, practical, and to-the-point introduction to observational research, unusually focusing solely on observation. Quite a few of our examples are about public spaces. Jan Gehl and Brigitte Svarre's *How to study public life* (2013, Island press) is an accessible, generously illustrated guide. It also has some great examples of creative approaches to presenting the results. Finally, we edited a special section called 'Inside the notebook' (2024) for the journal *Area*. That offers a series of practical reflections on taking fieldnotes, with each contributor starting with an image from their notebooks, so you can immediately see the variety of forms these notes might take.

Chapter 4. Taking Part: Considering the Benefits of Getting Involved Ourselves

There are a bunch of very good introductions to doing participant observation and ethnographic research – the broad method headings under which taking part usually gets absorbed. Kathleen Musante and Billie Dewalt's *Participant observation: A guide for fieldworkers,* 2nd edition (2010, New York: Rowman Altamira) is a thorough and accessible introductory guide written from the perspective of cultural anthropology. Another classic text is Martyn Hammersley and Paul Atkinson's *Ethnography: Principles in practice*, 4th edition (2019, Routledge) which offers a more sociological and education studies take. Mike Crang and Ian Cook's *Doing ethnographies* (2007, SAGE), written by two fellow human geographers, is also excellent (see in particular Chapter 4 'Participant observation'). And of course, Spradley's already mentioned *Participant observation* is full of great tips for taking part (or participating as he'd have it). For a more concise introduction to the practicalities of taking part, Chapter 6 'Learning to do participant observation' in Annette Lareau's *Listening to people: A practical guide to interviewing, participant observation, data analysis and writing it all up* (2021, University of Chicago Press) is fantastic, to the point, and full of useful concrete advice. Similarly, Chapter 5 'Hanging out' in John Levi Martin's *Thinking through methods: A social science primer* (2017, University of Chicago Press) is another engaging, no-nonsense guide to taking part. To find examples of researchers taking part to find out about social worlds, we'd also recommend having a look through the journals *Ethnography*, *Journal of Contemporary Ethnography*, and *Journal of Autoethnography*.

Chapter 5. Staging Talk: How to Do and Imagine Interviews

Interviews are used by many social researchers and there's a huge literature on working with them. A comprehensive and accessible overview is provided by Svend Kvale and Steinar Brinkmann in *Interviews: Learning the craft of qualitative research interviewing*, 3rd edition (2014, SAGE). Herbert Rubin and Irene Rubin's *Qualitative interviewing: The art of hearing data*, 3rd edition (2012, SAGE) is another excellent, detailed guide to in-depth interviewing. For those who think of themselves as working in a more ethnographic register, Martyn Hammersley and Paul Atkinson's *Ethnography: Principles in practice* and Mike Crang and Ian Cook's *Doing ethnographies* both address interviewing. Spradley's companion to his *Participant observation*, *The ethnographic interview* (1979, Waveland Press), is focused on interviews and excellent. To start thinking in more detail about how talk works as a contextual social interaction, Elizabeth Stokoe's *Talk: The science of conversation* (2018, Little, Brown) is an engaging introduction. For a more detailed collection of studies on everyday talk, have a look at Paul Drew and John Heritage's *Talk at work: Interaction in institutional settings* (1992, Cambridge University Press). For those who really want to dig into interviewing, Jaber Gubrium, James Holstein, Amir Marvasti, and Karyn McKinney's (eds) *The SAGE handbook of interview research: The complexity of the craft*, 2nd edition (2012, SAGE) covers the topic from pretty much every angle. Finally, for some concrete examples of how researchers stage their talk in a range of contexts, have a look at the articles collected in the 'Working with the spoken word' special section of the journal *Area* (2023, 55). We edited this with the aim of demystifying the process and sharing tips between researchers with different levels of experience.

Chapter 6. Engaging People: Seeing Social Research as a Relationship

The most helpful book for writing this chapter was Mario Luis Small and Jessica McCrory Calarco's *Qualitative literacy: A guide to evaluating ethnographic and interview research* (2022, University of California Press). Small and Calarco do a great job of explaining the process of developing self-awareness as a researcher (what others might call self-reflexivity), and why it is so central for doing good social research; Chapters 1 'Cognitive empathy', and 5 'Self-awareness' are particularly worth a look. We also found Annette Lareau's *Listening to people* really helpful here too. For those struggling with questions of positionality, her discussion of the advantages and disadvantages of being an insider or outsider is great (see pages 27–9 and 151–3). A really engaging – and influential – in-depth examination of how the relationship between interviewer and interviewee changes through an interview is developed by James Holstein and Jaber Gubrium in *The active interview* (1995, SAGE).

Chapter 7. Asking Questions: Exploring a Basic Act that Features in Many Methods

An excellent comprehensive overview of survey research can be found in Floyd Fowler Jr's *Survey research methods*, 5th edition (2013, SAGE). A slightly denser and more technical guide that's a good companion to Fowler is Robert Grove et al.'s *Survey methodology* (2004, Wiley). For those after a more concise introduction to surveys and questionnaire design, Jan Eichorn's *Survey sampling and design* (2015, SAGE) is excellent (and much less expensive!). Robert Weiss's *Learning from strangers: The art and method of qualitative interview studies* (1994, Free Press) is a wonderfully clear practical guide to asking questions in in-depth interviews. Chapter 4 'Learning to interview', in Annette Lareau's *Listening to people*, has some great advice on designing interview guides and other nitty-gritty strategies for asking questions. If you're interested in digging deeper into some of the gnarly interactional questions raised by the interview format, Elliott Mishler's *Research interviewing: Context and narrative* (1986, Harvard University Press) is well worth a read. Our reflection on images is based on the 'Images' chapter in Becker's *Tricks of the trade*.

Chapter 8. Playing with Words: Strategies for Identifying and Exploring Patterns

A great resource for thinking about coding and analysis is Matthew Miles and Michael Huberman's *Qualitative data analysis: An expanded sourcebook*, 4th edition (2019, SAGE). Much of the discussion in this chapter overlaps with the much broader term 'discourse analysis'. An excellent, comprehensive introduction and overview of this is provided in Barbara Johnstone and Jennifer Andrus's *Discourse analysis*, 4th edition (2024, Wiley). Grounded theory is popular with many social researchers and involves paying close attention to emergent patterns in a researcher's material as they go along. Juliet Corbin and Anselm Strauss's *Basics of qualitative research techniques and procedures for developing grounded theory*, 4th edition (2015, SAGE) is an accessible entry point into this approach. We've only scratched the surface in terms of coding strategies in this chapter (because we wanted to get across the basic idea). But there are many strategies to consider. Jonny Saldana's *The coding manual for qualitative researchers* (2021, SAGE) does a great job of going through those. For the practicalities of doing discourse analysis, we think Gordon Waitt's chapter 'Doing discourse analysis' in *Qualitative methods in human geography* (I. Hay (ed.), 2005, Oxford University Press) is a good practical introduction but, for those interested in all the possibilities (there are many), we'd recommend a dive into the journals *Discourse and Society* or *Discourse Studies*.

Chapter 9. Looking at Pictures: Ways of Getting Drawn into Social Worlds

A great place to start thinking about photographs is Douglas Harper's *Visual sociology*, 2nd edition (2023, Routledge). This provides a clear, comprehensive introduction to using photography when studying social worlds by a master in the field. In thinking through photography as a fieldnote technique we drew inspiration from Becker's *Telling about society*, especially Chapters 3 and 11. Alan (Latham, with Derek McCormack) explored the use of photographic 'audits' and 'lists' in the short article 'Thinking with images in non-representational cities: Vignettes from Berlin' (2009, *Area, 41*(3), 252–62). Gillian Rose's *Visual methodologies: An introduction to researching with visual materials*, 5th edition (2023, SAGE) offers a comprehensive overview of how social researchers work with images. Likewise, Sarah Pink's *Visual ethnography*, 4th edition (2021, SAGE) offers an ethnographic take on working with visual material – including using video. Caroline Knowles and Paul Sweetman's edited collection *Picturing the social landscape* (2004, Routledge) provides a nice variety of case studies on the different ways social researchers work with photography. To further explore them, have a look at the journals *Visual Studies* (which was co-founded by Doug Harper) and *Visual Anthropology* (which is bound to the discipline of anthropology but still worth reading even if you aren't an anthropologist).

Chapter 10. Choosing: How Thinking About Cases and Samples Can Make for Innovative Projects

The starting point for this chapter was Chapter 3, 'Sampling', in Becker's *Tricks of the trade*. This does a great job of setting out the fundamental representational problem that sits at the heart of all social research – which part of the social world do we choose to stand in for the whole? Not all social research is case study based, but an awful lot is. In thinking about cases, we've found the collection *What is a case? Exploring the foundations of social inquiry* (1992, Cambridge University Press) edited by Charles Raglin and Howard Becker really helpful. Becker developed some of his thinking on cases further in *What about Mozart? What about murder? Reasoning from cases* (2014, University of Chicago Press). This is a book that pulls off the unlikely feat of making methodological reasoning fun. Mario Luis Small's 'How many cases do I need? On science and the logic of case selection in field based research' (2009, *Ethnography 10*, 5–38) is an excellent reflection on sampling size and qualitative research, as is Mitch Duneier's 'How not to lie with ethnography' (2011, *Sociological Methodology*, 41(1), 1–11). For those really interested in sampling strategies, Charles Raglin's *The comparative method: Moving beyond qualitative and quantitative strategies* (1987/2014, University of California Press) and *Redesigning social inquiry: Fuzzy sets and beyond* (2009, University of Chicago Press) develop provocative ideas about how social researchers might go about their work. Finally, Jennifer Mason is refreshingly honest about all things methods and her chapter on sampling in *Qualitative researching*, 3rd edition (2017, SAGE) would be an excellent way of getting a bit more context to some of the ideas in this chapter.

Chapter 11. Writing: How to Present the Material We've Collected

As you know, Howard Becker's *Telling about society* is one of our favourite books; it provides an original take on how social researchers might present their empirical material to others, and it encourages us to be inventive and resourceful. It's a great resource when you come to writing-up too. Mario Luis Small and Jessica McCrory Calarco's *Qualitative literacy: A guide to evaluating ethnographic and interview research* is less expansive in scope but provides an excellent – and accessible – set of reflections on the qualities that make for a rigorous and persuasive piece of finished social research. Writing can be a challenge. In *Writing for social scientists* (1986, University of Chicago Press) Becker provides a no-nonsense guide to taking a piece of social research writing from an initial idea to a finished article, dissertation, or term paper. For those of you who have to write a dissertation there are dozens of 'how-to' guides out there. But if you're going to read something, Umberto Eco's *How to write a thesis* (1985, MIT Press) is hard to beat – it's beautifully written (Eco was a best-selling novelist as well as an academic) and full of sage advice like 'You must write the thesis you are able to write' and 'Citing a book from which you copied a sentence is paying a debt'. Revising is key to good writing. William Germano's *On revision* (2021, University of Chicago Press) is an engaging guide to revising and editing by a former editor at a major academic publishing house. Finally, Roy Peter Clark's *Writing tools: 55 essential strategies for every writer* (2008, Little, Brown Spark) is chock-full of good advice on how to get writing done; its tips are straightforward, and they work!

Finally, there are many super interesting journals devoted to all things method. For those interested in surveys and questionnaires the *Journal of Survey Statistics and Methodology* is excellent. The *International Journal of Social Research*

Methodology is a broad-based journal that publishes articles on quantitative and qualitative methods. Similarly *Methodological Innovations Online* (open access) addresses debates across the full range of social research methods. Both *Sociological Methods & Research* and *Sociological Methodology* also have many articles on surveys – focusing on their use by sociologists – but ones on using mixed methods and a whole range of other research approaches too. *The International Journal of Qualitative Methods* (open access), *Qualitative Research*, and *Qualitative Inquiry* publish articles from a wide range of disciplines on research methods such as interviews, focus groups, participant observation, as well as a whole range of more cutting-edge approaches. *The Qualitative Report* has some nicely candid accounts of how it is to put certain methods into practice. For those interested in how social researchers work with discourse, *Discourse Studies* and *Discourse and Society* have lots of interesting examples. *Narrative Inquiry* is a journal devoted to ways of studying narrative. *Visual Studies* and *Visual Anthropology* are two excellent journals focused on visual methods. Finally, for readers interested in observation, taking part, participant observation, interviewing, and all the other techniques that get collected under the banner of ethnography, the journals *Ethnography, Journal of Contemporary Ethnography, Field Methods,* and *Journal of Autoethnography* offer a treasure trove of fascinating examples.

REFERENCES

Adams-Hutcheson, G. & Longhurst, R. (2017). 'At least in person there would have been a cup of tea': interviewing via Skype. *Area, 49*(2), 148–55. https://doi.org/10.1111/area.12306

Back, L. (2004). Listening with our eyes: Portraiture as urban encounter. In C. Knowles & P. Sweetman (eds), *Picturing the social landscape: Visual methods and the sociological imagination* (pp. 132–46). Routledge.

Baker, S. & Edwards, R. (eds) (2012). *How many qualitative interviews is enough? Expert voices and early career reflections on sampling and cases in qualitative research.* UK National Centre for Research Methods.

Becker, H. (1974). Photography and sociology. *Studies in the Anthropology of Visual Communications, 1*(1), 3–26. https://repository.upenn.edu/svc/vol1/iss1/3

Becker, H. (1986). *Writing for social scientists: How to start and finish your thesis, book, or article.* University of Chicago Press.

Becker, H. (1998). *Tricks of the trade: How to think about your research while you're doing it.* University of Chicago Press.

Becker, H. (2007). *Telling about society.* University of Chicago Press.

Becker, H. (2009). How to find out how to do qualitative research. *International Journal of Communication, 3*(9), 545–53. https://ijoc.org/index.php/ijoc/article/view/550

Becker, H. (2012). Commentary. In S. Baker & R. Edwards (eds), *How many qualitative interviews is enough? Expert voices and early career reflections on sampling and cases in qualitative research* (p. 15). UK National Centre for Research Methods.

Becker, H. (2014) *What about Mozart? What about murder? Reasoning from cases.* University of Chicago Press.

Belotto, M.J. (2018). Data analysis methods for qualitative research: Managing the challenges of coding, interrater reliability, and thematic analysis. *The Qualitative Report, 23*(11), 2622–33. https://doi.org/10.46743/2160-3715/2018.3492

Billig, M. (2013). *Learn to write badly: How to succeed in the social sciences.* Cambridge University Press.

Bissell, D. (2009). Conceptualising differently-mobile passengers: Geographies of everyday encumbrance in the railway station. *Social and Cultural Geography, 10*, 173–95. https://doi.org/10.1080/14649360802652137

Bissell, D. (2014). Encountering stressed bodies: Slow creep transformations and tipping points of commuting mobilities. *Geoforum, 51*, 191–201. https://doi.org/10.1016/j.geoforum.2013.11.007

Bissell, D. (2023). Questioning quotation: Writing about interview experiences without using quotes. *Area, 55*(2), 191–6. https://doi.org/10.1111/area.12854

Boonzaier, F. & de la Rey, C. (2003) 'He's a man, and I'm a woman': Cultural constructions of masculinity and femininity in South African women's narratives of violence. *Violence against Women, 9*(8), 1003–29. https://doi.org/10.1177/10778012032551

Bourgois, P. (2003). *In search of respect: Selling crack in El Barrio*, 2nd edn. Cambridge University Press.

Browne, A. (2016). Can people talk together about their practices? Focus groups, humour, and the sensitive dynamics of everyday life. *Area, 48*(2), 198–205. https://doi.org/10.1111/area.12250

Chiweshe, M., Mavuso, J. & Macleod, C. (2017). Reproductive justice in context: South African and Zimbabwean women's narratives of their abortion decision. *Feminism & Psychology, 27*(2), 203–24. https://doi.org/10.1177/0959353517699234

Clark, R.P. (2008). *Writing tools: 55 essential strategies for every writer*. Little, Brown Spark.

Corbin, J. & Strauss, A. (2015). *Basics of qualitative research techniques and procedures for developing Grounded Theory*, 4th edn. SAGE.

Corburn, J. (2002). Combining community-based research and local knowledge to confront asthma and subsistence-fishing hazards in Greenpoint/Williamsburg, Brooklyn, New York. *Environmental Health Perspectives, 110*(suppl 2), 241–8.

Cramer, K. (2016). *The politics of resentment: Rural consciousness in Wisconsin and the rise of Scott Walker*. University of Chicago Press.

Crang, M. & Cook, I. (2007). *Doing ethnographies*. SAGE.

Day, R. & Hitchings, R. (2011). 'Only old ladies would do that': age stigma and older people's strategies for dealing with winter cold. *Health and Place, 17*(4), 885–94. https://doi.org/10.1016/j.healthplace.2011.04.011

DeLand, M. (2012). Suspending narrative arrangements: the case of pick-up basketball. *The Annals of the American Academy of Political and Social Science, 642*(1), 96–108. https://doi.org/10.1177/0002716212438201

DeWalt, K. and DeWalt, B. (2011). *Participant observation: A guide for fieldworkers*, 2nd edn. AltaMira Press.

Dittmer, J. (2009). Textual and discourse analysis. In D. Delyser, S. Herbert, S. Aitken, M. Crang & L. McDowell (eds), *The SAGE handbook of qualitative geography* (pp. 274–86). SAGE.

Doughty, K. (2013). Walking together: The embodied and mobile production of a therapeutic landscape. *Health and Place, 24*, 140–6. https://doi.org/10.1016/j.healthplace.2013.08.009

Dowling, R. (2000) Power, subjectivity and ethics in qualitative research. In I. Hay (ed.), *Qualitative research methods in human geography* (pp. 23–36). Oxford University Press.

Drew, P. & Heritage, J. (eds) (1992). *Talk at work: Interaction in institutional settings*. Cambridge University Press.

Duncan, T. (2007). *Working tourists: Identity formation in a leisure space*. Doctoral dissertation, University of London.

Duneier, M. (2011). How not to lie with ethnography. *Sociological Methodology, 41*(1), 1–11. https://doi.org/10.1111/j.1467-9531.2011.01249.x

Eco, U. (1985). *How to write a thesis*. MIT Press.

Eichorn, J. (2015). *Survey sampling and design*. SAGE.

Eldh, A., Årestedt, L. & Berterö, C. (2020). Quotations in qualitative studies: Reflections on constituents, custom, and purpose. *International Journal of Qualitative Methods*, *19*, 1–6. https://doi.org/10.1177/1609406920969268

Eliasoph, N. (1998). *Avoiding politics: How Americans produce apathy in everyday life*. Cambridge University Press.

Elliott, V. (2018). Thinking about the coding process in qualitative data analysis. *The Qualitative Report*, *23*(11), 2850–61. https://doi.org/10.46743/2160-3715/2018.3560

Emmerson, R., Fretz, R. & Shaw, L. (2011). *Writing ethnographic fieldnotes*, 2nd edn. Chicago University Press.

England, K. (1994). Getting personal: Reflexivity, positionality, and feminist research. *The professional geographer*, *46*(1), 80–9. https://doi.org/10.1111/j.0033-0124.1994.00080.x

Fowler, F. (2013). *Survey research methods*, 5th edn. SAGE.

Gehl, J. & Svarre, B. (2013). *How to study public life*. Island Press.

Germano, W. (2021). *On revision: the only writing that counts*. University of Chicago Press.

Gill, S. (2004). *A book of field studies*. Chris Boot.

Goffman, E. (1959) *The presentation of self in everyday life*. Doubleday.

Grootaert, C. (ed.) (2004). *Measuring social capital: An integrated questionnaire* (No. 18). World Bank Publications.

Grove, R., Fowler, F., Couper, M., Lepkowski, J., Singer, E. & Tourangeau, R. (2004). *Survey methodology*. Wiley.

Gubrium, J. & Holstein, J. (2001). *Handbook of interview research: context and method*. SAGE.

Gubrium, J., Holstein, J., Marvasti, A. & McKinney, K. (eds) (2012). *The SAGE handbook of interview research: The complexity of the craft*, 2nd edn. SAGE.

Hall, S.M., McIntosh, K., Neitzert, E., Pottinger, L., Sandhu, K., Stephenson, M-A, Reed, H. & Taylor, L. (2017). *Intersecting inequalities: The impact of austerity on Black and minority ethnic women in the UK*. The Women's Budget Group, Runnymede Trust, Coventry Women's Voices, RECLAIM.

Hammersley, M. & Atkinson, P. (2019). *Ethnography: Principles in practice*, 4th edn. Routledge.

Harper, D. (1987). *Working knowledge: Skill and community in a small shop*. University of Chicago Press.

Harper, D. (2002). Talking about pictures: A case for photo elicitation. *Visual Studies*, *17*(1), 13–26. https://doi.org/10.1080/14725860220137345

Harper, D. (2023). *Visual sociology*, 2nd edn. Routledge.

Hitchings, R. (2009). *Indoor office workers and outdoor nature: A research report*. University College London.

Hitchings, R. (2011). Researching air-conditioning addiction and ways of puncturing practice: Professional office workers and the decision to go outside. *Environment and Planning A*, *43*(12), 2838–56. https://doi.org/10.1068/a43574

Hitchings, R. (2021). *The unsettling outdoors: Environmental estrangement in everyday life*. Wiley (Chapter 5).

Hitchings, R. (2022). Understanding air-conditioned lives: qualitative insights from Doha. *Buildings and Cities*, *3*(1), 28–41. doi: 10.5334/bc.155

Hitchings, R. (2023). Agreeing about smartphones: Making opinions in online focus groups. *Area*, *55*(2), 210–14. https://doi.org/10.1111/area.12850

Hitchings, R. & Latham, A. (2017). How 'social' is recreational running? Findings from a qualitative study in London and implications for public health promotion. *Health and Place*, *46*, 337–43. doi: 10.1016/j.healthplace.2016.10.003

Hitchings, R. & Latham, A. (2020a). Qualitative methods I: On current conventions in interview research. *Progress in Human Geography*, *44*(2), 389–98. https://doi.org/10.1177/0309132519856412

Hitchings, R. & Latham, A. (2020b). Qualitative methods II: On the presentation of 'geographical ethnography'. *Progress in Human Geography*, *44*(5), 972–80. https://doi.org/10.1177/0309132519879986

Hitchings, R., Browne, A. & Jack, T. (2018). Should there be more showers at the summer music festival? Studying the contextual dependence of resource consuming conventions and lessons for sustainable tourism. *Journal of Sustainable Tourism*, *26*(3), 496–514. https://doi.org/10.1080/09669582.2017.1360316

Hochschild, H. (2016). *Strangers in their own land: Anger and mourning on the American right*. The New Press.

Hodgson, A. & Hitchings, R. (2018). Urban air pollution perception through the experience of social practices: Talking about breathing with recreational runners in London. *Health &Place*, *53*, 26–33. https://doi.org/10.1016/j.healthplace.2018.07.009

Holm, G. (2020). Photography as a research method. In P. Leavy (ed.), *The Oxford handbook of qualitative methods* (pp. 569–600). Oxford University Press.

Holstein, J. & Gubrium, J. (1995). *The active interview*. SAGE.

Hommels, A. (2008). *Unbuilding cities*. MIT Press.

Hughes, R. & Huby, M. (2004). The construction and interpretation of vignettes in social research. *Social Work and Social Sciences Review*, *11*(1), 36–51. doi: https://doi.org/10.1921/swssr.v11i1.428

Israel, M. & Hay, I. (2006). *Research ethics for social scientists*. SAGE.

Johnson, O. (2024, March 7). Malcolm in the middle (well, in the beginning), *Logging the World Substack*. https://bristoliver.substack.com/p/malcolm-in-the-middle-well-at-the?utm_source=post-email-title&publication_id=1174206&post_id=142383179&utm_campaign=email-post-title&isFreemail=true&r=9bdbk&triedRedirect=true

Johnstone, B. & Andrus, J. (2024). *Discourse analysis,* 4th edn. Wiley.

Katz, J. (1997). Ethnography's warrants. *Sociological Methods & Research*, *25*(4), 391–423. https://doi.org/ 10.1177/0049124197025004002

Katz, J. (2012). Ethnography's expanding warrants. *The Annals of the American Academy of Political and Social Science 642*(1), 258–75. DOI:10.1177/0002716212437342.

Klinenberg, E. (2002). *Heatwave: A social autopsy of disaster in Chicago*. University of Chicago.

Knowles, C. & Harper, D. (2009). *Hong Kong: Migrant lives, landscapes, and journeys*. University of Chicago Press.

Knowles, C. & Sweetman, P. (eds) (2004). *Picturing the social landscape: Visual methods and the sociological imagination*. Routledge.

Kvale, S. & Steinar Brinkmann, S. (2014). *Interviews: Learning the craft of qualitative research interviewing*, 3rd edn. SAGE.

Lareau, A. (2021). *Listening to people: A practical guide to interviewing, participant observation, data analysis and writing it all up*. University of Chicago Press.

Latham, A. (2003a). Urbanity, lifestyle and making sense of the new urban cultural economy: Notes from Auckland, New Zealand. *Urban Studies*, *40*(9), 1699–724. https://doi.org/10.1080/0042098032000106564

Latham, A. (2003b). Research, performance, and doing human geography: Some reflections on the diary-photograph, diary-interview method. *Environment and Planning A*, *35*(11), 1993–2017. https://doi.org/10.1068/a3587

Latham, A. (2006). Sociality and the cosmopolitan imagination: National, cosmopolitan and local imaginaries in Auckland, New Zealand. In J. Binney, J. Holloway, S. Millington & C. Young (eds), *Cosmopolitan urbanism* (pp. 101–23). Routledge.

Latham, A. (2020). Diagramming the social: Exploring the legacy of Torsten Hägerstrand's diagrammatic landscapes. *Landscape Research*, *45*(6), 699–711. doi: 10.1080/01426397.2020.1749579.

Latham, A. & McCormack, D.P. (2009). Thinking with images in non-representational cities: Vignettes from Berlin. *Area*, *41*(3), 252–62. https://doi.org/10.1111/j.1475-4762.2008.00868.x

Latham, A., Nattrass, M. & Hitchings, R. (2024). Thinking through an ethnography of infrastructure: Commonsensical reasoning and road sharing in Carlisle, UK. *Transactions of the Institute of British Geographers*. Forthcoming.

Laurier, E. & Philo, C. (2006). Cold shoulders and napkins handed: Gestures of responsibility. *Transactions of the Institute of British Geographers*, *31*(2), 193–207. https://doi.org/10.1111/j.1475-5661.2006.00205.x

Layton, J. (2022). *Urban public sports facilities: social infrastructure and the public life of cities*. Doctoral dissertation, University College London.

Lim, J. (2003). *Ethics and embodiment in racialised, ethnicised and sexualised practice*. Doctoral dissertation, University College London.

Liu, Q. (2023). Analysis of governmental open letters mobilizing residents in China during the COVID-19 pandemic. *Discourse and Society*, *34*(1), 77–95. doi: 10.1177/09579265221116980

Longhurst, R., Johnston, L. & Ho, E. (2009). A visceral approach: Cooking 'at home' with migrant women in Hamilton, New Zealand. *Transactions of the Institute of British Geographers*, *34*(3), 333–45. https://doi.org/10.1111/j.1475-5661.2009.00349.x

Lowenhaupt Tsing, A. (2015). *The mushroom at the end of the world: On the possibility of life in capitalist ruins*. Princeton University Press.

Martin, J.L. (2017). *Thinking through methods: A social science primer*. University of Chicago Press.

Mason, J. (2002). *Qualitative researching*, 2nd edn. SAGE.

Mason, J. (2018). *Qualitative researching*, 3rd edn. SAGE.

Mason, M. (2010). Sample size and saturation in PhD studies using qualitative interviews. *Forum Qualitative Sozialforschung*, *11*(3). https://doi.org/10.17169/fqs-11.3.1428

Menzel, P. (1994). *Material world: A global family portrait*. Counterpoint.

Mercer, C., Page, B. & Evans, M. (2008). *Development and the African diaspora: Place and the politics of home.* Zed Books.

Middleton, J. (2024). Analytical leapfrogging: A conference presentation about caring on the move. *Area*. Forthcoming.

Miles, M. & Huberman, M. (2019). *Qualitative data analysis: An expanded sourcebook,* 4th edn. SAGE.

Mishler, E. (1986). *Research interviewing: Context and narrative.* Harvard University Press.

Mollison, J. (2010). *Where children sleep.* Chris Boot.

Morse, J. (2010). 'Cherry picking': Writing from thin data. *Qualitative Health Research, 20*(1), 3. doi:10.1177/1049732309354285

Musante, K. & Dewalt, B. (2010). *Participant observation: A guide for fieldworkers,* 2nd edn. Rowman Altamira.

Nathan, S., Newman, C. & Lancaster, K. (2019). Qualitative interviewing. In P. Liamputtong (ed.), *Handbook of research methods in health sciences* (pp. 391–410). Springer.

Nippert-Eng, C. (2015). *Watching closely: A guide to ethnographic observation.* Oxford University Press.

Oakley, A. (1981). Interviewing women: A contradiction in terms? In H. Robert (ed.), *Doing Feminist Research* (pp. 30–61). Routledge and Kegan Paul.

Ocejo, R. (2007). *Masters of craft: Old jobs in the new urban economy.* Princeton University Press.

Olive, J.L. (2014). Reflecting on the tensions between emic and etic perspectives in life history research: Lessons learned. *Forum Qualitative Sozialforschung, 15*(2). https://doi.org/10.17169/fqs-15.2.2072

Osborne, T. & Rose, N. (1999). Do the social sciences create phenomena? The example of public opinion research. *British Journal of Sociology, 50*(3), 367–96. https://doi.org/10.1111/j.1468-4446.1999.00367.x

Pavlidis, A. & Fullagar, S. (2015). The pain and pleasure of roller derby: Thinking through affect and subjectification. *International Journal of Cultural Studies, 18*(5), 483–99. https://doi.org/10.1177/1367877913519309

Pink, S. (2021). *Visual ethnography,* 4th edn. SAGE.

Raglin, C. (1987/2014). *The comparative method: Moving beyond qualitative and quantitative strategies.* University of California Press.

Raglin, C. (2009). *Redesigning social inquiry: Fuzzy sets and beyond.* University of Chicago Press.

Raglin, C. & Becker, H. (eds) (1992). *What is a case?: Exploring the foundations of social inquiry.* Cambridge University Press.

Reeves, R., Greiffenhagen, C. & Laurier, E. (2016). Video gaming as practical accomplishment: Ethnomethodology, conversation analysis, and play. *Topics in Cognitive Science, 9*(2), 308–42. https://doi.org/10.1111/tops.12234

Rivas, C. (2012). Coding and analysing qualitative data. In C. Seale (ed.), *Researching society and culture.* SAGE.

Rivoal, I. & Salazar, N. (2013). Contemporary ethnographic practice and the value of serendipity. *Social Anthropology, 21*(2), 178–85. https://doi.org/10.1111/1469-8676.12026

Robinson, O. (2014). Sampling in interview-based qualitative research: A theoretical and practical guide. *Qualitative Research in Psychology*, *11*(1), 25–41. https://doi.org/10.1080/14780887.2013.801543

Rose, G. (2023). *Visual methodologies: An introduction to researching with visual materials*, 5th edn. SAGE.

Rubin, H. & Rubin, I. (2012). *Qualitative interviewing: The art of hearing data*, 3rd edn. SAGE.

Ryan, L. & Golden, A. (2006). 'Tick the Box Please': A reflexive approach to doing quantitative social research. *Sociology*, *40*(6), 1191–200. https://doi.org/10.1177/0038038506072287

Sacks, H. (1992). *Lectures on conversation: Volumes I and II*. Blackwell.

Sadati, A., Iman, M., Lankarani, K. & Derakhshan, S. (2016). A critical ethnography of doctor–patient interaction in southern Iran. *Indian Journal of Medical Ethics*, *1*(3), 147–55. doi: 10.20529/IJME.2016.042. PMID: 27474695

Saldana, J. (2021). *The coding manual for qualitative researchers*. SAGE.

Schaeffer, N. & Presser, S. (2003). The science of asking questions. *Annual Review of Sociology*, *29*, 65–88. DOI:10.1146/annurev.soc.29.110702.110112

Schwanen, T. (2007). Matter(s) of interest: Artefacts, spacing and timing. *Geografiska Annaler: Series B, Human Geography*, *89*(1), 9–22. https://doi.org/10.1111/j.1468-0467.2007.00236.x

Seamon, D. (2015). Body-subject, time-space routines, and place-ballets. In A. Buttimer & D. Seamon (eds), *The human experience of space and place* (pp. 148–65). Routledge.

Sennett, R. (2006). *The culture of the new capitalism*. Yale University Press.

Shove, E. (2003). *Comfort, cleanliness and convenience: The social organization of normality*. Berg.

Silverman, D. (2013). *A very short, fairly interesting and reasonably cheap book about qualitative research*. SAGE.

Silverman, D. (2015). *Interpreting qualitative data*, 5th edn. SAGE.

Small, M.L. (2009). 'How many cases do I need?' On science and the logic of case selection in field based research. *Ethnography*, *10*, 5–38. https://doi.org/10.1177/1466138108099586

Small, M.L. & Calarco, J.M. (2022). *Qualitative literacy: A guide to evaluating ethnographic and interview research*. University of California Press.

Spradley, J. (1979). *The ethnographic interview*. Waveland Press.

Spradley, J. (1980). *Participant observation*. Holt, Rinehart and Winston.

Staller, K. (2015). Moving beyond description in qualitative analysis: Finding applied advice. *Qualitative Social Work*, *14*(6), 731–40. doi:10.1177/1473325015612859

Staller, K. (2021). Big enough? Sampling in qualitative inquiry. *Qualitative Social Work*, *20*(4), 897–904. https://doi.org/10.1177/14733250211024516

Staller, K. (2022). Confusing questions in qualitative inquiry: Research, interview, and analysis *Qualitative Social Work, 21*(2), 227–34. https://doi.org/10.1177/14733250221080533

Stokoe, E. (2018). *Talk: The science of conversation*. Little, Brown.

Suchar, C.S. (1988). Photographing the changing material culture of a gentrified community. *Visual studies*, *3*(2), 17–21. https://doi.org/10.1080/14725868808583618

Suchar, C.S. (1993). The Jordaan: Community change and gentrification in Amsterdam. *Visual Studies*, *8*(1), 41–51. https://doi.org/10.1080/14725869308583712

Svarre, B. & Gehl, J. (2013). *How to study public life*. Island Press.

Swidler, A. (2001). *Talk of love: How culture matters*. University of California Press.

Tavory, I. & Timmermans, S. (2014) *Abductive analysis: Theorising qualitative research*. University of Chicago Press.

Temsah, M.-H., Aljamaan, F., Malki, K.H., Alhasan, K., Altamimi, I., Aljarbou, R., Bazuhair, F., Alsubaihin, A., Abdulmajeed, N. &, Alshahrani, F.S. (2023) ChatGPT and the future of digital health: A study on healthcare workers' perceptions and expectations. *Healthcare*, *11*(13), 1812. https://doi.org/10.3390/healthcare11131812

Thieme, T. (2021). 'Youth are redrawing the map': Temporalities and terrains of the hustle economy in Mathare, Nairobi. *Africa*, *91*(1), 35–56. doi:10.1017/S0001972020000832

Thorpe, S. (2023). *How young people talk about climate change in everyday life: A photo-elicitation focus group study of London students*. MSc Dissertation, University College London.

Tilly, C. (2006). *Why? What happens when people give reasons ... and why?* Princeton University Press.

Trouille, D. (2021). *Fútbol in the park: Immigrants, soccer, and the creation of social ties*. University of Chicago Press.

van Teeffelen, T. (1994). Racism and metaphor: The Palestinian-Israeli conflict in popular literature. *Discourse & Society*, *5*(3), 381–405. https://doi.org/10.1177/0957926594005003006

Waitt, G. (2005). Doing discourse analysis. In I. Hay (ed.), *Qualitative Methods in Human Geography* (pp. 163–91). Oxford University Press.

Waitt, G. (2010). Doing Foucauldian discourse analysis: Revealing social realities. In I. Hay (ed.), *Qualitative research methods in human geography* (pp. 217–40). SAGE.

Weiss, R. (1994). *Learning from strangers: The art and method of qualitative interview studies*. Free Press.

Wilkinson-Weber, C.M. (1999). *Embroidering lives: Women's work and skill in the Lucknow embroidery industry*. SUNY Press.

Yantseva, V. (2023). Discursive construction of migrant otherness on Facebook: A distributional semantics approach. *Discourse and Society 34*(2), 236–54. https://doi.org/10.1177/09579265221117014

Yoon, I.J. (1997). *On my own: Korean businesses and race relations in America*. University of Chicago Press.

Zaman, S. (2008). Native among the natives: Physician anthropologist doing hospital ethnography at home. *Journal of Contemporary Ethnography*, *37*(2), 135–54. https://doi.org/10.1177/0891241607312495

AFTERWORD

This book was written together in cafes across Islington, at Russell's dining table, in Alan's basement workroom, during a we'd 'better bloody get this book done' writing retreat in Hay-on-Wye, as well as very occasionally in our UCL offices. A lot of time was spent working out what we wanted to say, and how to say it. We spent hours arguing over tone, wording, and syntax. Russell died a few weeks after the final manuscript was finished. He cared deeply about research methods — about doing social research well. This book is full of his wisdom about research. But it is also full of the enthusiasm and delight that was key to who he was. I hope this book inspires readers to approach research with Russell's sense of wonder and inventiveness. He is missed.

INDEX

Page references to Figures contain the letter 'f'

analytical leapfrogging, 200
Andrus, J., *Discourse analysis*, 215
Area (journal), 213, 214
artificial intelligence (AI), 200, 201
Atkinson, P., *Ethnography: Principles in practice*, 213, 214
Auckland inner-city neighbourhood, New Zealand
　engagement with research subjects, 81–3, 87–8, 89*f*, 197, 198
　examples of engaging others, 144
　Field Studies, 144*f*
　photography, use of, 144, 145, 146, 161
　recruitment flyer, 87–8, 89*f*
audiences, speaking to, 4, 18
　appealing to, 189
　characteristics, 19
　convincing, 169
　defining, 8, 191–4
　dissertations, 193
　engagement with, 17, 25, 193
　make up of, 172
　matters found acceptable to, 172, 173
　particular audiences, addressing, 8, 14
　photography, with, 145, 160, 161, 165
　reaching, 19, 20, 74
　researcher seen to be making an effort, 60
　sample choice, 179
　storytelling, 90
　thinking about, 170
　understanding of, 172
　and warrants, 212
　in writing, 8, 19, 191–4

Back, L., 162
Becker, H., 57, 107, 108–109, 120, 160, 170, 173, 193, 201–203, 206–207, 211–12
　Telling about society, 212, 216, 217
　Tricks of the trade: How to think about your research while you're doing it, 211, 215, 216
　What about Mozart? What about murder? Reasoning from cases, 216–17
　What is a case?: Exploring the foundations of social inquiry, 216

Bissel, D., 24n1, 98, 194
　Encountering stressed bodies: Slow creep transformations and tipping points of commuting mobilities, 93–4
Blumer, H., 107, 108–109
Boonzaier, F., 78
Bourgois, P., 107
Brinkmann, S., *Interviews: Learning the craft of qualitative research interviewing*, 214

Calarco, J.M., 41, 87, 119, 195, 197, 200
　Qualitative literacy: A guide to evaluating ethnographic and interview research, 214, 217
cameras, 146, 148, 163
　automatic, 144
　disposable, 158
　installing, for observation research, 37, 38–9
　video, 37
　see also photographs/illustrations
Cameroon, 113
cases and samples
　audiences, speaking to, 170, 172
　being able to know when researchers have done enough, 172–3
　different methods/arguments, 173–6
　　making a call based on what is available, 175
　　matters of importance, 175–6
　　shorter interactions and bigger numbers, 176
　　telling the story and seeing what you think, 174–5
　　wait and see, 174
　examples of issues discussed
　　mistreatment of migrants, 178
　　urban change, reflecting in TV shows, 178
　human populations
　　experiences, 186–7
　　interactions, 184–5
　　practices, 186
　making innovative projects, 7–8, 167–89, 216–17

making the most of what is available, 182–4
political/controversial statements, 167
pragmatism, 175
reactions of student researchers, 170–1
scientific versus humanities backgrounds, students from, 97, 170–1
seeing what others are up to, 170–3
selection of cases to study, 168–70
variation in numbers interviewed, 171
see also samples/sampling
China
COVID-19 pandemic, government letters about, 137–8
Chiweshe, M., 78
Clark, R. P., *Writing tools: 55 essential strategies for every writer*, 217
climate change, 18, 179, 202
activities adding to, 169
asking questions, 108, 109, 112
defining, 108
denial of, 80
engagement with research subjects, 95, 97
in everyday life, 157
gender, views on according to, 167
global, 155–6
human driven, 105
in the media, 157
perception that most people don't understand, 177–8
photography, use of, 155–7, 156*f*
young people's thoughts on, 155–7
coding, 127–9, 132
of chunks of texts, in interviews, 132
comparison of two codes, 134–6
'Going without Urban Nature,' 135–6
'Shoes,' 136
defining, 127
etic and emic, 127–8, 129, 131
good quality codes, 129
insider and outsider, 128
list of codes, 134
see also words, playing with
communication *see* discourse; interviews; language; talking; writing
computer games, 36–7
Confucius, 45
convenience stores, 43, 46
conversations *see* talking
Cook, I., 36, 133–4
Doing ethnographies, 213, 214
Corbin, J., *Basics of qualitative research techniques and procedures for developing grounded theory*, 215
Cramer, K., 119
The Politics of Resentment, 104

Crang, M., 36, 39, 134, 213, 214
Doing ethnographies, 213, 214
crime, 12, 15
cultural anthropology, 213
cultural narratives, 78

data
analysis, 213
collecting, 17, 173
defining, 17
'enough,' 172
forms of, 20
functions of, 17–19
graphs or maps, informing, 18
numerical, 115
questionnaire, 119
'rich,' 6
survey sources, from, 105
Day, R., 156, 158, 159
de la Rey, C., 78
DeLand, Michael, 53
Dewalt, B., *Participant observation: A guide for fieldworkers*, 213
diagrams, using, 202–203
discourse
defining, 136–7
discourse analysis, 139, 215–16
discourse hunting, 139–40
generalized, 206
student discourses, 137
working with, 218
see also interviews; talking; writing
Discourse and Society (journal), 218
Discourse Studies (journal), 218
dissertations, 9, 25, 98, 119, 128, 160, 172, 208, 217
audiences for, 193
good quality, producing, 193
masters level, example of, 156–7
supervision of students, 183
undergraduate level, 207
Doughty, K., 67
Dowling, R., 85
Drew, P., *Talk at work: Interaction in institutional settings*, 214
Duneier, M., 'How not to lie with ethnography,' 217

eavesdropping, 36
analytical, 39
Eco, U., *How to write a thesis*, 217
'eco-anxiety,' 157
Eichorn, J., *Survey sampling and design*, 215
Eliasoph, N., 75
Emmerson, R., 40
Writing ethnographic fieldnotes, 212–13

empathy, 86–7
engagement with research subjects, 6, 81–100, 214–15
   analytical aspects, 96–8
   examples of engaging others
      Auckland inner-city neighbourhood, 81–3, 87–8, 89*f*, 144, 145, 197, 198
      being a 'research robot,' 96
      Hong Kong, life as a migrant domestic worker, 91–3, 94, 164*f*, 194
      job interview exercise, 83–4
      photography, use of, 144, 145
      Sydney, life of a long distance commuter, 93–5
      termination of research relationship, 98–9
      urban regeneration, London, 96–8
   existing characteristics, working with (big 'P' positionality), 84–6
   gaining access, 82
   getting other people to help, 88–91
      Auckland example recruitment flyer, 87–8, 89*f*
      'honorarium,' 89–90
   how to engage with research subjects, 82, 100*f*
   length of time taken, 176
   reasons for people becoming part of a social research project, 90
   reframing positionality question, 86–7
   self-awareness (small 'p' positionality), 87–8
   women interviewing women, 85–6
   see also interviews; questions; talking
England, K., 85
ethical challenges, 37, 85, 89, 98, 165
ethnicity, reports on, 19
ethnography, 174, 192, 212, 217, 218
   see also fieldnotes
Ethnography (journal), 213, 218

facts, collecting, 104–106
Field Methods (journal), 218
field studies, 143–4
fieldnotes
   examples
      Berlin café, 29–31, 30*f*, 32*f*
      birdwatching, 31
      comparison of, 29–34
      objects, use of, 35
   photography as, 146–7, 216
   practical reflections, 213
   thinking about language, 34
   writing, 28–34, 30*f*, 32*f*
   see also notebooks/note-taking; writing
focus groups, interviews, 16
football *see* soccer

Fowler, F., *Survey research methods*, 215
Fretz, R., *Writing ethnographic fieldnotes*, 212–13
Fullagar, S., 45

gays and lesbians *see* LGBTQ community
Gehl, J., *How to study Public Life*, 24n1, 213
gentrification, 178
Germano, W., *On revision*, 217
Gill, S., 143–4
   A book of field studies, 143
Gladwell, M., 193
Goffman, E., 84
graphs, 18, 19, 170
grocery stores, 43–4
grounded theory, 215
groups
   identity, handling in group situations, 37–8
   interaction patterns, 38
   overlapping, 17
   witnessing/giving voice to, 15–16
Grove, R., *Survey methodology*, 215
Gubrium, J.
   The active interview, 215
   The SAGE handbook of interview research: The complexity of the craft, 214

Hall, Sarah M., 16
   Intersecting inequalities: The impact of austerity on Black and minority ethnic women, 13
Hammersley, M., *Ethnography: Principles in practice*, 213, 214
Harper, D., 53–4, 164, 194, 196
   Hong Kong: Migrant Lives, Landscapes and Journeys, 92
   Visual sociology, 216
   Working knowledge, 45
   see also Knowles, C.
Heritage, J., *Talk at work: Interaction in institutional settings*, 214
Hitchings, K., 65*f*
Hitchings, R., 23*f*, 52*f*, 53*f*, 65–7, 69, 77, 106*f*, 109*f*, 110*f*, 112–13, 125, 129, 157, 159, 180, 182, 185, 196, 197, 207, 212
   code list, 128
   flow chart by, 132, 133*f*
   interview transcription, 126–7, 129–30, 135–6
   photographs by, 29*f*, 30*f*, 32*f*, 70*f*, 112*f*, 153*f*, 186*f*, 187*f*
Hochschild, A., 75
Hodgson, A., 180, 181, 186
Holstein, J.
   The active interview, 215
   The SAGE handbook of interview research: The complexity of the craft, 214

Hommels, A., *Unbuilding Cities*, 104
homosexuality *see* LGBTQ community
Huberman, M., *Qualitative data analysis*, 215
'hustle economy,' 198–9

identity, handling in group situations, 37–8
immigrants on social media, talking about, 137
in-depth interviews, 15, 19, 174, 214, 215
India, embroidery industry, 55
infrastructure, 192
injustice, highlighting, 12–13, 16–17
inspirational people, 8, 211–18
International Journal of Qualitative Methods, 218
International Journal of Social Research Methodology, 217–18
interviews, 6, 214
    active, 64
    aide-mémoire *see* schedules *below*
    asking questions, 6, 75
    challengers, 79
    conventions, 130
    as conversations with a purpose, 74
    coverage of topics, 71
    debating in, 76
    in-depth, 15, 19, 174, 214, 215
    different ways of seeing, 71–3
    discoverers, 79
    effective, ensuring, 5–6, 72, 74, 80
    excerpts from, 126, 127, 129–30
    focus group, 16
    formal, 55
    fruitcake analogy, 74
    imagining, 71, 79–80, 214
        as a challenge, 75–6
        as storytelling, 77–8
    imposing a framework, 66, 68
    insight, depth of, 73
    interview samples in human geography, 171*f*
    laughter, 130
    listeners, 79
    lunchtimes, 131
    monologues, 79
    paper versus screen, use of, 69
    patterns in, 67, 134
    pauses, 72, 79
    peer pressure, 130
    physical environment of conversations, 62, 65–8
        car, 66
        coffee shop, 66
        countryside paths, 67
        domestic gardens, 66–7
    police, 74
    preamble, 69–71
    presentation of material, 201–202
    push backs/rejection of questions, 79–80
    reasons for, 63, 66
    'richness' in research material, assumption of, 6, 80
    and role of researcher, 6
    schedules, 61, 69–70, 70*f*, 117*f*, 160
    scribbles and marks, making, 71
    seen as challenges, 75–6
    semi-structured, 69, 95
    sequence of questions, 71
    as shared discovery, 76–7
    short, 95, 97
    showing an interest, 72
    skilled, 65, 68, 76
    standard models, 71
    staying on track, 73
    structured, 69
    styles, 78
    'sweet spot' in social research, as, 170
    talking in, 63, 67, 74, 77
    texts, coding of chunks of, 132
    themes
        abortion, narratives of, 78
        LGBTQ community, 38, 82, 85, 88
        living in London, 61–2
    tips for, 71–3
    transcription of, 67, 126
    types of interactions, 73–4
    unstructured, 69
    use of material, 195–6
    variety of interview approaches, 74–5
    whether difficult, 64–5
    women interviewing women, 85–6
    see also questions; quotations; talking

Johnstone, B., *Discourse analysis*, 215
Journal of Autoethnography, 213, 218
Journal of Contemporary Ethnography, 213, 218
Journal of Survey Statistics and Methodology, 217
journalism, 131–2
journals, 213, 214, 216–18

Katz, Jack, 14
    'Ethnography's warrants,' 212
Klinenberg, Eric, *Heatwave: A social autopsy of disaster in Chicago*, 12, 15, 19
Knowles, C., 93, 94, 98, 164, 194–6
    Hong Kong: Migrant Lives, Landscapes and Journeys, 92
    Picturing the social landscape, 216
    see also Harper, D.
Kvale, S., *Interviews: Learning the craft of qualitative research interviewing*, 214

language, 124, 199, 213
    controlling, 84
    everyday, 90
    and interviews, 5–6

learning, 36, 192
see also interviews; talking
Lareau, A., *Listening to people: A practical guide to interviewing, participant observation, data analysis and writing it all up*, 213–15
Latham, A., 53*f*
Laurier, E., 184–5
Layton, J., 162, 163*f*
lectures, 62, 140, 176
LGBTQ community, 38, 82, 85, 88
Longhurst, R., 51, 69
Lowenhaupt Tsing, A., 55, 57

McCormack, D., 216
McKinney, K., *The SAGE handbook of interview research: The complexity of the craft*, 214
maps, 18, 19
Martin, J.L., *Thinking through methods: A social science primer*, 213
Marvasti, A., *The SAGE handbook of interview research: The complexity of the craft*, 214
Mason, J., 29
 Qualitative researching, 217
Menzel, P., *Material world: A global family portrait*, 154
Methodological Innovations Online, 218
Middleton, J., 200
Miles, M., *Qualitative data analysis*, 215
Mishler, E., *Research interviewing: Context and narrative*, 215
Mollison, J., *Where children sleep*, 154
Musante, K., *Participant observation: A guide for fieldworkers*, 213
music festivals, summer, 112–13, 162, 163*f*, 185–6

Narrative Inquiry (journal), 218
Nattrass, M., 191
naturalistic observation/research, 26, 38, 106
neighbourhood change, material culture, 163–4
Nippert-Eng, C., *Watching closely: A guide to ethnographic observation*, 213
notebooks/note-taking
 benefits of using, 7
 breaking things down into categories for, 49
 example contents, 30–1
 examples, strengths and weaknesses, 32–4
 fieldnotes, writing, 28, 30–1
 not having a notebook, 29
 reactions in researcher, eliciting, 39
 study of notebooks, 29
 taking notes whilst participating in social research, 57–60
  example of Tara, 58–60
 use of, 28, 30–1
 see also fieldnotes
novels, and Israel-Palestine conflict, 138–9

Oakley, A., 85
observation of public spaces, value of studying social life through, 5, 21–41, 212–13
 bags and social life, 35–6
 cameras, installing, 37, 38–9
 detail, noticing, 34–5
 feeling that nothing is happening, 40–1
 feeling uncomfortable, coping with, 39–40
 fieldnotes, writing, 28–34, 30*f*, 32*f*
 on-the-ground observation, 15
 group situations, handling identity in, 37–8
 list making and thinking about the words, 34–6
 listening in at the same time, 36–9
 location of research, 26–8
  patterns of interaction or movement observed, 28
  somewhere researcher happy to be, 27
  somewhere where interesting events occur, 27–8
 looking at people from a bench, analogy of, 21–2
 naturalistic observation, 26, 38
 online social life, understanding, 36–7
 passenger movement diagrams, 24n1
 people watching, 26, 39
 pure observation versus pure participation, 52
 reasons to use
  not knowing yet what is important, 24–5
  not wanting to disturb things, 25
  suspecting people won't talk about certain things, 26
  suspecting that people can't talk about certain things, 25–6
  thinking the detail will help later, 25
 reflections on examples, 38–9
 smartphones, use of, 23–4, 25, 26
 social scene for observation, 26
 straightforward, whether, 41
 two chosen groups exercise, 22–4
  assigning of people to colours, 22–3
  full-lines and dashed lines, use of, 23–4
  urban park, watching two types of people moving around, 23–4, 23*f*
 visualisation, 22
Ocejo, R., *Masters of craft*, 45
online social life, understanding, 36–7
opinions, collecting, 104–106, 109

participant observation, 44, 94
participation of researcher in social research, 43–60, 213
 and asking questions, 51
 breaking things down into categories for note-taking, 49

copying/imitating others, learning from, 44
developing a sense of what to notice, 49–50
illustrative examples
    cooking versus the cook, 50–2
    embroidery, professional, 55–6
    e-scooters in Stockholm, 46–8, 47*f*, 51, 56
    exotic mushrooms, selling, 54–5
    membership versus non-membership, 52–3
    shopping, methods of, 43–4
    soccer field and social ties, 56–7
learning about activity and about people with whom we interact, 50
participant observation, 44
pure participation verus pure observation, 52
roles of researchers, 53–4
taking part
    defining, 45–6
    effectiveness in research, 60
    enjoyment of researcher, 60
    identity of researcher, 52–4
    motivations for, 5, 45–6
    noticing how one feels, 46
    tips for, 48–9
    when to take part, 54–7
    whilst taking notes, 57–60
patterns, identifying/exploring, 215–16
    in collected material, 7, 126, 127
    deference, 38
    emergent, in a researcher's material, 215
    in everyday life, 130
    flowcharts, making, 132–3
    inequality or injustice, 12
    interaction, 28
    interviews/interview transcripts, 67, 134
    new, finding, 52, 128
    patterns of living, 195
    patterns of mobility, 203
    in photographs, 145, 154
    slowing down in order to see, 125, 128, 131–2, 139, 145
    social life, 26, 33
    software use, 140
    surveys, 175
    talking, 37
    in words *see* words
Pavlidis, A., 45
personal involvement of social researchers *see* participation of researcher in social research
Philo, C., 184–5
photo-elicitation, 155, 159–60, 166
photographs/illustrations, 143–66, 216
    asking others to take photographs for us, 154–60
    asking researcher to 'take a quick photo' of environment at 6.30 pm last night, 154–5
    how older people keep warm in the winter, 157–9, 158*f*
    photo-elicitation suggestions, 155, 159–60, 166
    young people's thoughts on climate change, 155–7
Auckland inner-city neighbourhood example, 144, 145, 146, 161
audits, 216
benefits of using, 7, 145, 146–7, 166
detail, seeing potential in, 143–5
determining how things are used, 150–2
determining how things change, 152–4
diagrams, using, 202–203
different kinds, determining, 148–50
ethical issues, 165
everyday life, of, 147
as evidence in social research, 160, 162
as fieldnotes, 146–7
limits of, 144–5
looking at, 143–66
as notetaking, 145
objects, use of, 151–2
photographic audit, 150
settings, changes in, 153–4
sharing over social media, 146
and smartphone use, 146, 147, 154, 157, 159, 166
social signalling, 152
storytelling/making arguments with, 160–5
    affective demonstration, 162
    animating/explicating the narrative, 161
    bearing witness, 162–5
    evidencing an argument, 162
time-lapse photography, 152
variation, exploring, 150
Viennese windows example, 148, 149*f*, 150
see also cameras
pictures *see* photographs/illustrations
Pink, S., *Visual ethnography*, 216
place ballet, 152
positionality
    big 'P' (how to work with our existing characteristics), 84–6, 87
    defining, 85
    fixed, 53
    importance of, 85
    reframing question, 86–7
    small 'P' (self-awareness), 87–8
presentation of material, 8, 64, 77, 90
    audience, defining, 191–4
    final, 14, 145
    in flowchart form, 132–3
    graphs, 18, 170

interviews, 92
photo-elicitation, 155, 159–60, 166
quotations *see* quotations
study results, 14, 193, 200
'tropes' of, 19
vignettes, 8
in writing, 191–210, 217–18
see also self-presentation

Qing Liu, 137
Qualitative Inquiry (journal), 218
The Qualitative Report (journal), 218
Qualitative Research (journal), 218
questionnaires, 108, 110*f*, 114, 115, 118, 119
completed, 175
designing, 111, 118, 215
on 'eating out,' 114–15
'image issues,' 110, 111
in journals, 217
on refugees in the UK, 110
short, 120
and surveys, 102, 108n1, 215, 217
working with, 121
see also questions; surveys; writing
questions, 101–121, 215
asking someone why they did something, 120
asking someone's opinion, 120–1
climate change, 157
different purposes, for, 115–18
drawing out a worldview, 103–104
examples, 105
failure to answer, 102
hierarchy of effectiveness, 105–106
on love, 117, 118
and naturalistic research, 106
open-ended, 103
over research projects, 118–20
and participation in social research, 51
perils of asking, 101
probing, 78
prompt for conversations, 103
questioning styles, 106*f*
reasons for use by social researchers, 102–106
rejection of, 79–80
sequence of, 71
'so what' questions, 14
styles of questioning, 6, 106*f*
survey situations, 111–14
taking an opinion poll, 101–102
as a way of collecting facts and opinions, 104–106
as a way of finding out what happened, 104
ways of asking, 6–7
see also interviews; talking

quotations, 8, 12–13, 19, 64, 87, 92–3, 102, 174, 208
authentic, 195
avoiding, 195–6
collection of, 135
cultures, 197
direct, 195
editing, 195
and engagement with research subjects, 132
extended, 194, 195, 196
getting to the heart of the issue, 171
individual interviewees/respondents, avoiding referring to, 196–7
injustice, highlighting, 16
'juiciest quote,' making the most of, 131
notetaking, 58
numbers needed, 197
quotation cultures, 197
quoting at length, 194–5
report writing, 19
research papers, 102
saturation, reaching, 172
selecting, 195, 197
styles, 195
use of, 136
using, 193
vignettes, 197, 199
ways of using, 193
words, playing with, 129
see also interviews; words, playing with; writing

Raglin, C.
The comparative method: Moving beyond qualitative and quantitative strategies, 217
Redesigning social inquiry: Fuzzy sets and beyond, 217
What is a case?: Exploring the foundations of social inquiry, 216
recording of research subjects, 37
Reeves, R., 36
relationship, seeing social research as, 6, 81–100
termination of, 98–9
reports, research
photography, use of, 7
report writing, 19
Research and *Sociological Methodology* (journal), 218
research subjects
engagement with *see* engagement with research subjects
Rose, G., *Visual methodologies*, 216
Rubin, H., *Qualitative interviewing: The art of hearing data*, 214
Rubin, I., *Qualitative interviewing: The art of hearing data*, 214
rural consciousness, 104

Sadati, A., 27
Saldana, J., *The coding manual for qualitative researchers*, 215
samples/sampling
    acceptable sampling methods, 167, 168
    assumptions, 8
    concerns, overcoming
        seeing existing research as an opportunity, 188–9
        something not previously done, relating to, 188
    'convenience' samples, 184
    formal, 189
    interview samples in human geography, 171*f*
    opportunities for unusual samples, 179–82
        defining who cares about shared experience, 181–2
        defining who cares about urban air pollution, 180–1
        making the most of what is available, 182–4
        types of student researcher, 183–4
    'proper' samples, 179
    'spread' of sample sizes, 171
    turning answers into samples, 176–9
    unusual, spotting opportunities for, 179–82
    'usual sampling suspects,' 184
    see also cases and samples
Schwanen, T., 202–203
Seamon, D., 152
security scanners, in supermarkets, 44
self-awareness (small 'p' positionality), 86–8, 91
self-presentation, 26, 29, 114, 136, 162
    conversations/interviews, 62, 63, 75
    engagement with research subjects, 82–4, 87, 88, 94, 97, 99
    see also presentation of material
Sennett, R., 104
    The Culture of the New Capitalism, 103
Shaw, L., *Writing ethnographic fieldnotes*, 212–13
shopping, methods of, 43–4
Shove, E., 195–6
silences, listening for, 139
Silverman, D., *A very short, fairly interesting and reasonably cheap book about qualitative research*, 212
Small, M.L., 41, 87, 119, 195, 197, 200
    Qualitative literacy: A guide to evaluating ethnographic and interview research, 214, 217
smartphones, use of
    observation of public spaces, 34, 35
    participation of researcher in social research, 43
    and photography, 146, 147, 154, 157, 159, 166

soccer, 11, 14, 16–19, 56–7
social capital, 117
social media, talking about immigrants on, 137, 140
social research
    authenticity, 54
    failed projects, 85
    motivations for, 3, 13–14
    non-contentious purpose and methods for doing, 15
    purpose of *see* warrants (purpose) of research
    seeing as a craft, 3
    seeing as a relationship, 6, 81–100, 214–15
        termination of, 98–9
    as studying social life, 3
    styles, 11
    thinking of as an adventure, 2, 3
    warrants of, 14–17
        taking for granted, 14–15
        whether delivering on, 20
    who to compare, 177
    see also social researchers
social researchers, student
    anxiety, feelings of, 2
    articles by, 169
    dissertations *see* dissertations
    ethical challenges for, 37, 85, 89, 98, 100, 165
    family background, variations in, 13
    handling of situations, 1–2
    image of, 106–111
    indifference of, 2, 39–40, 72
    interpretative, 105
    interviews by *see* interviews
    master level research, 3, 9, 13, 49
    methodology, 2, 4
    patterns, identifying/exploring *see* patterns, identifying/exploring
    personal involvement, motivations for, 5, 43–60
    photography, use of *see* photographs/illustrations
    practical points, understanding, 5
    presentation of self *see* self-presentation
    questions, asking *see* questions
    roles assumed, 95–6
    'taken for granted' ideas students have about themselves
        as brainbox, 123–4
        as customers, 124
        as revellers, 124
    trust building, 5
    types of student researcher, 183–4
    undergraduate level, 207
    working with words *see* words
    writing *see* presentation of material; writing
    see also social research

Sociological Methods (journal), 218
Spradley, J., 26
   Participant Observation, 212–14
statistics, 172, 200–202
Stockholm, Sweden, e-scooters in, 46–8, 47*f*, 51, 56
Stokoe, E., *Talk: The science of conversation*, 214
storytelling, 17
Strauss, A., *Basics of qualitative research techniques and procedures for developing grounded theory*, 215
student researchers *see* social researchers, student
Suchar, C., 163–4
supermarkets, 44
surveys, 6, 100
   ambiguity, avoiding, 114
   articles on, 218
   asking questions, 102, 106, 110, 111–14, 115, 118
   data sources, 105
   designing, 176
   embedded in contemporary life, 108
   examples
      migrant workers and money sent back home, 113–14
      summer music festival, showering at, 112–13, 185–6, 196
   presentation of results, 175, 193, 195, 200
   and questionnaires, 108n1, 215, 217
   questions with no second chance, 114–15
   standard urban food consumption, 105
   see also questionnaires; questions
Svarre, B., *How to study Public Life*, 24n1, 213
Sweetman, P., *Picturing the social landscape*, 216
Swindler, A., 117, 118

talking, 61–80, 214
   about immigrants on social media, 137
   context, importance of, 68
   conversation analysis, 37
   defining what is happening, 61–3
      physical context, 62–3
      self-presentation, 62
      social context, 62
   fundamental to social research, 5
   keeping up the flow of conversation, 68–71
   methods of communication, 73–4
   motivations for
      learning from the reactions of others, 64
      seeing things from another's perspective, 64
      understanding how something works, 63–4
   questions as a prompt for conversations, 103
   self-presentation, 62, 63, 75
   skilled, 75
   use of in a social research project, 5–6
   see also discourse; interviews; words, playing with; writing
Temsah, M.-H., 200
thesis, preparing, 98, 193, 217
   PhD, 160, 207
Thieme, T., 198–9
Thorpe, Sophie, 156–7
Trouille, David, 17, 18, 56, 57
   Fútbol in the park: Immigrants, soccer, and the creation of social ties, 11, 16

urban life
   air pollution, 180–1
   change, reflecting in TV shows, 178–9
   example of 'going without urban nature,' 135–6
   food consumption, standard, 105
   role of stores in, 46
   urban park, watching two types of people moving around in, 23–4, 23*f*
   urban regeneration, London, 96–8

van Teeffelen, T., 138
vignettes, 8, 197–200
Visual Anthropology (journal), 218
Visual Studies (journal), 216, 218

Waitt, G., 'Doing Discourse Analysis,' 215–16
warrants (purpose) of research, 8, 11–20, 212
   and audiences, 212
   being clear about, 4
   differences in, 14–15
   evidence, pieces of, 11–14
   group, witnessing/giving voice to, 15–16
   informing government policy, 14
   injustice, highlighting, 16–17
   interviews, 63
   and photography, 165
   primary, 206–207
   questioning vested interests, 14
   social research, 14–17
      taking for granted, 14–15
      whether delivering on warrant, 20
   understanding/deepening, 15
   and writing, 193–4
Weiss, R., *Learning from strangers: The art and method of qualitative interview studies*, 215
Wilkinson-Weber, C., 55–6
women
   Black/ethnic minority, 16, 17
   interviewing others, 85–6
   migrant women in New Zealand, 51
words, playing with, 123–42, 215
   'already existing' collections, examples
      COVID-19 pandemic, government letters about, 137–8, 140–1

immigrants on social media, talking about, 137, 140
popular novels and Israel–Palestine conflict, 138–9, 141
already generated, analysis, 125–7
codes, 7, 127–9, 132
exploring of ideas, 136
flowcharts, making, 132–3
interview transcription, 126
observation of public spaces, 34–6
parts of projects unsuccessful, next steps, 134–6
   example of 'going without urban nature,' 135–6
   example of 'shoes,' 136
patterns, exploring, 7, 125–8, 130–4, 140–1
   'cherry picking,' 131–2
   in coding of chunks of texts, 132
   journalism, 131–2
   software, useful, 133–4
produced versus found words, 141–2
studies focused on, 136–41
and writing, 8
see also talking; writing

World Bank, 116, 118

writing
aims of, 8
audience, defining, 8, 191–4
diagrams, using, 202–203
different devices, considering, 204
of fieldnotes, 28–34, 30*f*, 32*f*
good or bad, 193
images we live and write by, 204–205
improving, 209–210
numbers and statistics, including, 200–202
presentation of material, 191–210
quality of, 17
references, numbers of, 208
of reports, 19
strategies, 8
theories as just simplifications, 205–207
vignettes, 8, 197–200
'worry writing,' 39
see also discourse; notebooks/note-taking; quotations

Yantseva, V., 137
Yoon, I.-J., 44

Zaman, S., 27